This book belongs to

_____

From

_____

Date

_____

In the Light of His Glory

CHRISTIAN ART
PUBLISHERS

Published by Christian Art Publishers
PO Box 1599, Vereeniging, 1930, RSA

© 2017
Second edition 2020

Written by Jimi le Roux

Designed by Christian Art Publishers

Images used under license from Shutterstock.com

Printed in China

ISBN 978-1-4321-3168-5

20 21 22 23 24 25 26 27 28 29 – 10 9 8 7 6 5 4 3 2 1

Introduction

"Arise, shine, for your light has come, and the glory of the Lord has risen upon you."

Isaiah 60:1

God's promises carry us and help us to rise above our circumstances. They give us strength, hope, endurance and the unshakable confidence that God is in control.

In the Light of His Glory, God's promises in the book of Isaiah. These promises teach us about God's love for His people, His will for our lives and the future He has planned for us. They help us to better understand the Almighty and His wonderful purpose for our lives.

Take a few minutes every day to be still before the Lord. Read the key Scripture verse and devotion, meditate on the personal promise God has for you and pray the prayer at the end of each devotion.

Use the promises as inspiration and encouragement as you allow God's Word to lead you in the way you should go. Be blessed as you carry the message of each devotion with you throughout your day.

May God bless you!

~ *Jimi le Roux*

January

Invitation to a Fresh Start

"I, the LORD, invite you to come and talk it over. Your sins are scarlet red, but they will be whiter than snow or wool."

Isaiah 1:18 CEV

Israel's corrupt and cruel leaders had strayed far from God. The ordinary folk were joining them in droves with their idolatry. The worst was that the people wanted to worship God at the same time: they just continued sacrificing to Him, singing songs and raising their hands to Him in prayer. Isaiah assured them in the most direct of terms that that would never work! However, he gave them a promise: if they came to God, their sins – scarlet as they were – would be washed away and they would be made pure and blameless again.

Today, God promises us the same! Remember, our sin primarily is not in our misdeeds as such, but in our obstinacy and hypocrisy. Sinful deeds are merely the results of our defiance. Listen: God completely knows your weaknesses and failings, but He waits on you and me to wholly turn to Him, to include Him in our struggles and our sins. If you come to Him, humbly and sincerely, He will establish you into a new relationship with Him and give you a fresh start. With Him you have a wonderful new year ahead!

Lord, You know me through and through. You know my sin.
You also know that I really want to live my life with You! Amen.

If you come to God in earnest and are willing
to share your life with Him, He promises you a new beginning –
and a wonderful year with Him.

Enjoy the Blessings

If you are willing and obedient, you shall eat the good of the land.
Isaiah 1:19 ESV

It's interesting that this verse refers to two separate actions in its condition. The first is to be willing to obey God. It has to do with the right attitude, a right heart: a heart that loves God and wants to please Him, even though it doesn't always succeed. It's willing and it's trying! Remember that God is firstly interested in our heart. A right heart is the prerequisite for true obedience – mere outward observance or cold compliance by someone whose heart is far from Him, doesn't please God. The question therefore is: do you love God; do you want to do His will?

Then comes the second action: to obey as such. Obedience is important, so let's obey! However, according to Scripture and our experience, our compliance to God's will is always lacking. We are human and weak: we want to obey, but we rarely make it! Because of this God sent His obedient Son who fully complied on our behalf. Our obedience now is not to merit anything before the Father, but just to show our love to Him. The verse concludes with the sure promise of blessing! Take your promise, but tell me: are you willing today to love God?

Lord, I want to love You and I do love You.
I want to obey – help me to obey! Amen.

If your heart is right and you truly want to serve God,
He promises that you will reap the rewards of your obedience –
even in your everyday life.

Melt and then Shine

"I will turn My hand against you and will smelt away your dross as with lye and remove all your alloy."

Isaiah 1:25 ESV

God showed His people their sins – godlessness, unrighteousness, corruption, greed, etc. Nothing has changed, has it? Then He gave a promise: He would intervene! They were after all His people, and He remained committed to His covenant with them. Therefore – ironically – He would "turn His hand against them." When God's hand is passive in our lives, nothing happens, but that would mean that God doesn't care. However, He does care and He does intervene! Therefore His mighty hand moves. Remember, God's hand moving isn't always pleasant, but it's always good for us.

Here He promises to cleanse His people. Lead was often found in the silver ore and had to be burnt off. The artisans would melt the silver and scoop away the dross containing the impurities. Lye (potash and natron) were used to accelerate the process. The pure silver that wouldn't oxidize was then left behind. God says He will work with us in the same way: the lead will be worked out of our lives so that the silver can remain. Don't become disheartened by this! Oh no, it is the most worthwhile attention God can give us! Listen: God is actively involved in your life! That is why these things happen.

Lord, I see Your hand moving in my life.
Finish what You have started! Amen.

God promises He is constantly at work in your life.
He is busy cleaning out the impurities in your life
and transforming you into something beautiful.

You Will See Zion

Zion shall be redeemed by justice, and those in her who repent, by righteousness.

Isaiah 1:27 ESV

God promised to deal with His people. They were far from where they should be, but He loved them. They were His children! Therefore He intervened. He wanted to restore Israel to "Zion": Jerusalem as a Holy City, as the habitation of God – in which we also see the "New Jerusalem" that the Bible speaks of. God promised that it would happen!

The same goes for us. God has an image in mind of what we should become – a worthy and shining temple of God, full of love and grace, reflecting His glory! He doesn't want to take away our individuality – no, that's what He so loves in us – but He wants to take away that which is wrong in us. We often live a false life and He wants to bring us to our true selves – hallelujah! He wants to make us more of how we should be, more us! He's at the moment actively busy with exactly that – He already brought us to Christ and is now busy transforming our lives. We should actively work together with God in this; "daily conversion" means to commit yourself again and again willingly and purposefully to God's involvement.

Lord, I'm still not where I should be,
but I'm further than where I was.
Continue to work in my life! Amen.

God promises to restore your life into a worthy temple for Him.
God is transforming you every day. Allow Him to work in you.

You Will See the Fulfillment

Many people will come and say, "Let's go to the mountain of the LORD God of Jacob and worship in His temple."

Isaiah 2:3 CEV

God's promise was that Israel would be restored and that Jerusalem, or Zion, would take its place as the capital of the world. God would rule from there! Isaiah foresaw that people from all nations would come to worship and seek Him there. We might believe that this will happen literally on that day when God joins us and the New Jerusalem is established forever. Yes, then God will wipe away all tears and we'll live in His love forever!

But for now, take note: the fulfillment of this prophecy – by an unknown prophet around 700 BC in a tiny corner of the world – has already started. In fact, the whole of history made a shift in order to accommodate it! This "unimportant" country and the "unknown" God of Israel took the center-stage of the world scene in Jesus Christ. History literally started to hinge around Him!

Today billions of followers (let alone the billions of the past) look to Jerusalem as the Holy City, the place of His revelation – just as the prophet said. What is the lesson? God's promises are true, true, true!

Thank You, Lord, for making every promise true! Amen.

If God made a promise, it will be fulfilled.
Nothing can stand in the way of it coming to pass.
You can fully trust that God will keep His promises.

You'll Not Always Fight

He will settle arguments between nations. They will pound their swords and their spears into rakes and shovels; they will never make war or attack one another.

Isaiah 2:4 CEV

What Isaiah wrote here was a promise. Peace is the future! All strife and struggle is only temporary – in the world and also in your life. All the misery that conflict and war brings, the anguish and the tears would come to an end. God would step in and restore order! Justice and peace, love and grace, dignity and respect would be reinstated. Take note: this has already started in Jesus Christ! When God's Son, the "Prince of Peace" was born, the angels sang, "Peace on earth, good will to all men."

Indeed, Christ's message is one of love, even for our enemies. He said, "Blessed are the peacemakers." He Himself brings peace into the hearts of all who follow Him – and that's only the start! When He returns, He will establish peace to the whole world. Wars will cease, as the prophet said, and the weapons of war will be melted down.

Do you also get so tired of all the fighting, the never-ending quarrels, the unnecessary hostility? Do what you can about it, but remember: it won't be forever.

Come, Lord! We await Your peace! Amen.

God promises an end to the struggle –
and your personal struggle too. You will enjoy peace –
not only in eternity, but already now in your heart.

You'll See Them Fall

And the haughtiness of man shall be humbled, and the lofty pride of men shall be brought low, and the LORD alone will be exalted in that day.

Isaiah 2:17 ESV

The Day of the Lord (in Hebrew: *Yom Yahweh*) is a prominent theme in biblical prophecy. When God intervenes in history – on the last day – it will be a day of judgment for the godless and for hardened sinners. It is interesting that Isaiah described them as "proud" and "haughty", or arrogant. That is absolutely the scriptural view of what sin is at its core. Pride is the first sin, because it disconnects us from God. It believes it doesn't need God; it refuses to bow before Him. On that day though, the arrogant will bow, says the Bible. That's why it's important that we learn to bow to God in this life already, to humble ourselves.

Remember, the very beginning of a relationship with God, ground zero, is to acknowledge our need and put our hand out for Him to take. Yes, it's a humbling thing to do, but remember that Jesus said, "Blessed are the poor in spirit", which refers to exactly such an attitude. For the humble the Day of the Lord will come as a deliverance – that's a promise!

Lord, I need You and I put out my hand to You.
Please take it! Amen.

God promises a future judgment over all. However, if you have already humbled yourself before the Lord, that day will be one of joyful redemption for you.

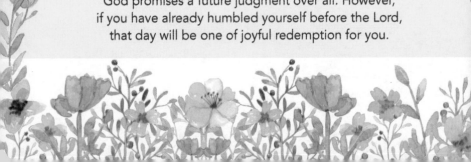

You'll Enjoy the Fruit

Tell the righteous that it shall be well with them, for they shall eat the fruit of their deeds.

Isaiah 3:10 ESV

Isaiah predicted dark days for the godless of his time. He especially aimed at the corrupt spiritual and political leaders, although the common folk were joining them *en masse*. This whole chapter is straightforward doom and gloom, but then the prophet turned to the righteous. For them he had a promise right out of God's heart! Let's phrase that message as follows: when the tree is good, the fruit will be good – there can be no exceptions. The righteous will bear good fruit! It's a natural and spiritual law.

Scripture says it's the Holy Spirit that works in us to bear the fruit of love, joy, peace, patience, etc. That is the fruit that pleases God! If we find more love, joy, peace and so on in our lives, we can know that God is present and working in us, and we're really transforming into loving and grateful and fully-alive beings! Take hold of His promise and keep pursuing your growth.

*Holy Spirit, take charge of my life and bear
the fruit in me that will give glory to God. Amen.*

If you are righteous before God, in other words,
if you have truly accepted Christ and want to follow Him,
He promises you good fruit in your life. Everyone will see it.

You'll Enter the Kingdom

And he who is left in Zion and remains in Jerusalem will be called holy, everyone who has been recorded for life in Jerusalem.

Isaiah 4:3 ESV

When God has finished judging His people, only the righteous will remain. Then God will rule in a new way. New values will be lived by. That's what Jesus calls the kingdom of God. In the old Jerusalem holiness was an external matter: Jews were in principle holier than other nations, Jewish men more so than women, Levites more than ordinary men, priests more than Levites and the high priest was the holiest of men. Also geographically holiness was accorded to Jerusalem as a city (more holy than other cities), then the Temple court with its increasingly holy areas for Gentiles, women and men, then the Sanctuary itself and ultimately the Holiest of Holies. None of this would remain, says Isaiah. In that day all whose hearts are focused on God will be called holy (*kadosh*).

God will raise up a new nation for Himself, the prophet says, a holy priesthood of ordinary people! Where He resides in a heart, He makes it holy. He establishes His kingdom among ordinary and sincere folk. That's you and me, if we serve Him! We already live in that Kingdom, but one day the kingdom of God will break through in its fullness. If we remain sincere and dependent, He – the Holy God – will work a great work through us!

Lord, I am unworthy of Your holiness,
yet You establish Your kingdom in my heart ... thank You! Amen.

If you truly serve God, He promises to establish
His kingdom in your life. Everything will change –
you will start looking and acting more and more like Him.

You'll See the Cloud

Then the LORD will cover the whole city and its meeting places
with a thick cloud each day and with a flaming fire each night.
God's own glory will be like a huge tent that covers everything.

Isaiah 4:5 CEV

Isaiah was talking about the Day of the Lord, when God would intervene
physically. On that day He will remove all sin – everything remaining will
be holy. When is that day? That day has already started! See it like this: the
end times started when the Messiah, Jesus Christ, introduced the Messianic
Era with His appearing. Many end time promises were fulfilled! God indeed
became man and entered the world personally. The Kingdom came "near"
as Jesus said. However, Jesus also said not everything would happen immediately. There would be an overlap of time.

The end has started, but it's not yet finished. The nations must first be
brought in (amongst other things) and then the (final) end will come. That
will be the Day of the Lord, the return of Christ. We already experience
spiritually what one day will come physically. Read again what Isaiah said:
God establishes His presence and protection over every believer like the
cloud of old, like a canopy (the word there is *chuppa*) over you. Yes, you
are also covered – look up with your mind's eye, perceive it in faith! It's a
promise.

Thank You, Lord, for the protection of the cloud,
for the guidance of the fiery pillar through the desert. Amen.

God promises to keep you safe under His fiery pillar of protection
that He personally places over you. You can simply relax.

He'll Hide You

There will be a booth for shade by day from the heat, and for a refuge and a shelter from the storm and rain.

Isaiah 4:6 ESV

What a wonderful promise! The prophet was describing the time when the kingdom of God would come near, which started with Jesus – according to His own words. God will always provide shelter for us, a refuge. Take note that in this verse there's no promise that there won't be heat, or storms, or rain – no, the adversities will be there, but in the adversities there will be a wonderful resting place, a hiding place. The Hebrew word here carries with it the connotation of a secret hideout, of concealment.

Elsewhere in the Bible God also describes the protection of His church in much the same way. A hideaway, friend, is God's promise to you! Sometimes we just need to close the door behind us and regain our composure. When things are bad, we sometimes want to disappear somewhere where no one will find us – even if it's just for a little while.

Sometimes we just need time alone with God. Some pull a Jewish prayer shawl (a *talit*) over their heads when they feel like that. Whatever happens – whatever the storm, whatever the flood – with God we will be safe.

Thank You, Lord, for being my resting place, my hideaway. Amen.

God promises that you can find refuge with Him in times of adversity. He will immediately provide you with shelter.

Your Eyes Will See Him

In the year that King Uzziah died I saw the Lord sitting upon a throne, high and lifted up; and the train of His robe filled the temple.

Isaiah 6:1 ESV

Isaiah had an experience that he would never forget. In spite of the warning that no one could see God and live, he saw God! Isaiah's experience is described like a vision, a dream: on a very high throne he saw God. What God looked like couldn't be described exactly, because in front of him, filling the whole temple was God's robe. He also remembered the fiery seraphs, their loud voices, the doorposts that shook and the smoke in the room. What does it mean? Well, Jewish commentators believe that what Isaiah saw, was God's "glory" or *Shekinah*, His manifestation or visible presence, which was around Him like a robe. More importantly, John states that Isaiah saw Christ, who is God's glorious revelation (see John 12:41).

To us, Christ is God made manifest! Let's take it one step further: the Bible promises that one day we too will see Him like He is, in His glory, with our very own eyes! Until then we can experience something of His glory in our prayer, our worship, our lives.

Jesus, one day I will see You in Your full glory, but today, let me experience just some of that glory in my prayer. Amen.

God promises that the day will come when you will see Him in all His glory – at His throne – along with all of His other children.

The Fire Will Touch You

It touched my lips with the hot coal and said, "This has touched your lips. Your sins are forgiven, and you are no longer guilty."

Isaiah 6:7 CEV

Isaiah experienced a vision of God on the throne. The powerful presence of the Lord, His holiness and glory, overwhelmed him in such a way that he immediately felt dirty, guilty! He knew that everything he did and said was unclean. So he shouted out for help *"I'm doomed!"* It's interesting that we don't need an argument about our sin and condition before God. Arguments and reasoning will not bring someone to repentance – it only leads to more arguments and excuses. However, meeting with God will immediately show us who and what we are and bring us to our knees.

On Isaiah's confession of sin an angel flew towards him with a coal from the altar. He touched his lips with it and declared him purified, forgiven. Because of the altar his sins were expiated and he became reconciled to God. The altar, of course, is the Cross of Christ. On that altar the Lamb of God offered Himself fully and finally for all our sins – past, present and future. On our own confession, the fire from that sacrifice will also completely cleanse us. That fire is still burning, do you want it?

Lord, come with Your living fire,
forgive me and brand me as Your own. Amen.

If you realize and admit your inadequacy
and brokenness before God, He promises you
immediate forgiveness because of the Cross of Christ.

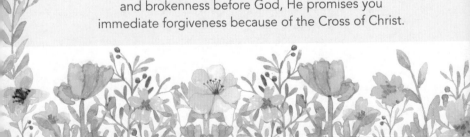

Go – God Sends You

"Whom shall I send, and who will go for us?" Then I said, "Here I am! Send me."

Isaiah 6:8 ESV

In Isaiah's vision he experienced God's holiness and his own sinfulness. An angel came and cleansed him with the fire from the altar that always burns between God and man. Then he heard God's voice for the first time – from the high and exalted throne it sounded, "Whom shall I send?" Isaiah was willing to go. Take note that Isaiah's answer was probably not out of eagerness to become a prophet – it turned out to be a very unpleasant and hard assignment! No, his feelings were not at stake here at all – the Almighty called and he had to comply. That's all. Actually there was no choice. It would've been unbelievably impudent, unthinkably rude, to just refuse God's order. No, the only answer God deserves is "yes".

You can try to run away from God's call, like Jonah did, but it will catch up with you and you will obey it in the end. Do you have a call from God? Yes, you have! Our general calling is to go and be ourselves to His glory, but you could also have some specific calling on your life. You cannot refuse.

Lord, here I am! I want to be more me – for You! Amen.

If you answer "yes" to God's calling,
He promises to use you in a special way.
You will be able to convey God's glory in your own way.

You Have Something He Can Use

"But just as stumps remain after trees have been cut down, some of My chosen ones will be left."

Isaiah 6:13 CEV

Isaiah got a message from God, but unfortunately the news was not good. God planned to withdraw and allow the land to be destroyed. He was not interested in sharing the limelight with every idol and false god one can think of. And so it happened, because soon afterwards the 10 "lost tribes" of Israel were captured and taken to Assyria, never to be heard of again. Eighty percent of the people of Israel were cut off – what a loss! God even said He would cut off the whole tree.

However, as it always is with God, the situation was not without hope. God says a stump will remain, and from that stump a new tree will grow. Indeed the remaining tribes of Judah and Benjamin became the new nation of the Judeans, which we today call the Jews. Paul came in New Testament times and said that the whole of the Christian Church was also grafted into that Jewish stump … what a huge tree it is now! The lesson today is this: God always finds something to work with. Your life is never in such pieces that He cannot make something completely new. He can! Just offer it to Him.

Lord, take the little that I have, take anything You want, and make something new in my life. Amen.

If you give yourself to the Lord, He promises that He can and will use something in your life. You will eventually come to realize what it is that God is using in you.

It Won't Happen

Thus says the LORD God: "It shall not stand, and it shall not come to pass."

Isaiah 7:7 ESV

Ahaz, the king of Judah, was anxious because the enemy was occupying his land. His troops had to retreat before the Arameans and had fallen back to the region around Jerusalem. In the meanwhile the enemy was ravaging the countryside. Ahaz heard the disconcerting news that the enemy already had a new king in mind for when they took over Jerusalem. He was shaking like a tree in the wind. Isaiah met him at the army encampment to give him God's word.

Read this verse again. Wonderful! The Lord then also said that the enemy was "only Damascus", which is ironic because Damascus was the big city of the region and most definitely a huge threat! But not for God. Isaiah was reframing the situation for Ahaz – giving him God's perspective. God looked down on Damascus and was not intimidated. He would put a stop to the Arameans. Then the threat disappeared.

I have learned that the things I have feared as threats in my life – health wise, financially, personally – have almost always disappeared later on. Don't fear. God is part of the picture!

Lord, thank You that this problem
is no problem for You. Amen.

God promises that He is indeed present in your life.
He has a different perspective on your problem
and He will handle it in His own way.

Faith Will Establish You

If ye will not believe, surely ye shall not be established.

Isaiah 7:9 KJV

When the Arameans invaded the country, Isaiah went to reassure king Ahaz. He said that God would save them from calamity. God wasn't intimidated by the enemy. Within years the Arameans would themselves fall before the much greater might of the upcoming Assyrians. Then he warned Ahaz to cling to these promises in faith.

Remember, a promise in itself is wonderful, but it's only half of the picture. God gives it to us to help us through the onslaughts and rough times. However, it must be accepted in our lives with faith. What does that mean? Remember that faith isn't just a theoretical truth in our minds, or even our hearts. Yes, that's where it takes root, but faith then converts into practice in our lives.

To become a life-giving power, faith should live in our words and in our deeds. Therefore: say what you believe to yourself, to others, to God in your prayers – for example, that God will intervene. Confess it! Then, live it! Act as if it's already so. Just carry on. Stand in faith until your situation changes.

Lord, I confess and believe that You are in this matter.
I will wait on You. Amen.

If you faithfully hold onto God's character in general
and to His promises in particular, God promises
that you will stand firm through the rough times.

You Can Ask for a Sign

Ask a sign of the LORD your God; let it be deep as Sheol or high as heaven.

Isaiah 7:11 ESV

Isaiah had a message for king Ahaz, who was afraid of the Arameans. God promised him salvation. Then Isaiah informed Ahaz that he may also ask God for a sign – something to encourage him in his need. Ahaz refused and said that he didn't want to "test" God. It sounds spiritual, but it angered Isaiah, because he knew that the king had already decided not to trust God – he had decided to go into an alliance with the Assyrians. But let's leave Ahaz for the moment.

May we ask God for a sign? Yes, of course we may! In our distress or insecurity we often have the need for guidance or encouragement. However, we should approach this with care – God is communicating indeed, but we can make mistakes in hearing. Take note:

If you hear God's encouragement – albeit from the Bible, a conversation, a sermon, something happening or perhaps something that you read somewhere – take it joyfully;

However, if it is a heavy word, or one with far-reaching implications, be careful. Take your time with it. Seek confirmation – discuss it with a spiritual mentor.

We have such a need for God in our lives! But be very patient – we're only human.

Lord, my need is not so much for a sign, but for You in my life! Amen.

If you sincerely ask for God's guidance and openly anticipate it,
He promises that you will receive it. However, be wise in your
deductions – discuss it with mature believers.

You'll Receive a Sign

> But the LORD will still give you proof. A virgin is pregnant; she will
> have a Son and will name Him Immanuel.
>
> *Isaiah 7:14* CEV

King Ahaz didn't want a sign from God, because he wasn't trusting God in his crisis – he had already made his own plan. Isaiah said that God was so tired of the royal house not consulting Him, but He would give them a sign anyway. With us it's the same, not so? When the crisis hits us, we are immediately, anxiously making plans. God isn't in the picture! Later on perhaps we'll remember to take the matter to Him. Still, God is always communicating, whether we're listening or not. It's like a radio station that's broadcasting around the clock, but only those who have their radios tuned to it can hear it.

We need to be much more attuned to God and what He's saying to us. If we focus our hearts on hearing from Him, we'll discern messages from God every day! They will come from the Bible, via other people, through circumstances, from something we've read on the side of a bus – sometimes the most unusual places – the signs are everywhere!

Lord, I know that I don't always listen,
but today I want to hear Your voice. Amen.

If you open your eyes to God's presence,
He promises that you will see it everywhere – in so many ways.

God Is There With You

Behold, the virgin shall conceive and bear a Son, and shall call His name Immanuel.

Isaiah 7:14 ESV

Isaiah had a message for King Ahaz, who was afraid of the enemy invading his country. He had to take notice of this sign: a woman would have a child and name Him – in that stressful time – Immanuel, which means "God is with us." What faith! That alone should have served as a sign for the fearful Ahaz.

There was, however, a second sign involved: before the child could even know the difference between good and bad the enemy would be totally destroyed. It happened exactly so – within years the whole scene changed, because God was with them! Finally, the sign had been seen, in the New Testament, as a prediction of the Messiah.

Jesus Christ is Immanuel: God that came to be with us – and who's still with us! So, if the enemy threatens us or trouble faces us, we can look at the sign: God has been born among us in the person of Jesus Christ. God loved us and took such pity on us that He wanted to come and be with us. He is also there with you.

Thank You, Lord, for coming to us – to me – today. Amen.

Jesus Christ is the manifestation of God's presence with us. He is also intimately and intensely involved with you through His Holy Spirit. It's a promise!

You Are Being Protected

"… it will sweep on into Judah, it will overflow and pass on, reaching even to the neck, and its outspread wings will fill the breadth of your land, O Immanuel."

Isaiah 8:8 ESV

Isaiah prophesied that the enemy would overrun the country. They would fly in like flies and wasps from Egypt and Assyria, and come and settle in all the cliffs and ravines of the mountains – and from there they would attack. It sounds like the plagues of Egypt – unleashed on Israel! It would come in like a flood sweeping over the land like a dark wing. It was an ominous prediction, evil even – like a nightmare! The message is very clear though: however dark the days that were predicted, in the same breath there was the promise that God would be with them.

Faith always leads to hope. Are you in the valley of the shadow of death? Are you experiencing turmoil and onslaught? You will not fear, because His rod and His staff protects you.

Thank You, Lord, for protecting me –
it gives me hope for full deliverance. Amen.

Even if you experience all sorts of attacks and adversity,
God promises to protect you. His specific promise today is:
"I am with you."

You Won't Fear

"I am the one you should fear and respect … Run to Me for protection."

Isaiah 8:13-14 CEV

Isaiah warned the people not to get carried away. They heard fearful rumors of a conspiracy against them – still having to do with the Arameans. He said they shouldn't be alarmed. Their fear should be towards God, not towards man. What he was trying to tell them was that they were listening to the wrong voices. We make the same mistake.

We lend our ears easily to the scary tales of people – and we hear such a lot of dreadful stories nowadays in the world! Fear easily steals our joy, our trust, our hope! It also takes away our love, because we struggle to love those who we fear or anger us.

We should change our input and start listening to God instead: what does He say in this situation? Is there really a reason for fear with Him in the picture? What role does our faith play then? No, fear is not a fitting disposition for a child of God! When we fear God, we needn't also fear man.

Lord, I choose not to fear –
let me hear Your voice! Amen.

God wants you to listen to Him rather than to people.
He promises that you will then experience safety, not fear.

You Have a Future

To the teaching and to the testimony! If they will not speak according to this word, it is because they have no dawn.

Isaiah 8:20 ESV

Oh, the people! See how they reacted to the threat of the enemy: they wallowed in fear, but managed to avoid God and then – the cherry on top – they turned to spiritualists and mediums! Can those already dead give guidance to the living? Isaiah was exasperated. He asked why people would consult with spirits of the dead, but not their own God? He cried out, "Back to the teaching and the testimony!" (of the *Torah*, their Scripture). For those who return to the Lord He promised a future, survival through their current circumstances.

That is your promise too. However, those who seek their help elsewhere – especially from the adversary – have a dark future ahead of them. For those He cannot promise a "dawn", in other words a sunrise, a tomorrow. They're in the dark and most likely will stay there. No friend – let the sun rise!

Lord, I turn my back on the darkness
and I seek Your light, Your will. Amen.

If you stay away from evil and seek help from God only,
He promises to give you a future, a new day. He gives you new hope!

Leave It to Him

"The holy God, who is the light of Israel, will turn into a fire."

Isaiah 10:17 CEV

The Israelites were afraid of the Arameans, their immediate neighbors, who were strong at that stage. The Lord said the Arameans were not to be feared because in turn they would succumb to the much greater power of the Assyrians – as would Israel itself, unfortunately. Yes, God used the Assyrians to punish Israel. But then God would turn on the Assyrians – their fate was also sealed! He would put a fire into them that would burn them out like a dry bush. And so it was.

Do we even remember the Assyrians? They were taken over by the Babylonians, under Nebuchadnezzar, who were in turn taken over by the Persians under Darius and Xerxes. Who ever thinks of them? The Persians were defeated by Alexander, who established the Greek empire and in turn had to give way to the Romans. It's all ancient history – all before the birth of Christ!

Let's now talk about your big threat. What is that in God's eyes? It's nothing. How important is that going to be in 10 years or 100 years from now? Leave the things that frighten you to God. Focus on today and focus on Him. That's all.

Lord, today I give away my small worries to a big God. Amen.

The Lord promises that your major problems,
which are small for Him, shall pass. Seasons come and seasons go,
but a relationship with God remains.

Your Promise, but New

For though your people Israel be as the sand of the sea, only a remnant of them will return.

Isaiah 10:22 ESV

God's promises are true – we can take that as a fact. We should, however, add the following: the way God fulfills His promises often differs from what we expected, or would have wanted. Look at today's verse. God originally promised Abraham that his descendants would be as many as the sand of the sea, and also that they would inherit the land (of Israel). Both promises were fulfilled. In Isaiah's time the Israelites were very populous in their two countries. However, since the conditions that accompanied God's promise were not met, God allowed for most of them to be lost from the nation. Only a remnant remained.

Does that mean that God isn't fulfilling His promises anymore? No, not at all. The fulfillment was there for everyone to see! Then He dealt with them in a new way, with new promises. God always works dynamically, always new – as it happens in any living relationship, not so? You and I are always in a vitally current relationship with God. What is He saying to you today?

Thank You, Lord, for sharing with me anew today. Amen.

God assures us that His promises will be fulfilled,
but He also wants a dynamic, sharing relationship with you.
He never stops speaking. Keep listening and seeking Him today.

The Spirit of the Lord Upon You

There shall come forth a shoot from the stump of Jesse, and a branch from his roots shall bear fruit. And the Spirit of the LORD shall rest upon Him.

Isaiah 11:1-2 ESV

Isaiah saw into the future and described what would happen. The tree of Israel would be cut down, but then a shoot would grow out from the stump. He was referring to the Messiah. He said that the "Spirit of the LORD", i.e. the "Spirit of Yahweh", would rest upon Him. When Christ (which means "Messiah") was born, the prophecy was fulfilled. The Spirit of the Lord was on Him, but then He also gave the same Spirit onto His disciples.

We are also recipients of that Spirit of the Lord! *Yahweh*, the covenant name of God, means I *am*, or I *will be*. It reminds us that the presence of the Almighty God in our lives is a given. Whatever we do, wherever we go, God is with us. Enter therefore, like Abraham, into a personal covenant with *Yahweh*! Then He will deposit His Spirit into your heart in order to be with you personally, as your trustworthy Partner, as the subtle voice in your heart.

Yes, I want to live in constant covenant with You, Lord!
Give me Your Spirit. Amen.

Yahweh, the Lord God, promises that through His Spirit, He will be with you personally and permanently – as your friend and your partner.

The Spirit of Wisdom

> There shall come forth a shoot from the stump of Jesse ... And the Spirit of the LORD shall rest upon Him, the Spirit of wisdom and understanding.
>
> *Isaiah 11:1-2 ESV*

Isaiah prophesied that the Messiah would be filled with the Holy Spirit, for whom He had seven names. Because of this, some people talk about the "sevenfold Spirit." The promise of the Spirit is also meant for us, because the Messiah poured out the same Spirit on His disciples.

Today we'll focus on the second name of the Spirit, i.e. the Spirit of wisdom. Wisdom is more than knowledge or experience; it is insight into life, into the bigger picture, into the heart of God. It also has to do with correct behavior. Wisdom is always practical!

The Bible distinguishes between heavenly wisdom and earthly wisdom and it is the former that is the work of the Spirit of wisdom – and the wisdom which we seek. The Spirit-filled person is a wise person: they have the right word for the right time and know how to act sensibly – what to do and when to do it, when to act and when to wait. How such wisdom is needed! You can start by not reacting impulsively. Wisdom is considered behavior.

Holy Spirit, give me Your wisdom. Amen.

God promises you the Spirit of wisdom. If you wait on Him,
He will lead you and teach you what to say and what to do.

The Spirit of Understanding

There shall come forth a shoot from the stump of Jesse ... And the Spirit of the LORD shall rest upon Him, the Spirit of wisdom and understanding.

Isaiah 11:1-2 ESV

Isaiah prophesied about the coming of the Messiah. He said that the sevenfold Spirit would be on Him. We're currently looking at the seven names of the Holy Spirit and today we discuss the third one: the Spirit of understanding.

The focus is definitely more on the intellect with this name – to comprehend, to know rationally. Sometimes there's an idea among Christians that a strong mind is not "spiritual", but rather "natural", or even "worldly." Shouldn't we rather focus on the promptings of the Spirit? That's not completely true.

There are three ways of approaching God, and each of us follows a way that is unique to us: (1) the way of the head, i.e. by study and teaching; (2) the way of the heart, i.e. by prayer and worship; and (3) the way of the hands, i.e. by service or activism. Let's not judge each other! A thorough understanding and exposition of sound doctrine prevents God's people from just following every other teaching. It's also wonderful if you sit with the Bible and the Holy Spirit comes and breaks it open in all its dimensions. Yes, that's Spirit-worked understanding!

Lord, enlighten my mind,
and open Your heart and will to me. Amen.

God promises you the Spirit of understanding. If you wait on Him, He will give you knowledge, insight and understanding on what the Word says and what God means.

The Spirit of Counsel

> And the Spirit of the LORD shall rest upon Him, the Spirit of wisdom and understanding, the Spirit of counsel and might.
>
> *Isaiah 11:2 ESV*

The Holy Spirit will rest on the Messiah, said Isaiah – and also on us, because the same Spirit was poured out at Pentecost. Isaiah gives the Spirit seven names and we're discussing the fourth name today, namely the Spirit of counsel.

The Holy Spirit is indeed called the Advocate, the Encourager, the Consoler, the Counselor. The Spirit is God who passionately defends you when you're accused; God who comes alongside you saying, "Yes, you can"; God who puts His hand on your shoulder when you cry and reassures you that everything will be all right; God who patiently listens and knows what you're going through, showing you new ways of handling things. That is the work of the Spirit! You and I are privileged to have such a Friend we can bother with our problems, our worries, our questions – with whom we can just be ourselves. His love for us is such that we can never, ever understand it! I pray that the guidance and counsel and support of the Spirit of God will be with you!

Holy Spirit, thank You for being with me
in such wonderful ways. Amen.

God promises you the Spirit of counsel. If you wait on Him,
He will give you advice, encourage you and lead you –
to deal with your circumstances.

The Spirit of Might

And the Spirit of the LORD shall rest upon Him, the Spirit of wisdom and understanding, the Spirit of counsel and might.

Isaiah 11:2 ESV

The fifth name of the Holy Spirit, of which we read in Isaiah, is the Spirit of might. Remember that Jesus said we'll receive power when the Spirit comes on us. Sometimes we're disappointed by our own lack of strength – when the big storm hits, we feel that we cannot handle it, that our fear has paralyzed us, that we have been robbed of the last ounce of power. We want to resist, but we cannot! That is completely normal and okay.

Here is God's promise: when fear hits you like a wave, you will be engulfed in it and completely feel it. That's okay. Then it will leave you. On the other side of your fear you will find God's power. If you have nothing left of your strength, that's okay. God's power is strongest in our weakness! That is why we have God in our lives – to become for us what we cannot be for ourselves.

Don't trust your feelings, because emotions are fickle. Hold onto God and His promises in faith. That will be your strength.

Thank You, Holy Spirit,
for Your strength when I am weak. Amen.

God promises you the Spirit of might. If you wait on Him,
He will encourage and inspire you, equip you and give you power –
regardless of the circumstances or your limitations.

The Spirit of Knowledge

And the Spirit of the LORD shall rest upon Him … the Spirit of knowledge and the fear of the LORD.

Isaiah 11:2 ESV

The sixth name of the Holy Spirit, that Isaiah mentioned, is the Spirit of knowledge. We already said that knowledge and reason – a sharp intellect – is a gift from God. However, the Spirit comes and adds to our natural abilities His supernatural ability: the gift of knowledge can be seen as specific, divine insight in a situation. Sometimes we just don't know what's happening, or what to do. Then we can ask the Holy Spirit – He can give us insight into the spiritual dynamics of things and guide us into how to pray or to act.

There's also a third level of knowledge that the Spirit gives and that is to know God. It still remains the biggest wonder that we can know God and get to know Him more and more. In the Bible to "know" someone is an intimate matter – it suggests unity. Also, to know someone requires a certain revelation, a personal revealing. We allow someone to get to know us. How wonderful that God reveals Himself to us through His Spirit!

Lord, You know me better than I know myself;
thank You that I may also know You! Amen.

God promises you the Spirit of knowledge.
If you wait on Him, He will reveal to you His special knowledge,
including the knowledge of God Himself.

February

The Fear of the Lord

And the Spirit of the LORD shall rest upon Him ... the Spirit of knowledge and the fear of the LORD.

Isaiah 11:2 ESV

Isaiah predicted that the Holy Spirit would be on the Messiah, and then he described the Spirit using seven names. Some therefore call Him the sevenfold Spirit, thinking also of the enigmatic "seven spirits" in front of God's throne in Revelation.

We have already discussed six of these names and today we come to the last: the Spirit of the fear of the Lord. To "fear" God is the Old Testament's description of a righteous person's stance towards the Almighty. It means to have deep reverence or respect for God, to recognize His might and demands – and, yes, to fear being found on His wrong side!

In the New Testament the whole perspective changes because of Jesus Christ. Jesus took the full burden of God's judgment on the cross, so if we are now "found in Christ", we are fully reconciled to God. Of course we'll always be in awe of Him and have deep respect for Him, but we're not children who are afraid of our Father. No, we love Him, and He loves us! Take that as a promise.

Holy Spirit, thank You for creating a relationship between God and me. Amen.

God promises you the Spirit of the fear of the Lord.
The Holy Spirit awakens in you a deep respect for God and,
above all an overwhelming love.

God Knows You

He shall not judge by what His eyes see, or decide disputes by what His ears hear.

Isaiah 11:3 ESV

Isaiah prophesied the coming of the Messiah-King and said that He would rule and judge fairly, impartially. Let's start by saying when the Messianic Era will be. The Messianic Era is now! Jesus came as the Messiah of God and as such ushered in the Messianic Era. With His coming, many Messianic prophesies were fulfilled. Many are still outstanding, though, because the Messianic Era, although already started, has not yet been concluded. The Messiah Himself said that these final things would happen at the end of the time, when He returns and eternity breaks into this realm.

In the meanwhile, we can already experience the kingdom of God. The Kingdom is already "near!" For example, we know this King – we know His kind heart and His just ways! He doesn't merely judge us outwardly – He knows us, by His Spirit, from the inside. He knows your thoughts, your emotions, your motives, your heart! He knows you better than you know yourself! No one is as near to you as He is. What's more: His knowledge of you is saturated by His love for you through Jesus Christ. We have nothing to fear of the King's judgment.

*Thank You, Lord, that You live inside of me
and that You know me! Amen.*

God promises that He knows you intimately and that He deals with you according to your own heart and mind. You can trust in His love.

Eternal Peace for You

Leopards will lie down with young goats, and wolves will rest with lambs.

Isaiah 11:6 CEV

Isaiah predicted the coming of the Messianic Era, which will be a time of peace. When Christ, the Prince of Peace, was born He brought a peace that no one could ever bring. Millions were reconciled with God and received His peace – the true peace – in their hearts – the "peace that surpasses all understanding."

Peace with God is more important than peace between countries, because a relationship with God comes first. The Jews of Jesus' time, however, expected the Messiah to physically bring salvation (from the Roman invaders), to physically rule in Jerusalem, to physically establish peace between countries. That's why Christ was rejected – as a failed Messiah! However, the early believers saw that these prophesies were fulfilled in a spiritual way. In Christ the lion and the lamb came together, as prophesied … because He was both. When Christ returns, He will usher in the "age to come," in which He will rule physically and set up eternal peace. Then the lion and the lamb will physically have peace! The lesson, however, is this: you don't have to wait for the Messiah to one day bring the peace you need – you can enter into that peace today!

Yes, Lord, I want to share in Your eternal peace today! Amen.

God promises that one day perfect peace will prevail, but He also wants to give you peace today. If you give everything over to Him, that peace will come down and rest on you.

You'll See the Glory

For the earth shall be full of the knowledge of the LORD as the waters cover the sea.

Isaiah 11:9 NKJV

The prophets often looked ahead and foresaw the day when everyone would know and serve God, when everyone's knee would bow, everyone's tongue would confess; when the glory of the Lord would fill the earth! Isn't God, after all, the Creator of it all, the Father of everyone?

Unfortunately, there will be those who turn their backs on the Creator, the Father, those who refuse Him. Therefore, according to prophecy, there will be a cleansing so that ultimately the whole earth will indeed know and serve Him. Then the glory of the Lord will cover the earth, "as the waters cover the sea."

Why does Isaiah tell the people these things? Well, he offers them hope amidst fear and hopelessness, and he wants them to be ready for God when He comes. We must be part of that remnant! Yes, be part of it.

Thank You, Lord, for new hope – and that You
will also save me on that day. Amen.

God promises that those who sincerely serve Him
will push through and experience how His glory fills the whole earth.
You will know God like never before!

You Will Be Counted

He … will assemble the banished of Israel, and gather the dispersed of Judah from the four corners of the earth.

Isaiah 11:12 ESV

Isaiah was talking about the Messianic Era. A feature of that era, which started with the coming of the Messiah, Jesus Christ, was that God would gather His people from all over the earth.

The New Testament has a lot to say about that as well. For example, Paul and the apostles add that God doesn't just want to gather a people from among the Jews, but also from the non-Jews. They are also part of God's family! The Old Testament was aimed only at the Jewish people, but the New Testament – the times of the Messiah – says that God has extended His covenant to the whole world. That's why we proclaim the gospel to the entire world today, to contribute to the ingathering of God's people. This will continue until the "full number" has been reached (which only God knows) and then the end will come.

Are you part of that number? Well, if you love God, you are counted in! The meaning of that is enormous! It means that we'll see each other one day, in that Jerusalem-of-God, before the throne. Hold on to that thought.

Thank You, Lord, that You're counting me in –
I look forward to that day! Amen.

If you follow Jesus and can sincerely say to God,
"I love You," then you are already joined with Him
and counted as having His salvation.

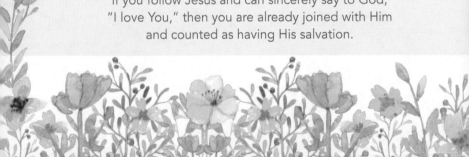

You'll Be on a Highway

There will be a highway from Assyria for the remnant that remains of His people.

Isaiah 11:16 ESV

Isaiah said that the people of Israel (the Northern kingdom) would go into captivity, but that a remnant would return. That will happen when the Messiah comes, and we therefore understand the prediction with reference to Jesus Christ. We may believe that in future there will be a large conversion of Jewish people to Christ – Paul expects it – but for now we see the meaning as spiritual.

Take the following spiritual lesson: Assyria stands for the godless world, the enemies of God, the life of captivity. However, the Messiah comes and builds a highway from there to Jerusalem. Christ makes it easy for us to come to God. With Him, the kingdom of God became near, accessible to all! We must make use of it – oh, take the highway to God that He provided!

Lord, I take this highway to You, to Zion, in faith. Amen.

God promises that He is not far. It's not difficult to reach Him.
Jesus Christ is the highway to God – choose Jesus
and you'll discover that God is in your life.

You Will Praise and Praise

In that day thou shalt say, O LORD, I will praise Thee.

Isaiah 12:1 KJV

Praising God has two sides to it. Praise rises naturally to God when we experience something beautiful or when something good happens in our lives. Then we just want to rejoice and give God the glory. Praise God indeed when you have received a blessing, because it's pure grace – many other people are struggling with such obstacles. Yes, let's praise God in our prayers, in our songs, in our journal entries, in our conversations with others – yes, let's not be shy.

Praise, however, can also enter a supernatural dimension and that's when we praise and give thanks in the absence of the benefits and the blessings, right when our days are still dark, when we're still struggling. When the shackles are chafing us at midnight, we can – like Paul and Silas – sing our songs of praise right there in the dungeon. In this way, praise becomes a powerful weapon of faith!

Isaiah looked ahead in this verse – to our day – and he promised, promised, promised that there would be an intervention from God in our lives, and then we would really praise God!

Thank You, Lord, for Your salvation –
I praise You even now … Amen.

God promises that He knows your situation.
He knows about your struggles and hurt.
He also promises that a day of great rejoicing awaits you.

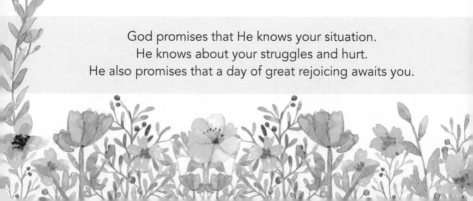

You Will Write a Song!

I will trust, and will not be afraid; for the LORD GOD is my strength and my song, and He has become my salvation.

Isaiah 12:2 ESV

This verse is one of only two places in Scripture where God is mentioned by His double name, literally *Yah Yahweh* (rendered here as the Lord God), to emphasize and underline His mighty presence and salvation. Isaiah quoted these words from the song the Israelites sang after they had come through the Red Sea unscathed, the Egyptians drowning behind them. The double name was of course also for poetic purposes, and Isaiah was absolutely inspired in this short but beautiful chapter as he rejoiced in God's future provision and salvation.

God will intervene mightily and take us through the danger to safety. When that happens, His strength will also become your song, as you exult in Him! Yes, you will also sing – perhaps even write your own song! Don't say you can't – the Holy Spirit will inspire you if you wait on Him in your quiet time, your pen in hand …

You, Lord, are my strength and song: the danger now behind me song, the waters standing tall beside me song, the dry ground warm beneath me song, the promised land before me song; the hand of God is always over me – You're always my salvation song! Amen.

God promises to take you through your circumstances the same way He took the Israelites through the Red Sea. Then you will also rejoice.

Stream of Living Water

With joy you will draw water from the wells of salvation.

Isaiah 12:3 ESV

There are times in your life that your well is dry – times when there's just never enough, when all your expectations disappoint you. With our prayers we try to draw some blessing from God, but sometimes it's as if the blessings never reach us. It's like the dry and dusty parts of Palestine where a lack of water can quickly become a real crisis. Perhaps we draw only small amounts of water, because, like the Samaritan woman, we don't believe we're worthy of more.

Isaiah told the people that those times were over. He assured them that a time would come when there would be water in abundance. We too will draw that abundance of water with joy! God's salvation will be like a stream of living water.

Salvation means more than an escape from harm; in the Bible it refers especially to God's favor, blessing, harmony, abundance, peace, *shalom*! Keep on drawing water from the well – a mighty stream is already rushing in.

Thank You, Lord, for a place of abundance – with You! Amen.

If you desire to draw spiritual water from God,
He promises in time to bless you abundantly.
The fountain will bubble with living water.

God Is Here to Help You

Sing, people of Zion! Celebrate the greatness of the holy LORD of Israel. God is here to help you.

Isaiah 12:6 CEV

Everyone in Zion should praise God. The words translated as "sing" and "celebrate" in this verse have connotations of shouting or crying out. This jubilation is set in the Messianic Era, which means it is also meant for us: God is also with us, with you! Remember that this promise was fulfilled in Jesus Christ. He was Emmanuel – *God with us*. In Him, God came to us.

The description "Holy Lord of Israel" reminds us that God is holy and that He expects holiness. Let us add something about that. Holiness isn't something seen primarily on the outside, for example, in what you wear or whether you drink or smoke. That's the way the Pharisees reasoned. Holiness is being like God, because God is holy. Holiness is behaving more and more like Him.

What are God's characteristics? Well, God is loving, God is merciful, God is just. God is patient and kind. That is how we should become! Let's become more like God – that should be our goal!

Lord, make me holy. Help me to be more like You. Amen.

God promises that He is with you today
and that His presence as the Holy God also makes you holy –
in other words, more like Him.

Unbelievable, but Believe It

"It will never be inhabited or lived in for all generations; no Arab will pitch his tent there; no shepherds will make their flocks lie down there."

Isaiah 13:20 ESV

Isaiah was prophesying against the heathen nations, because they oppressed God's people, among other things. Today, let's take the lesson not to be too judgmental toward other believers. When you're immature in Christ, you easily condemn other Christians left and right. This one is heretical, that one is spiritually dead and others are too extreme. Everyone is wrong, except for you! As you grow, you learn to say less and less about others. Of course you may believe what you believe and of course you may motivate it, but we know that others also believe for a reason.

Isaiah predicted that the great city of Babylon, the center of the civilized world, would be destroyed and laid to waste – a desolate heap of rubble. Only jackals and hyenas would live there. It's actually such an unbelievable statement – like saying New York will be ruined completely and that not one person will live there ever again. Well, this "ridiculous" prediction came true. Babylon has been, for millennia, nothing more than a ruin. It's currently being restored somewhat as a tourist attraction. Trust God's promises – He never lies!

Lord, if You say so, it will be so.
Your promises to me are true! Amen.

If you are confident that God has made you a promise,
know that it is possible, regardless of how impossible it sounds.
With God all things are possible!

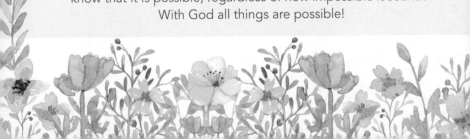

Did You See It? Believe It

The LORD will have mercy on Israel and will let them be His chosen people once again. He will bring them back to their own land.

Isaiah 14:1 CEV

Isaiah knew that the northern state of Israel would be taken off the map – and that's what happened. Possibly he looked far into the future and foresaw that the southern state of Judah would also fall – he warned them against it, anyway.

But then Isaiah also promised that there would be a return, a remnant that God would use for new work. See now how God's promises were fulfilled time and again (remember, in prophecy we work with recurring themes, with types and shadows):

- God-fearing Israelites fled to Judah and avoided the Assyrian captivity
- God let a remnant of Jews return to Israel after the Babylonian captivity
- In 1948, God permitted Jews return to their land, now the modern state of Israel
- God will work a great return of Jews to Jesus the Messiah in the end times.

The first three have already happened – the fourth is yet to come. Think about its meaning for your own life: God's promises come to fulfillment – sometimes bit by bit. Let's also continue praying for the covenant people and for the Holy Land. Yes, let's pray and work for its peace.

Thank You, Lord, for fulfilling Your promises – one at a time. Amen.

God promises that He is at work –
just look at the history of Israel. This must make you realize today
that God's unstoppable plan *will* be carried out.

Evil Will Fall

You, the bright morning star, have fallen from the sky! You brought down other nations; now you are brought down.

Isaiah 14:12 CEV

Isaiah looked ahead to the time when the king of Babylon would fall. On that day he would arrive in Hades, where the phantoms of the dead would be amazed that such a great king (whom Isaiah equated with the morning star) could fall so low.

Many believe that because the word "morning star" in Latin is *lucifer*, and because the whole passage was applied to the devil since ancient times, he was also called "Lucifer," but this isn't exactly what the Bible says. However, similarities can be drawn between the king of Babylon and the devil. The most important one is their fall. Babylon was the greatest empire on earth and its king the mightiest man ever, but God simply pushed him from his position.

Nothing can stand between God and His will. The contrast in this verse is obvious: the king fell from the highest throne imaginable to the lowest low, right into the pit of Hades. That's also the story of the devil – from heaven to hell. God will *not* allow him to stop us.

Thank You, Lord, for being in control –
You alone decide what happens. Amen.

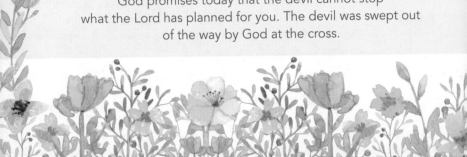

God promises today that the devil cannot stop
what the Lord has planned for you. The devil was swept out
of the way by God at the cross.

Pride Leads to Death

"You have said, 'I will ascend into heaven, I will exalt my throne above the stars of God; I will also sit on the mount of the congregation on the farthest sides of the north; I will ascend above the heights of the clouds, I will be like the Most High.'"

Isaiah 14:13-14 NKJV

Isaiah was speaking here of the king of Babylon, but this passage has also been seen since the earliest times as referring to the devil. Perhaps we can say that the king is a type of or symbol of the devil.

There are things we can learn from these verses about him, and about sin and our sinful nature. For example, in this quotation the king's sin is his ego – it's all just me, me, me. Five times the king says, "I will do this and I will do that …"

In exactly the same way, the devil is also arrogant, trying to be like God. That was also the theme with the fall of man – "you'll be like God" (see Genesis 3) … And isn't it also the motive of today's humanistic world, in which man has replaced God and become his own god? What God asks from us is exactly the opposite: humility, subjection, obedience, service! That is the cross that we need to take up daily.

*Lord, teach me the cross of humility –
the one You also bore. Amen.*

God promises today that if you are humble
and submit to Him, you'll escape the trap of the devil.
God Himself will lift you up at the right time.

The Enemy Is Defeated

"But you are brought down to Sheol, to the far reaches of the pit."
Isaiah 14:15 ESV

The Old Testament doesn't teach much about an afterlife. By the time of the New Testament, however, it was commonly accepted that there would be a resurrection, either unto reward or unto punishment. The Pharisees believed it, as did Jesus. In this passage we see a picture of the Old Testament view of the dead in *Sheol* (or *Hades*, in Greek): vague descriptions of a dark place underneath the earth, a shadowy existence of phantoms that are asleep, or sometimes awake and moving about, man at his weakest and most feeble … a very depressing picture. That was the end for the mightiest man on earth, the king of the greatest empire, Babylon! Isaiah used it to add perspective for the Israelites on their enemy.

We fear only because we cannot see far enough into the future, friend. If we accept that this passage can be taken as a metaphor for Satan, the archenemy, we can know this: his end is in hell (*Gehenna*), the place farthest from God that you can imagine. If he bothers you, remind yourself and him of his future.

Lord, let me see so far that I needn't fear at all. Amen.

God promises today that your end is with Him,
and Satan's end is in hell. If it looks to you like the enemy is winning,
just look a bit farther into the future.

Who Will Stop Him?

"I, the LORD All-Powerful, have made these plans. No one can stop Me now!"

Isaiah 14:27 CEV

Isaiah prophesied over the nations and then turned to the Assyrians, who were the biggest threat at that time. Here he proclaimed the following: yes, the Assyrians would take over the world, but then their end would come as well. Today the ruins of Nineveh, once the capital of the biggest empire ever, are merely a tourist site in Mosul, a city in Iraq.

Let's ask the following question: if God has decided something, who will stop Him? If He has decided that you are the object of His love, or favor, or protection, or blessing – will the devil stop Him? Will your enemies? Will you? Paul makes it very clear that *nothing* will separate us from the love of God – no height or depth or angel or spirit or power or authority, not even death will prevent you from receiving the *full* blessing that God intended for you (see Romans 8:38-39). Listen: God loves you, He has decided to bless you and He *will* save you. That is the gospel, the good news that we proclaim. Just react to it by saying, "Yes, Lord! Thank You! I accept Your grace."

Lord, I do accept Your gift of love with gratitude! Amen.

If you are feeling down or discouraged today,
God promises that He loves you, He blesses you with His
presence and He will deliver you. Believe it by confessing it!

Surrender Your Enemies to God

Cry and weep in the gates of your towns, you Philistines! Smoke blows in from the north, and every soldier is ready.

Isaiah 14:31 CEV

Isaiah was prophesying against all the enemy nations that surrounded Israel. The Philistines were probably the Israelites' most pernicious enemy – a small but powerful nation right alongside them against the sea.

The Philistines were already there when the Israelite tribes entered Canaan and they could never be subdued for any long period. On the contrary, they constantly posed a threat to Israel from their land and their five cities: Ashdod, Ashkelon, Ekron, Gaza and Gath. It is the greatest irony that the name of their land *Philistia* (in Hebrew *Peleshet*) became the name of the whole region – *Palestine* – and that the current "Palestinians," although a different people, continue to attack the Israelis from Gaza (Ashkelon today being an Israeli city).

One doesn't know what to make of it – it's thousands of years later! Isaiah shows the Philistines that their end will come – which happened when the Romans (much later) attacked from the north and wiped them out as a people. Don't bother too much about your so-called enemies. Surrender them to God's will and move on.

Lord, deal with the enemies in my life in Your way –
I surrender them to You now. Amen.

God promises today that your enemies are no problem for Him.
Do what is necessary, but do not invest too much emotion into it.
Surrender it to God.

You Know, Everything Can Change

Moab's messengers say to the people of Judah, "Be kind and help us! ... Hide our refugees! Don't turn them away."

Isaiah 16:3 CEV

Isaiah went on to prophesy against the Moabites, one of their neighboring nations. Sometimes they had peace, but at other times there would be a bloody war. Isaiah warned them of the coming doom and said that something strange would happen in that day: the Moabites would pour over the border asking for help. The old enemies would come with gifts and be full of compliments!

That's the way it happens, not so? People are at odds now and things are said – but then time lapses, attitudes change and maturity and distance bring new perspective. People often realize that they acted hastily and immaturely. They regret what was said and want to be friends again. How should one react to that? Remember, peace and reconciliation is always God's will. True peace and reconciliation, that is – with hearts that are sincere. Never doubt that God is always for sincere forgiveness! Do you have a broken relationship? Don't set it in stone. Leave it open and see what happens. Everything can still change, especially with God.

Lord, I'm still uncomfortable with some people,
but I leave this matter to You. Amen.

If you are struggling with a broken
and wounded relationship, give it to God. He promises
to heal your pain and even bring reconciliation.

Your Promises
Still Unfulfilled?

*An oracle concerning Damascus. Behold, Damascus will cease to
be a city and will become a heap of ruins.*

Isaiah 17:1 ESV

For chapters and chapters, Isaiah prophesied against the neighboring nations. We only touch on it here and there since we focus in this devotional on God's promises. Often we see how God's promises and predictions were fulfilled in detail, but this verse is different. Damascus, the capital of the Arameans, was still standing – and thriving. It withstood many attacks, but the prophecy wasn't fulfilled precisely, as yet.

Centuries later, Paul committed himself to Jesus in that city and until Islam came to the fore in the 7th century, Damascus was a patently Christian city. Today Damascus is the capital of Syria, with 2 million inhabitants, of which about 10% of the population are still Christian.

What are we to make of the unfulfilled prophecy – 2,700 years later? Does it remind you of promises that you are also still waiting on? Do not worry! Two or three thousand years (let alone your few years) is no big thing for God. Damascus will be destroyed some day and the prophecy will come to pass. Your promises will also be fulfilled. Just wait – if God said it, He will do it!

Lord, I am still waiting in faith.
I know You will intervene on my behalf! Amen.

If you are waiting on a promise from God, do not be too
concerned about time. God promises it will come to pass and it will.
Remember that God's view is different from yours.

Your Enemy Can Come to God

At that time tribute will be brought to the LORD of hosts from a people tall and smooth, from a people feared near and far, a nation mighty and conquering.

Isaiah 18:7 ESV

Next, Isaiah turned to the Cushites – the Ethiopians. He described their appearance as tall, smooth and "shining." According to him, they were feared all around. They too, with the whole world, would come under God's judgment. Afterward only those who were right with God would remain. They would then go to Jerusalem to worship God there. That had already started, of course, when the Christian faith took hold in Ethiopia shortly after Christ's death. At least 40 million Ethiopians today are Christian and worship the God of Israel.

What is evident, however, in this passage is how people's hearts are softened when they serve God. Sometimes we deal with intimidating people in our lives – we feel threatened by their attitude, words or actions. Do you feel threatened by some people? Give the situation to God. He will be their judge. Don't think that hard people cannot also repent and start serving God – it has happened countless times! They may even come and tell you they are sorry for their previous behavior.

Lord, I pray for the following people's relationship with You … [list the names]. Amen.

If there are people in your life who intimidate you, you can give the situation to God. He promises to take your case. He will come to your defense.

God Loves Your Enemy

The LORD will show the Egyptians who He is, and they will know and worship the LORD.

Isaiah 19:21 CEV

The Egyptians were Israel's old, old enemies. Remember, Israel were captives in Egypt for 400 years. Only after the 10 plagues hit were they allowed to escape the "house of bondage" and flee to Canaan. In this passage Isaiah predicted that Egypt would come to know God. They too would be His people, and He would be their God. How amazing!

Today there are 12 million orthodox Christians in Egypt – after Mark established the church there shortly after Jesus' death. Even so, the Christians there still expect a major revival for Christ in their country. In any case, we again see how God makes friends out of enemies – not just friends, but loved ones, children of God. The Jews must've been uncomfortable with this prediction of salvation – perhaps they would rather have wanted a prediction of punishment on their old foe! Isaiah did foresee punishment on them (as on all), but thereafter proclaimed restoration and reconciliation. That's how God's heart works. Doesn't He also love the Egyptians? Of course He does. He doesn't only love me – He also loves my enemies! His will is always forgiveness, restitution and healing. Always! Perhaps it will take time for you (and your enemies) to get to that point – but it remains a fact, God's fact.

I know that You love my enemies.
I still struggle to love some people, Lord! Amen.

God asks you to be patient concerning your enemies –
that you hand them over to Him.
He promises to deal with them on your behalf.

A Naked Prophet and You

About this same time the LORD had told me, "Isaiah, take off every-thing, including your sandals!" I did this and went around naked and barefoot.

Isaiah 20:2 CEV

The king of Assyria invaded the Philistine city of Ashdod. The Philistines hoped that Egypt or Ethiopia would come to their rescue, but Isaiah said they could forget it. Then he did something strange – God instructed him to take off his clothes and walk naked (probably in his undergarment). By doing that, he was saying that Egypt as well as Ethiopia would themselves be vanquished and stripped as bare as he was. This indeed happened in 670 and 667 BC. Isaiah walked around like this for three years.

Elsewhere in the Bible we also see prophets acting strangely. Over the years peculiar people have told me peculiar things that they believe God told them. Sometimes such "prophets" made me feel uneasy. Still I would generally accept what they said, or at least consider it carefully. One shouldn't stare oneself blind at the channel God uses, because God can use whomever He wants. He can speak to you through a charismatic young pastor, an old-school minister, a hypocritical Christian, a complete stranger, your unbelieving husband or even your child. God is speaking – we should be listening!

Speak, Lord, I am listening. Amen.

God promises to talk to you. He can use whom He chooses – do not look at the person He uses, but rather ask yourself if there might be a message in it for you.

You Must Be Ready

They prepare the table, they spread the rugs, they eat, they drink.
Arise, O princes; oil the shield!

Isaiah 21:5 ESV

The great power of the Assyrians was rising against the nations and Isaiah was sounding the warning. Like a typical prophet he could already see it before his eyes, like a nightmare. The kings of the nations would be celebrating in their palaces when the alarms would sound: "The country has been invaded. Officers – report at once! Soldiers – prepare your weapons!"

Images like these were used in later prophesies again and again as the prophets warned the people to prepare for God. Jesus also said that people would be eating and drinking when suddenly the end will be upon them.

The message is clear that we should be ready. How are we to stay ready? Well, we'll be ready when we stay in a relationship with God – when His Holy Spirit remains burning in us like the wise virgins' lamps (see Matthew 25:1-13). Then we won't be caught unaware. We'll know what to do in any circumstance; we'll receive guidance, promises and faith. Stay in a relationship with God! What is a relationship? It is communication.

Lord, I want to remain close to You.
Then I'll be ready for anything. Amen.

Life is full of surprises, but God promises you will be ready
to handle anything if you remain in a relationship with Him.

Seek the Keys

"I will place on his shoulder the key of the house of David. He shall open, and none shall shut; and he shall shut, and none shall open."

Isaiah 22:22 ESV

In this verse, Isaiah was actually talking about a certain official (Eliakim), whom God appointed in the government. However, his exact words echo further in Jesus' announcement that He would give to His disciples the "keys of the kingdom."

We believe that this authority is given not just to Peter or the apostles but to all disciples; in other words, to all believers. It's the same authority that Jesus gives His followers to act "in His name." What does it mean to act "in Jesus' name"? Well, what it doesn't mean is that one can pray for whatever one wants and then add (loudly) "in Jesus' name" – being the "key" to get anything! Alas, Jesus never gave such a key!

To act in Jesus' name means to act on Jesus' behalf. He gives us full authority and a mandate to continue with the work of the Kingdom as His representatives, as ambassadors. In essence, it means to continue doing what He has done, and continue praying the way He prayed. It's about the Kingdom, not about us! Be Jesus to someone today.

Lord, what would You have done today?
Help me to do the same. Amen.

God promises that you can act in His authority and power, but in doing so He expects you to promote His interests, not your own.

The Trappings of the World

At the end of seventy years, it will happen to Tyre as in the song of the prostitute.

Isaiah 23:15 ESV

Isaiah prophesied against the cities of the Phoenicians, who were successful merchants. Their ships traveled all over the world, laden with valuable goods. In Scripture, the image of the big city, full of businesspeople and pleasure seekers, is not always a good one. In the Bible, such an image is often a symbol of the "world," the system that turned its back on God.

People are easily lured away by the world's glitz and glamour, which make them forget about God. Accordingly, Isaiah compares the city to a prostitute, who tempts people with all sorts of promises and takes their money, but doesn't offer them anything enduring in return. In Revelation, the same image is used for the whole worldly system as "Babylon, mother of harlots;" in other words, life's greatest seduction.

In our modern world it also is all about materialism and fame. People give their whole lives to make money or to be part of the "in-crowd." However, God reminds us that this is only temporary. We do live *in* the world, but we do not live *for* the world. We live for Him.

Thank You, Lord, for this wonderful life –
keep me from losing my way. Amen.

The Lord gives us life to live – and thrive –
but never without Him. He promises that a life with Him
is much more fulfilling and fun than a life without Him.

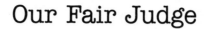

Our Fair Judge

From the ends of the earth we hear songs of praise, of glory to the
Righteous One.

Isaiah 24:16 ESV

The prophet Isaiah was now in top gear. Like something out of a nightmare,
he described the unraveling of the world: the earth shaking, the light of the
sun and moon rapidly receding. Then, in the midst of the chaos, a song will
be heard. It will come from the east, the west – from all corners of the earth.
It will be the song of the survivors, the "remnant" of God who will be saved
from destruction. They will sing the praises of the "Righteous One," or the
"God of Justice" as one translation puts it. Yes, God *is* the just God and He
is the Judge of judges. He *is* also the One who demands from us perfect
justice and righteousness.

We should never fear that God might not be fair in His judgments. No,
He is more just than any judge could ever be. Remember that fairness does
not mean that a judge simply pardons all criminals and lets them go. That is
not justice. Justice does involve punishment. However, we praise God that
His punishment was meted out to Christ on the cross. Those who accept
that in faith are not judged again.

Lord Jesus, thank You for saving me –
now and forever. Amen.

The Bible warns of Judgment Day, but God promises
that He will judge fairly. More than that – you know
that those whose lives are in Christ will not be judged.

Bind the Evil One

On that day the LORD will punish the host of heaven, in heaven, and the kings of the earth, on the earth.

Isaiah 24:21 ESV

On the Day of the Lord, when God will intervene on earth, He will bring an end to the evil powers. The Bible teaches that God's children wrestle against such powers. It's interesting that Isaiah predicted in the verse that follows that these powers – together with earthly powers – would be bound and punished. We already experience the binding of the evil one:

Christ triumphed over the evil one on the cross. He is still acting up, but his power is limited and his time is almost up

Christ gives us authority to rule over the enemy. His place, according to Scripture, is under our feet. Resist him in Jesus' name!

The power of the enemy can best be overcome by living in such a way that he has no hold over us. Ban him from your life by living away from him, not toward him. Remember, the enemy mainly uses one weapon against you, and that is fear. Even this weapon is based on lies.

Thank You, Lord, for Your full
and final victory over Satan. Amen.

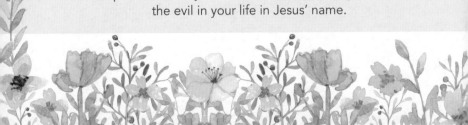

Evil is a reality in the Bible, but the victory over evil is, too.
God promises that you can bind and effectively overcome
the evil in your life in Jesus' name.

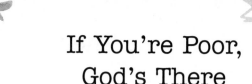

If You're Poor, God's There

For Thou hast been a strength to the poor, a strength to the needy in his distress, a refuge from the storm, a shadow from the heat.

Isaiah 25:4 KJV

Isaiah rejoiced over God's goodness, knowing He would personally intervene in the world and put everything right. God does not just put up with injustice. We needn't think that bad people will get away with their deeds. Crime, corruption, fraud and untruth do not pay.

At the end of everything, the Judge will come and everyone will appear before Him. He will demand accountability, and punishment and reward will be fairly allotted. Then – when the judgment is over – justice will reign on Earth.

Remember, justice and fairness is God's heart – He sides with those who are treated unjustly and unfairly. God is on the side of the downtrodden, the needy, the dependent. Blessed, says Jesus, are those who struggle, because God is there with them. The Bible also has a special word for the poor. They have few resources to fall back onto, but God is their resource, their strength and their sanctuary. He will help them! That is your promise if you are also struggling today.

Thank You, Lord, for being with me always –
thank You for being my Source. Amen.

Life is often difficult due to personal, social, economic or political circumstances, but God promises that He is on the side of the needy and poor (in spirit)?

God Will Be There

The humble will rejoice in the LORD; the needy will rejoice in the Holy One of Israel.

Isaiah 29:19 NIV

God is the God of the needy. Jesus' preaching started with the words, "Blessed are the poor in spirit" (Matthew 5:3), meaning those who realize how dependent they are on God. Then He named examples of need, sorrow and injustice. Blessed are they, Jesus said, because God is with them.

God's presence is the first important point to recognize. Some people turn their backs on God in their need, not understanding why He has allowed their hardship. That is not a good choice because then we have to deal with our challenges on our own. Personally, in my need, I want to be with God! In the difficult times I want to share my heart, my concerns and my anxieties with Him! That's what Isaiah meant when he said that God is our refuge and our shelter.

The second point to remember is that we really can expect God's help. Faith is practical and our need is real. Something real needs to happen in our need! Look to God for that, friend. He will be your refuge and help.

Lord, I need You today –
be my refuge and my help. Amen.

Challenges and crises are a part of life, but God promises
to always remain close to us and to help us in a myriad of ways.
Are you in a crisis or going through a difficult time?

March

You Are Going to Jerusalem

On this mountain the LORD of hosts will make for all peoples a feast of rich food, a feast of well-aged wine.

Isaiah 25:6 ESV

Isaiah rejoiced in the day when God would intervene and set everything right. He described it as a celebration. The food would be the best: rich delicacies and well-aged, fine wines. It would be in Zion, which is Jerusalem, the place of God's presence and government. All the nations would be there, *sans* the godless and the sinful – only the God-fearing and the righteous.

I believe that such a day will one day come, but in the meanwhile we already share in this spiritual reality. Jewish people end the Passover each year with "next year in Jerusalem!" which expresses the hope that the Messiah will come in the interim, restore the temple and have the people return to the Holy Land. As Christians, however, we believe that the Messiah *did* come, *did* restore the spiritual house of God and at this moment *is* gathering in His people from all over the world. Through a relationship with God, the celebration has already begun! Everyone can be part of it, and Holy Communion is the church's reminder of that feast. However, we still await the ultimate marriage supper of the Lamb, when Jesus returns. With an eye on that, we close with the words, "See you in Jerusalem!"

Thank You, Lord, for the celebration
of a relationship with You! Amen.

There's a celebratory feast awaiting us one day, but God promises you can already experience this festivity. You can experience it through the celebration of a living relationship with Him.

All Are Going to Jerusalem

> He will swallow up on this mountain the covering that is cast over all peoples, the veil that is spread over all nations.
>
> *Isaiah 25:7* ESV

Isaiah predicted the coming of the Day of the Lord. For the godless, it will be the terrible "judgment day;" but for the righteous, a joyous day of salvation. They will celebrate a victory feast with God! Isaiah was looking forward to the fact that all the nations would be present. He said that on that day, the veil covering the nations, which blinded them to the true God, would be removed. Their inability to recognize their own gods and idols as false had led to many sins, but no more!

On that day – in the New Jerusalem – the world would be one before God. All nations, cultures and languages would be represented before the throne. Remember, God loves all nations equally, even though He once chose one nation to reveal Himself to and to use as an example for all the world. Yes, we'll be there as well, but at present we still assist in gathering in this "peculiar people," God's chosen ones, from the nations. You can also help with this task!

Lord, thank You that there'll be complete harmony on that day –
give us love for each other today as well. Amen.

God promises that He loves all nations and people equally and that He is assembling people from all the nations for His kingdom. Since we help in this, it is also necessary that you and I are able to love all people and nations.

You Will Live Forever in Jerusalem

The LORD All-Powerful will destroy the power of death and wipe away all tears.

Isaiah 25:8 CEV

Isaiah was looking forward to the day that God would say "enough" – when He would draw a line under history! Time will stop and we'll continue to live in a new dimension, in a new heaven and earth. God will be with us personally. The old Jerusalem will become the New Jerusalem, the true Zion – where He will rule. Faith will become sight – remember, faith is only the way we live this life, not the next. It will add new meaning to the concept of a "relationship with God" when He's right there, not so? All tears will be wiped away and death will be "swallowed up" by life, says the Bible.

These are all topics that are used again and again in the New Testament. Let's underline this for today: we have a living hope for eternity! We literally believe that our immortal souls will live with God forever, directly in His love. Forever! Doesn't that reframe everything that happens here, especially the tears, the heartache, the pain? Come now, stop crying. Look up, smile – the best is still ahead!

Thank You, loving Father,
that everything ends with You. Amen.

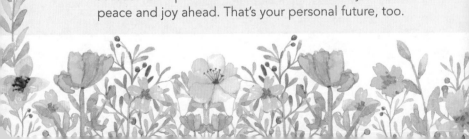

This life with its tears, illness and death is only temporary, because God promises that there is an eternity of love, peace and joy ahead. That's your personal future, too.

You Will Look Back and Rejoice

At that time, people will say, "The LORD has saved us! Let's celebrate. We waited and hoped – now our God is here."

Isaiah 25:9 CEV

On the Day of the Lord, the believers will see that they were right to trust God. Remember that faith is often tentative – it operates in the space where there isn't proof. Remember, the moment you have proof of something, the need to believe it disappears. The opposite of faith is therefore certainty. That's exactly the way we experience it. Faith as an absolute conviction is rare – a real spiritual gift.

Usually we believe with some amount of certainty, but on the edges of our faith we wish and hope that it really will be so! It's as if our faith has to fight a small shadow of doubt – and when we ask for something and do not receive, that shadow of doubt grows. Some may even lose their faith. Isaiah said that our faith would be confirmed when we reach the end and look back. On that last day we'll see and confirm and rejoice in the fact that every promise was true and that we were right in trusting God. Yes – keep your faith!

Thank You, Lord, for that day.
Help me to persevere to the end. Amen.

We do sometimes experience uncertainty and doubt,
but God promises that if you persevere in faith,
you will be able to look back and see that He was trustworthy.

You in God's City

Our city is protected. The LORD is our fortress, and He gives us victory.

Isaiah 26:1 CEV

We have said that the image of the "city" in Scripture isn't always a good one. Often the city serves as a metaphor for the godless world. The "worldly city" is a temptress, a prostitute who lures people away from God, because in our world of materialism, there is little place for Him.

In the Bible, Babylon (or Babel) serves as a symbol for the godless world. However, in the Bible there is also mention of another city, which is the opposite – the "city of God." In Scripture, Jerusalem (or Zion) stands for that godly city – in which He is the center. In the New Testament it is called the "New Jerusalem." The godly city is the home of God's children – where they find rest, where they're safe, where they have plenty. It's as strong as a fortress and abounds with streams and fruit trees.

Most importantly, this city is the place where God is – He resides there, in His heavenly sanctuary. In that city He is preparing a place for you and me – forever!

Thank You, Lord, for preparing a place for me –
right there with You. Amen.

Our journey through this life and this earth is often tiring,
but God promises that one day you will arrive
at the heavenly city and rest there forever.

Your Path Is Smooth and Level Path

Our LORD, You always do right, and You make the path smooth for those who obey You.

Isaiah 26:7 CEV

In the Old Testament, those who were right with God were called the righteous. They loved Him and did what He asked. In today's verse we read that those who obey the Lord will have a smooth path. Isaiah meant that God levels it out for them. Over and over again the Word says that God will make our paths straight when we serve Him.

Perhaps you're saying: "No, my path isn't particularly straight or easy – especially not at the moment!" That might be so. Yes, in this life bad things do happen to even the most dedicated children of God. But the promise from the Bible remains true. It doesn't mean that life's path will always be level, 100% of the way, with never ever a hitch at all. No, the road with God winds up and down and has twists and turns. It crosses mountains from time to time – even deserts. But it always remains a better path, a smoother path – a more blessed path – than any path without God. Without God our path is dark and hopeless. May your path be straight, friend – smoothed out – but remember that God will be with you wherever your path takes you.

Lord, I want to stay with You,
wherever this path leads. Amen.

God promises that the path with Him is a path
that is more even and smooth than any other.
You don't even have to try out a different route!

You Have Everything You Need

O LORD, You will ordain peace for us, for You have indeed done for us all our works.

Isaiah 26:12 ESV

With reference to the enigmatic words, "You have done for us all our works," we need to share a profound truth, which is at the very heart of what faith is. It is key to our spiritual life and will lead to deep, inexplicable peace, as this verse also states.

This truth is that God provides us with everything we need. It can also be stated as follows: "At this moment I have everything I need." It is also the sentiment of Psalm 23, where David says, "I shall not want" or "I will never be in need." Our natural identity, or ego, protests against such a notion and points to all the things we apparently *do* need – we need this and we need that! The more our ego dominates, the more needs we see. The spiritual person, however, by faith sees that God is all they need: that everything is supplied at this moment, that He is 100% in control and can be fully trusted. It *is* possible to surrender, and trust Him. God will provide, whatever happens. The end will be good, because for us the end is with God; God is the end! Even death is no longer an enemy. This is radical faith – and not so easy to accomplish – but it leads to radical peace.

Thank You, Lord, that I can surrender my situation and my life radically to You. Amen.

Although it may appear that there are things that you need that you still don't have in your life – according to yourself or the world – God promises that with Him you have all you really need.

Your Territory Will Enlarge

You have increased the nation, O LORD, You have increased the nation … You have enlarged all the borders of the land.

Isaiah 26:15 ESV

Isaiah was speaking in faith – the nation hadn't yet increased and the borders hadn't been enlarged. On the contrary, the enemy had amassed on the borders, ready to pour in, conquer the land and take the people away from it. Isaiah predicted all their enemies' downfall as well – for him there was no avoiding it and he was already looking far beyond that. He saw that the enemy also would fall and disappear, that the people would return to their land one day and that they would be prosperous once again. God would intervene! That is what he was rejoicing about.

Isn't that what faith is? Seeing what the eye as yet cannot see and already rejoicing in it, already behaving as if it's an accomplished fact? That's faith, yes. Indeed, the Israelites did return to their land. Even today, 2,700 years later, they are still a people to be reckoned with – what a miracle! This is the application: to look beyond the current circumstances and see the future. See God intervening, restoring, blessing, increasing your territory. See this and rejoice!

Thank You, Lord, for Your help –
make haste to help me! Amen.

Although you might not have everything you need right now, you can already "see" in faith how the Lord will provide for you, and rejoice about this fact. He promises that faith has a powerful effect.

You Will Live Again

Your dead shall live; their bodies shall rise. You who dwell in the dust, awake and sing for joy!

Isaiah 26:19 ESV

In the two preceding verses, Isaiah described his people's weakness in dramatic language. He said it was like a woman giving birth: she'd folded over as the contractions hit her and she screamed in pain. She was in anguish to give birth to something – but there was nothing. Nothing was being born! The people couldn't bring forth life on their own. Then God intervened. He went to the very depths of Hades and resurrected people there.

That's how God brings forth life – right from the dead – what a contrast! That's what God specializes in: creating life from lifelessness. Isaiah meant it figuratively, but he was also sowing the seeds for the belief later on that one day there would be a resurrection.

Let's apply this to our lives today. Perhaps there is soul-wrenching death in your heart, in your life, in a relationship, which drains you of energy. It's killing you in every sense of the word. Give it to the Lord, then let Him bring new life: powerful, vital, as never before!

Lord, You are the source of power in my life. Amen.

God promises that He can create new life out of your dead situations.
If you continue to ask and look for the signs in your life,
you will start seeing new growth.

God Is Busy with You

"I, the LORD, will protect it and always keep it watered. I will guard it day and night to keep it from harm."

Isaiah 27:3 CEV

Here and elsewhere, Scripture compares Israel to a vineyard. Isaiah said that God would protect His vineyard and water it. He would also pull out the weeds and burn off unwanted growth. After that, the vineyard would flourish again.

Jesus uses exactly the same metaphor with believers today. It's wonderful to realize that God is busy with us, He's working on us! He works in our hearts through His Holy Spirit. He uses everything that happens to us as part of the process.

God does not plan or ordain everything that happens to you, especially not the heartache, loss and calamities. No, God's not punishing you, because Jesus already took all of the punishment on the cross. Most often those things (the hardships of life) are just the realities of living in a sinful and broken world. However, God uses it – He works with it, He incorporates it as part of your growth, He changes it to your and others' advantage. He is making something beautiful of your life! How wonderful is that?

Lord, I want to be more conscious
of what You are doing in my life. Amen.

God promises that the bad things in your life are not His punishment.
However, He does want to harness and use everything
that happens in your life – even the bad things.

You Will Blossom and Bear Fruit

Someday Israel will take root like a vine. It will blossom and bear fruit that covers the earth.

Isaiah 27:6 CEV

Israel was described as God's vineyard. He worked His vineyard – weeding, pruning and uprooting where needed! Such work is necessary to yield better fruit, and that is what God is interested in. What does bearing fruit mean for us? Well, the fruit contains the DNA of the plant – the complete genetic material – packed in such a way as to survive, to spread and to reproduce. Bearing fruit is the whole purpose of the plant!

If we think of bearing fruit as Christians, it brings to mind our testimony, of reaching others for Christ, of Kingdom growth. Yes, it's our purpose as children of God to touch others as He would, to transplant God into the hearts of others – or at least facilitate that process. How does this occur? From the New Testament we learn that this happens through our love, joy and peace, patience, kindness, goodness, faithfulness, and humility and restraint. This is the DNA of the Spirit – this is the way God is! Yes, this is the fruit we bear, which is also our most essential testimony.

Lord, change me and bear Your fruit in me! Amen.

Jesus says, "Abide in Me" (John 15:7). If you remain faithful to God, He promises that your life will be fruitful and that others will see Him in you. In so doing, they will be drawn to Him.

You Will, If You ...

There's only one way that Israel's sin and guilt can be completely forgiven: They must crush the stones of every pagan altar and place of worship.

Isaiah 27:9 CEV

Isaiah warned the people like a true prophet of old. He didn't mince words! Due to their idolatry, Israel was far from God. Baal and Ashtoreth were worshiped by erecting stone pillars and wooden poles (as masculine and feminine principle, respectively) on the hills. There the people offered sacrifices and engaged in lurid lustful acts as a symbol of the fertility that the worship was to supposedly evoke.

Think of our own society where there isn't much place for God but emphasis is placed on money and lust! Let's emphasize the fact that God's blessing comes with a condition. When we focus through these devotions on God's promises, we shouldn't think that they come without conditions. However, if people would end their idolatry, then God's blessing will come. God's favor is the result of a sincere and intimate relationship with Him. Let's not ask Him to bless us from a distance, without any further regard for Him. Repent of your wrongdoings and put Him first in your life. Live with God – now that's a blessing!

Lord, help me to live closer to You. Amen.

If you seek God's blessing, it includes remaining in a genuine relationship with Him – that's the way to experience the blessing! If you do this, He promises that you will receive His blessings.

You Will Hear the Trumpet Call

A loud trumpet will be heard. Then the people of Israel who were dragged away to Assyria and Egypt will return to worship the LORD on His holy mountain in Jerusalem.

Isaiah 27:13 CEV

Isaiah warned that the Day of the Lord would come. First, the piercing sound of a ram's horn would be heard – a *shofar* or "trumpet" as it's translated. In biblical times, a *shofar* was blown to gain attention for an important event – a call to war perhaps, or the beginning of a feast or new moon. The *shofar* was also blown at the king's crowning, at special announcements at the palace or temple, or as part of worship. It is still blown in the Jewish religion and also informally in ours.

Isaiah said, as did Jesus and Paul, that at the end the "great shofar" will sound. One day, in the midst of the hustle and bustle, another sound will be heard, penetrating and incessant … that will be when God intervenes on earth! Remember, it will be a day of war, when God demolishes the enemy once and for all. It will be the day when God takes control of matters. It will be the day of our salvation. The Bible says we should look up to the clouds from time to time, waiting, expecting … Come, Lord Jesus!

Lord, make me conscious of Your coming,
and let me be ready. Amen.

God promises that one day you will hear
a piercing sound amid the noise – exactly how,
we do not know. This will herald the last day.

You Will Build on Solid Rock

"I'm laying a firm foundation for the city of Zion. It's a valuable cornerstone proven to be trustworthy; no one who trusts it will ever be disappointed."

Isaiah 28:16 CEV

Isaiah was angry with the spiritual leaders in Jerusalem. They had given themselves to drinking and parties. Isaiah said the prophets and priests were too intoxicated to interpret God's words, their tables covered with the vomit of their drunkenness (see verses 7-8) and yet they laughed at the approaching danger. They felt safe, because they bargained on an agreement they had made with the enemy. Isaiah had bad news for them. They hadn't taken God into account. God no longer had a need for such leaders and He was going to remove them. He would lay down a new cornerstone, or foundation, and on that foundation (which the New Testament identifies as Jesus Christ) He would raise up a new building. Righteousness and justice would rule in that new temple.

This is the lesson: don't build your life on sand. Money and pleasure have their place, but life is about much more than that. Those things are fleeting, transitory. Build your life solidly on God. Reach for that which has permanence and value, like a relationship with Him.

Lord, I do feel empty sometimes.
I want to build my relationship with You. Amen.

If you are sincere with God, and build your life on the rock Jesus Christ, God promises that you won't have to flee on Judgment Day. You will be saved.

He Knows How to Work with You

Does one crush grain for bread? No, he does not thresh it forever; when he drives his cart wheel over it with his horses, he does not crush it.

Isaiah 28:28 ESV

In these verses, Isaiah used the example of a farmer who knew what he was doing. He ploughed the ground in the right way and then sowed different crops: wheat, cumin and barley, with emmer on the sides. The yield was harvested at exactly the right time. It was threshed and ground, each according to its properties. Cumin and dill, for example, were not threshed out with a sledge, but struck with rods, so as not to harm the produce. Wheat was threshed by animals pulling a sledge, but only to separate the kernels, not to crush it to a powder.

Isaiah used this as a metaphor: his people were the land that God was working on. He ploughed it over and sowed His seed in it. They were the wheat that was threshed and ground. It may have been that God working with them was unpleasant, but – and this is the lesson – God knows what He is doing! Everything He does is to ensure a bountiful harvest, and so it is with us. The Lord wants you to trust Him today. He knows what He's doing.

Thank You, Lord. I trust You with my life! Amen.

God promises that He is working on you.
He knows what He is doing to ensure
a bountiful harvest in your life. There is no need to worry.

You Will See

In that day the deaf shall hear the words of a book, and out of their gloom and darkness the eyes of the blind shall see.

Isaiah 29:18 ESV

Isaiah spoke of the day that God would intervene on earth. Still, God won't just intervene on that one, final day in the future, He intervenes even now. Everything that is predicted for the End Times – such as the "signs of the times" – are already happening. They will become worse and worse and end in a climax on the last day. When Jesus heralded in the Messianic Era, He proved it by referring to the blind seeing and the deaf hearing. We live in that era and these things still happen!

There is also a spiritual truth here: Paul said that we currently see dimly, like a riddle in a mirror, but one day we'll see face to face. What does that mean? Well, we often struggle to see God's work in our lives – His interventions, His purposes. We live by the faith that it is so, that there is a plan. However, one day we will know it precisely. Then we'll see, and understand, how God worked with us – how perfect His plans were. You'll see for yourself!

Lord, thank You for working in my life – perfectly … Amen.

God's plan for our lives is already in progress
and He promises that one day we will understand
and witness His perfect ending.

You Will Be Free from These

For the ruthless shall come to nothing and the scoffer cease, and all who watch to do evil shall be cut off.

Isaiah 29:20 ESV

Isaiah was glad that God would "cut off" the following types of people:

Ruthless people are those who don't care about the feelings of others. They don't mind being cruel to others, sometimes even to children or animals. Terrible things happen to innocent people! But don't you worry – there is a Judge

Scoffers are those who make fun of everything – they do this in a negative and sad way (we all need fun and joy in our lives) because they are superficial. They have no depth, no empathy for others, no capacity for God and no understanding of life

The *evil* or *unrighteous* are those who do not love God, those who have no need for Him. Life is all about themselves: always and in all circumstances!

People like these are missing out on God's purposes. God wants people who live fully but who have overcome their preoccupation with themselves and can love others – and Him. That's the best life!

Lord, I want to live my life with You – and for You. Amen.

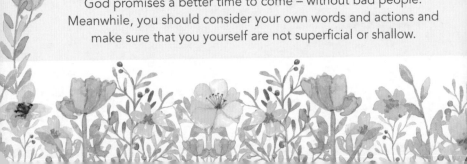

God promises a better time to come – without bad people. Meanwhile, you should consider your own words and actions and make sure that you yourself are not superficial or shallow.

Your Covenant Is Assured

"They will sanctify the Holy One of Jacob and will stand in awe of the God of Israel."

Isaiah 29:23 ESV

God made a covenant (a contract or agreement) with His people, Israel. It involved doing His will – as spelled out in the Law – which resulted in His blessings. The Sabbath and circumcision were the outward signs of that covenant. In the Bible, the covenant is referred to in typical words and terminology, such as the succinct phrase, "I will be their God and they will be My people," which sums it all up. Also, references to Abraham, Isaac and Jacob (who originally entered into covenant with God), or to God's covenant names – as in this verse – brings this divine contract to mind.

Do you also belong to this covenant? When you've accepted Jesus Christ, you are part of the exact same covenant, through Him, as was Abraham! That's the message from Paul, and a huge encouragement, because the covenant is our guarantee that God will never forsake us. For example, God punished the Israelites for their sin, but then brought them back. Why? Because of His covenant! Whatever happens, God will not leave you!

Thank You for the personal covenant between us, Lord! Amen.

God promises in accordance with His covenant to bless and save you. After all, He did seal the covenant with His own blood.

Your Strength Is in Returning

"In returning and rest you shall be saved; in quietness and in trust shall be your strength."

Isaiah 30:15 ESV

Isaiah reprimanded the people of Israel. They thought they could save themselves from the enemy by organizing this or that deal with enemies. However, they ignored God. Isaiah said their salvation should rather have been in returning to God, in resting in Him, in quietness and trust.

Does that mean we shouldn't do anything anymore? Shall we just wait for the miracle to happen? No, the Bible is clear that we do have a responsibility – it is important that we should do what we can and should do. However, some things only God can do. Once you have done your best, leave the rest in His hands. Then you can experience the peace and joy of trusting God. Let faith make you strong! Let's also learn to relax in God's presence. Once you have prayed to Him, stay in His presence for a while. Become completely still before Him. Quiet the many thoughts in your mind by focusing attention on your heart. Experience your heart burning with love for God – then hold that feeling for as long as you can. Did you feel it? Pure love and joy!

Lord, teach me to be still and to know
that You are God! Amen.

You do not have to do everything yourself –
that's why you have God in your life. If you quietly trust in Him,
He promises He will undertake for you.

Your Prayer Will Be Answered

He will surely be gracious to you at the sound of your cry. As soon as He hears it, He answers you.

Isaiah 30:19 ESV

We believe in the power of prayer. Prayer changes things! However, we need to put prayer in the right perspective – it's not really prayer that changes things, it's God who changes things, not so? We don't trust in our prayers as such – we trust in Him! We don't have a faith relationship with praying, but we do have a living relationship with God!

Prayer is only the way we express that trust, the communication by which we maintain the relationship with Him. Remember, no communication, no relationship! Prayer is to approach God, to speak with Him and to listen to Him. It's much more than simply words – especially hasty words that are purely about personal needs! Prayer is not getting God to do your will – no, prayer is to seek Him, enter His presence, find His will for you and share His love. Prayer is an attitude of longing for God, the wish to just be with Him. When we understand prayer this way, we'll realize that all prayers are answered.

Lord, like the disciples I ask You
to please teach me to pray! Amen.

If you sincerely seek God in prayer, He promises that you will experience His presence and receive His will and guidance for your life. Prayer is a discipline in which we must persevere.

You Will Hear the Voice

> Whether you turn to the right or to the left, you will hear a voice saying, "This is the road! Now follow it."
>
> *Isaiah 30:21 CEV*

In the future, Isaiah said, God would be nearer to His people. He would personally come and lead them. They would no longer stray like lost sheep. Whenever they strayed away, a voice would come to them, saying, "Here is the road – walk here." That time is already here, friend. When the Messiah came, He – Jesus Christ – announced, "The kingdom of God has drawn near" (Matthew 3:2). Yes, in Jesus Christ God came to us, here in the Messianic Era. Then He came even nearer to us: Christ sent the Holy Spirit onto us and into us. The Spirit is God-in-us – God living in our hearts, encouraging us, comforting us, warning us and guiding us. The Spirit is changing us from the inside out!

This coming of the Spirit was predicted as a sign of the End Times. It fulfills prophesies like these from Isaiah. You and I share in the privilege of the Holy Spirit! Yes, we can also listen to the guidance of the Spirit inside of us. Let's grow in that direction – hearing that voice!

Come, Holy Spirit. Fill me,
teach me, guide me. Amen.

God promises that He speaks and that He will speak to you.
You only need to make time and learn to listen.
Remember, He speaks in many different ways.

Your Seed Will Germinate

He will give rain for the seed with which you sow the ground, and bread, the produce of the ground, which will be rich and plenteous.

Isaiah 30:23 ESV

There is a "spiritual law" of sowing and reaping. Spiritual laws are not the same as physical laws, which can be implemented in an exact way. Spiritual principles are used by God in His own way. When we try to implement the principle of sowing and reaping for ourselves, for example, by sowing money in order to "harvest" a specific amount at a specific time, it doesn't work out. It's as if we try to implement spiritual things for carnal purposes, which is impossible – contrary. However, the principle remains a truth – if we sow, we will reap. God will provide a harvest, that's for sure! However, He will do it in His own way and time. He wants us to leave it with Him. We should just sow and then forget that we have.

Remember, we are called to a lifetime of sowing, of giving, of caring! Let's not do it for the reward – although the reward will be there. Look at today's verse: God's promise to you – again – is that He knows about your seed. There will be rain and yes, there will be a harvest. You will reap what you have sown.

Help me, Lord, to just sow.
I trust You with the seed. Amen.

If you live a life of sowing, God's promise today
is that you will reap a harvest. You do not have to worry
about the detail – it will germinate at the right time.

You Will Have Streaming Waters

On that day people will be slaughtered and towers destroyed, but streams of water will flow from high hills and towering mountains.

Isaiah 30:25 CEV

In Isaiah's vision he saw how enemy towers would fall on the Day of the Lord. Remember, the last war ever will bring judgment to all evildoers. Afterwards, God's blessing will be seen everywhere, like in the abundance of water that will stream from the hills and mountains. In Scripture, "towers" often symbolize bulwarks of sin and resistance to God, everything that actively opposes and excludes Him in the world. They also stand for spiritual strongholds that are put up against God. Remember that the hills and mountains were used for idolatry; that the enemy had the high ground, so to speak.

Think of an altar as a "high place" that is erected for idol worship. Similarly, in our personal lives, we create "high places" for false gods, which have undue importance. Now, if those towers were to fall, those same hills will overflow with God's goodness and mercy. From above God will anoint His people with His blessing. Think about these words – should you perhaps deal with some strongholds in your life?

*Yes, Lord, I need to deal with the following issues [name them].
In Jesus' name. Amen.*

If you take heed of the "high places" in your life –
the things you make sacrifices for – and renounce any ungodly
strongholds, God promises to give you the fullness of His blessings.

Your Light

The light of the moon will be as the light of the sun, and the light of the sun will be sevenfold, as the light of seven days, in the day when the Lord binds up the brokenness of His people, and heals the wounds inflicted by His blow.

Isaiah 30:26 ESV

Read this verse again and let the words and images sink in. Do you see God as the physician, sitting with His hurt and broken people, bandaging up their wounds? Beautiful!

The wounds were inflicted by God in the passive sense, meaning that He didn't stop the people from sinning and facing the consequences. Now, however, He puts a stop to it.

We realize again that the great and terrible Day of the Lord will for us be the day when God comes to fetch us, to rescue us, to help us up and to wipe away all our tears.

The signs concerning the sun, moon and stars that the prophets always associate with the coming of the Lord aren't meant literally – such light would kill us – but spiritually. God will be our light, coming to us in glory and shining like the sun. We will live in that light forever!

The purpose of verses like these is to encourage us to carry on. Be encouraged! Keep going faithfully until the day God comes for you!

Thank You for Your Word
and Your promises, Lord. Amen.

If you are experiencing hurt in your body or soul,
God promises to bandage your wounds and to heal you.
Then, for eternity, you will live, complete in His glory forever.

You Will Sing in the Night

You shall have a song as in the night when a holy feast is kept.
Isaiah 30:29 ESV

Isaiah was the greatest prophet of the Old Testament. He was such a visionary, writer and poet! He described the Day of the Lord in dramatic terms, the one image upon the other: God will come like the thunder, His words as a stream of fire. He will sift out the nations with a fine sieve. The storm of God's wrath will hit Assyria and it will tremble. Every one of God's blows will be accompanied by the sound of heavenly cymbals and harps (yes, even sound effects) – and the end of their king will be in the fiery pit that is being stoked as we speak … Wow!

Then, in the middle of all this drama and calamity comes this verse: in the night, the song of the righteous sounds. Yes, in the violent catastrophe God's people are calm, even happy. They sing and play the flute. What a contrast! What can we learn? We learn that God's children are safe, that this angry God is our Father who is coming to defend us. He will save us from danger and enemies, and take us home. Now that's something to sing about!

I praise You, Lord, for full salvation. Amen.

God promises that the end of the world will not be dreadful for you. It will be your deliverance, your salvation. You will sing and dance!

God Is like Your Mother

"I, the LORD All-Powerful, will protect Jerusalem like a mother bird circling over her nest."

Isaiah 31:5 CEV

Most images of God in the Bible are masculine, which is because the Bible was given in patriarchal times. Of course, wonderful meanings emerge when one thinks of God as King, God as Judge and especially God as Father. However, there are also some feminine images of God in the Bible (remember that God is Spirit and as such possesses no gender) and here we find one: God is like an eagle watching her nest. An enemy might think the nest is unprotected, but if they look up, they would see the mother bird circling high above, watching, ready to ward off any intruder. Isn't that beautiful?

The verse goes on to say that God protects us, saves us and "excuses" us – the last word meaning to "pass over" – this same term that is used for the Feast of the Passover, or *Pascha*. That adds something about the heart of a mother, doesn't it? Do you think you're all on your own – struggling along? Look up – God is there! Yes, God is very much like a Father, but He is also like a Mother: always available, always accepting, always ready to move the world to help their child.

Thank You, Lord, that You are also
like a mother to me. Amen.

If you thought that you are supposed to struggle along on your own, you're wrong, because God promises that He is watching over you with an eagle eye.

His Sword Is Your Sword

"The Assyrian shall fall by a sword, not of man; and a sword, not of man, shall devour him."

Isaiah 31:8 ESV

Isaiah said that on the last day, the enemy would be conquered by the sword, but not the sword of men – the sword of the Lord. In other words, not in humankind's own strength, but in the strength of God.

This verse makes us think of the instances in Scripture where the Word of God is referred to as a sword. Hebrews, for example, calls it a "double-edged sword" and Paul calls it the "sword of the Spirit" when he describes the Christian's armor. John, on the other hand, saw a vision of Jesus with a sword coming out of His mouth. We each need to learn to take up the Word of God as a weapon. How? Well, firstly we should know the Bible in order to trust its truths. Remember, faith = knowledge + trust. Therefore, read the Word (audibly is best), memorize it and meditate upon it. Let it enter your spirit.

Let the general Word become a specific word as the Spirit highlights certain parts for you personally. Then, stand on the Word, write it, say it, pray it and believe it! That's the way the Word's truth can become a trust-worthy weapon in your spiritual struggle.

Lord, help me to utilize Your Word more effectively. Amen.

God gives you His Word and promises that you can use it as a spiritual weapon and as a source for your spiritual growth. Learn to use it.

The Spirit in You

... Until the Spirit is poured upon us from on high, and the wilderness becomes a fruitful field, and the fruitful field is deemed a forest.

Isaiah 32:15 ESV

The Jews understood that at the end there wouldn't be just a once-off break between this age and the eternal one – the Messianic Era would come first, and fit in-between or overlap with both. The Messianic Era would be a special time in which certain things would happen. This includes the rule of the Messiah, peace and prosperity, the restoration of the temple, the gathering of the nations and – as Isaiah said here – the coming of the Spirit.

As Christians, we believe that Jesus the Messiah ushered in the Messianic Era. We believe that these things already happened or are about to happen, because we still live in that era. Let us add something about the outpouring of the Holy Spirit: the Spirit was poured out on the Church 2,000 years ago on Pentecost. And also on you! He is fully available to every child of God. Only, we should receive Him more fully and live out of His presence and power with more surrender. Open your heart to the Spirit's work without prescribing how it should be. Receive whatever happens (or doesn't happen) and start to live in His strength! Receive in faith and minister in faith. The onus is on you, not Him.

Thank You, Lord, for Your Spirit –
whom I receive right now. Amen.

God poured out His Spirit on His church and He promises that He will equip you and fill you with the Spirit. You just have to open your heart, receive Him and then live purposefully in His strength.

Your Strength for Today, and Every Day

O Lord, be gracious to us; we wait for You. Be our arm every morning, our salvation in the time of trouble.

Isaiah 33:2 ESV

This is yet another beautiful verse. God's "arm" every morning means God's daily strength – but what a beautiful picture! It focuses us on today. Yesterday is gone. Yes, we can do something about yesterday, but we have to do it today. Are there things in your life that weren't properly dealt with or adequately put to rest? Get to the point where you're free from the past: forgive people, ask for forgiveness, accept forgiveness! Forgive yourself radically as well – what you did when you were immature was immature; what else could be expected? You have learned the lessons, you have grown up – let it go and give it to God.

Also, to worry over the future is a waste of emotion, for we don't know what the future holds. We so often worry about things that will never occur, and the things that do happen we couldn't foresee at all. Yes, we can shape the future in a way, in the sense that we can plan for it and make provision for it. So, let's do – today – what we can, but then give our whole future into God's hands. That is faith! Ultimately, we only have today, and only strength for today. But that's all we need.

Lord, be my strength for today. Amen.

God does not want you to worry too much about yesterday
and tomorrow. He wants you to live for today and
He promises enough strength for today.

Your True Treasure

He will be the stability of your times, abundance of salvation, wisdom, and knowledge; the fear of the LORD is Zion's treasure.

Isaiah 33:6 ESV

Put this beautiful verse in your journal, because it tells us what our true treasure is. Jesus also spoke about it. Let's not seek our worth or wealth in money or possessions. We all do that, because it has the pretense of security, but our possessions can be taken from us in virtually overnight, or we from our possessions.

Jesus says they can also keep us away from our true wealth. Remember, our relationships are far more valuable than money. To share your life deeply, to give and receive love, to serve others – those are true riches! That is something that you can take into eternity.

Friend, your loved ones are your true silver and gold. The most valuable treasure imaginable, however, is living with God. To experience His full acceptance, forgiveness, redemption, to live according to His wisdom and purposes – that's living! Sell everything and obtain that, says Jesus!

Lord, You are my treasure,
my inheritance. Amen.

If you establish your confidence in money or try to find meaning through material goods, you will be disappointed. God promises that He is the fulfillment of your dreams, the treasure you are looking for.

Your Eyes Will See a King

With your own eyes you will see the glorious King; you will see His kingdom reaching far and wide.

Isaiah 33:17 CEV

Isaiah was reveling in the day that God would come and fix everything. He knew that difficult times were ahead for Israel: the destruction, the burnt cities, the thousands that would be killed, the abduction of the people to a far country, never to return, the families that would be torn apart for ever. All those things happened!

Isaiah, however, looked further than that and also saw the restoration – that there would be a wide new land and a King in glory. He guides the eyes of his readers to also see it, when he says, "with your own eyes you will see ..." We have already shown how God fulfilled these promises, although their complete fulfillment is still in the future. However, if we also fix our eyes on that fulfillment, if we can already see it in faith, we can withstand anything that lies between now and then. Remember: God's kingdom is not just for one day, it's also for *this* day. The kingdom will come and the kingdom has already come. We already experience God's reign and intervention! It's a reality for now, for the present, for your life! Bow now before the King and receive your fertile land.

*Thank You, Lord, for the inheritance
that I receive today. Amen.*

God promises you a wonderful inheritance,
a great reward. Keep your eye on the goal
and let the prize motivate you to run the race to the full!

April

Your Eyes Will See Zion

> Look to Mount Zion where we celebrate our religious festivals. You will see Jerusalem, secure as a tent with pegs that cannot be pulled up.
>
> *Isaiah 33:20* CEV

Isaiah wanted his readers to look away from their crisis. When a crisis hits us, we are most often so caught up by what is happening that we cannot think straight. We sink into a pit of worry and fear, or we become obsessed by anger or the injustice of it all. Soon we are trapped in a vortex of dark thoughts, in which things seem far more serious than they are. That is a dangerous place to be, because such thinking can drag down our emotions, drain our energy and prevent us from doing anything constructive.

Break that vicious circle! Scripture's answer is to look away radically. We need to see past our circumstances. For such a purpose, Isaiah painted a picture of the New Jerusalem for the Israelites. He wanted them to focus on that. Remember, crises will pass. They are temporary, insignificant in comparison to what awaits us. Nothing can really keep you away from God or His purpose! Nothing can ultimately go wrong. Just focus on Him.

Lord, my eyes are turned to You. Amen.

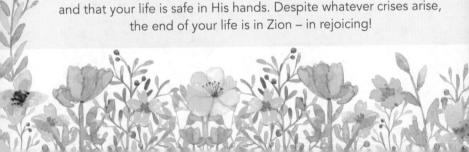

God promises that your end goal lies with Him
and that your life is safe in His hands. Despite whatever crises arise,
the end of your life is in Zion – in rejoicing!

You Won't Be Sick

And no inhabitant will say, "I am sick"; the people who dwell there will be forgiven their iniquity.

Isaiah 33:24 ESV

Isaiah was sharing about the Day of the Lord. On that day, there will be judgment, but also salvation. God will personally rule in Jerusalem, which the New Testament calls the "New Jerusalem." Isaiah mentioned wonderful things about the city, which is echoed in the New Testament: the temple, the streams of water, the abundant fruit, peace and prosperity, eternal joy … In today's verse Isaiah said that there will be no sicknesses.

Take note that Isaiah associated sickness with sin ("iniquity"), which is a common theme in the Bible. Generally, sin is at the root of all sickness, suffering and death. The intention is not to imply that you are sick because of a specific sin, but that sin and sickness are two sides of the same coin, that they belong in the same category. Both illustrate humankind's failure, our imperfection before God. We must be saved from both of these – and God will do that, said Isaiah. We already experience something of the kingdom of God. We *can* receive healing from sickness. Yes, we can – we can! Let's ask.

Thank You, Lord, for healing me;
and for one day healing me perfectly! Amen.

God promises you complete healing with Him one day,
but you should know that there is already
healing available now in His name.

Heaven Will Roll Back

All the host of heaven shall rot away, and the skies roll up like a scroll. All their host shall fall, as leaves fall from the vine.

Isaiah 34:4 ESV

The Day of the Lord will be the last ordinary day on earth. The prophets all say that the sun, moon and stars will stop shining on that day. The sun will darken and the moon will be as blood. Isaiah said that they will melt away, that the stars will wilt and fall off like dry leaves. Of the heavens itself – i.e. the blue skies – he said that they will roll up like a scroll. Remember, they saw the blue expanse above us as something that was stretched out over the earth, like a canvas or a dome. Against that backdrop the sun, moon and stars went about in their tracks.

We do believe that there will be a last day, but we also need to view these images figuratively. The heavenly bodies in those times were gods – they were worshiped, and the Hebrews wanted to convey that God would wipe them away, strike them off the map. What will we experience when the last day arrives and the sky rolls back? We don't know, but we do know that we'll be safe, with God, forever! We believe in eternal life!

Thank You, Lord, that I will be safe,
whatever happens. Amen.

God promises that there is eternal life and that after their death,
His children will rise again at the Second Coming
and will abide with Him forever.

Elsewhere, All Is Evil

Wildcats and hyenas will hunt together, demons will scream to demons, and creatures of the night will live among the ruins.

Isaiah 34:14 CEV

When God is done judging the nations and saving His people, only a barren and burnt landscape will remain. Dramatically and poetically, Isaiah told us what he saw: in the empty palaces and fortresses, thorns, nettles and thistles would grow. Instead of kings and princes living there, it would be inhabited by all the unclean animals (for the Jews) that one can think of: owls, crows, jackals, ostriches, wild dogs, hyenas, vultures, snakes.

That's still nothing! Then the demons would move in: the satyr (a field god) and "Lilith" are mentioned (a female demon, a type of vampire bent on hurting people at night). Yes, that's what it looks like where God is absent – pity the person who has to live in such a scenario! Let's make an application for today: there's a life with God, and a life without God. Both have eternal consequences.

The message of the Bible is that we should choose a life with God, which will lead into all eternity. Yes, that's a promise!

Lord, I choose a life with You! Amen.

God promises that the future with Him is good.
A future without God, however, is not good – it is shared with all that is evil and unclean. Make sure that your future is with Him.

Flowers Will Grow for You

Thirsty deserts will be glad; barren lands will celebrate and blossom with flowers.

Isaiah 35:1 CEV

Isaiah said that where God withdrew, everything turned to a wasteland. Chaos reigned. On the other hand, where God took control, the desert became a garden. Water began to flow, greenery sprang up and fields of flowers appeared. The original language referred here to a certain flower that no one knows anymore, so the different translations refer to a daffodil, narcissus, rose, lily or type of iris. It doesn't matter – the point is that beautiful flowers will flourish where once only barren land had been.

This verse brings to mind a well-known saying. When someone has been hurt or suffered emotional loss, people assure them – as encouragement – that the wound will heal, that "the grass will grow over it" again or that "the flowers will bloom over it" again. Have you heard that? Let's just share the following with those who are carrying a heavy burden: give yourself enough time to heal. Also, work actively with your hurt – talk about it, get closure, and grant or obtain forgiveness. Intentionally give the matter to God: "lay it at the foot of the cross," as the Christians of old would say. Let the flowers grow over it again.

Lord, help me to heal,
and turn my tears into beauty. Amen.

If you are experiencing inner pain, or the shock of rejection, trauma or loss, God promises that you will experience healing. Remember to give yourself enough time for the healing process.

Strengthen Your Hand

Say to those who have an anxious heart, "Be strong; fear not! Behold, your God will come with vengeance, with the recompense of God. He will come and save you."

Isaiah 35:4 ESV

This whole chapter in Isaiah is so beautiful – take time to read it slowly. It's only ten verses long, but it is pure poetry, fresh water for the soul! In these verses, Isaiah had a message for those with "weak hands;" in other words, those who had given up trying, who had "feeble knees" and who were barely stumbling on, tired to death. These are people who cannot go on anymore, who are on the verge of falling out of the race.

Are you at such a place? Don't lose heart – be strong! God is still at your side! What's more, God will come to change things, Isaiah said. Take note that he said both sides are involved in changing things. If God doesn't intervene, nothing will happen. However, despite our weariness, we need to strengthen our hands and knees and try once more. God works through us, remember, and also through our work. Yes, you may be exhausted and discouraged right now. But get up again! Keep your faith. Try once more.

Lord, help me as I try once again. Amen.

If you are discouraged and exhausted,
God promises to come to your aid. If you try again
you'll see that you can go on; you will find the strength.

Streams in Your Desert

For waters break forth in the wilderness, and streams in the desert.

Isaiah 35:6 ESV

Sometimes one feels inwardly dried out – fruitless and joyless, cut off even from your own inner being. Your life carries on, day by day, but the passion, the joy is not there. You don't *live*, you just exist. You just do what must be done. You feel alienated from God, as if He is far away and your prayers just disappear into the void.

Is this your experience? Then you're in the spiritual desert. What you need is the renewing of the Holy Spirit. He is the revitalizing streams of living water running in the desert, which will quicken your soul. Take note: if everything carries on the way it has, nothing will change at all. So, *you* must draw the line and make time to meet with God. Don't expect something specific and also don't think some once-off "hit" will do the trick. No, open yourself up over a period of time to God's presence. Make time in your day for prayer (ten minutes is a good start) and stick to it. Read a chapter in the Bible during your lunch break and play worship music as you drive. Just become more conscious of Him during your day! Then persevere with that, and the refreshing stream will break through!

Come, Holy Spirit – give me new life! Amen.

If you feel personally and spiritually drained,
God promises that there is renewed energy available to you.
He specializes in making streams flow in the desert.

Your Road Will Change

A good road will be there, and it will be named "God's Sacred Highway." It will be for God's people; no one unfit to worship God will walk on that road.

Isaiah 35:8 CEV

Life is often compared to a road or a journey. This comparison is also very common in the Bible. Jesus said, for example, that the path of the righteous is a narrow one. It means that if you serve God, you might encounter opposition, because a life lived for Him is often contrary to the life and values of the world around you.

Living with and for God involves choices, and some might not be popular with everyone. That's okay, though, because we don't live for the expectations of others; we live for the expectation of God. You can even experience real hardship, or ridicule and rejection, and you might wonder if it wouldn't be better to just join the others on the broad way. Don't consider that. Isaiah said that your road will change later on. The straight and narrow road will eventually become a highway, a freeway to heaven! The broad way that seems so attractive now will change as well and become very steep and extremely difficult, and take you to a place where you didn't want to be.

Lord, I want to stay on Your path! Amen.

God says that you are blessed if you experience exclusion or ridicule because of wanting to serve Him. He promises that the narrow way is the right way and will take you straight to Him.

You Will Return

The people the LORD has rescued will come back singing as they enter Zion. Happiness will be a crown they will always wear.

Isaiah 35:10 CEV

Back in the day when my generation was young – in the previous century! – we sang this verse:

Therefore the redeemed of the Lord shall return, and come with singing unto Zion; and everlasting joy shall be upon their head. What beautiful words of overcoming, hope, belief and steadfastness; all those years in captivity until one day the news broke – they were returning to Jerusalem! With singing and rejoicing, the procession would enter the city.

In the Bible, the topic of "returning" is an important one. Remember, as a nation Israel has "returned" twice: once out of Egypt and once out of Babylon – and today from all over the world. It's an important symbol for us, too: our life is also a journey to the Promised Land and the New Jerusalem. Here is the promise: the day will come when we will arrive, when we will enter the city with singing, with "everlasting joy"! So – live your life and do what you must do. Chase after your dreams. But also keep your eyes on the ultimate goal, and that goal is Him, one day, forever!

Lord, thank You for waiting for me
in the New Jerusalem! Amen.

Start imagining your joyful entry into the New Jerusalem, for God promised that day will come!

Focus on God, Not Your Problem

Don't be fooled by Hezekiah. He can't save you. Don't trust him when he tells you that the LORD will protect you from the king of Assyria.

Isaiah 36:14-15 CEV

Do you remember that Isaiah prophesied in the time when the Assyrians were threatening Israel's borders? Well, now they had invaded: the enemy had passed through the Northern Kingdom and taken out the people like weeds from a garden. Now they were in the Southern Kingdom, Judea. The second largest city, Lachish, was already taken.

An inscription in Nineveh, still seen today, testifies of this battle, in which the enemy built a ramp up to the city wall. Then they surrounded Jerusalem. King Hezekiah sent out a delegation to meet with the aide-de-camp of King Sennacherib. It is shocking what happened next: not in their own Aramaic, but in ordinary Judean, the enemy officer has his message shouted out to the city's inhabitants: *surrender so that we can remove you from this land! No one can save you! Your God will not save you – in fact your God told us to come for you!* Hezekiah, together with the whole city, was confused about the message, because in a sense the enemy was correct … hadn't the prophet warned them all along that God had ordained this? Would God save them from this calamity? What would He do? How about in your life?

Lord, what is Your will for me? Amen.

Often God gives us a clue or an answer to what we're searching for, but we stay focused on the problem. God promises that He will always come to your rescue, sometimes in ways you least expect.

Will You Save Me, Lord?

They said to him, "Thus says Hezekiah, 'This day is a day of distress, of rebuke, and of disgrace.'"

Isaiah 37:3 ESV

Sennacherib's forces had surrounded Jerusalem. It was usually just a question of time before famine forced a city to surrender. The enemy's official message to Jerusalem was that the Lord, the God of Israel Himself, had sent them to come and take the whole city. The king was absolutely confused about this. This was exactly what Isaiah warned them about, but they could not believe that surrendering was really God's will.

He called for Isaiah, asking him to pray for them. "It may be that the Lord your God will hear" (verse 4). Then things took a turn for the worse. The enemy king received notice that the Pharaoh of Egypt was on the way with an army – he wanted to finish off the matter immediately. Then he wrote threatening letters to Hezekiah, commanding his immediate surrender and telling him not to trust in his God, for they will not be saved. Hezekiah took the enemy's letters and went to the temple. There he spread them out before the Lord and prayed a wonderful prayer of true humility and faith. Friend, go to the Lord, spread out those unpaid accounts, those letters of demand, those test results or problems before Him. Fall on your knees and pray!

Lord, will You save me from this situation? Amen.

Things often seem overwhelming and impossible to us,
but God promises to bring deliverance.
Bring your concerns to Him, and trust Him.

The Lord Will Save You!

"Hezekiah, you prayed to Me about King Sennacherib of Assyria.
Now this is what I say to that king."

Isaiah 37:21 CEV

The enemy had surrounded Jerusalem and no provisions were coming in.
Hezekiah was in the temple, praying to God about the threatening letters
he had received from Sennacherib, demanding their immediate surrender.
He humbled himself in sackcloth and ashes and pleaded for salvation. Then
Isaiah sent him this answer: God has heard your prayer! God's message was
that Jerusalem wouldn't fall then – only much later.

The rest of the message is God taunting the enemy; God laughing at
Sennacherib. Nothing would come of the siege: "The king of Assyria won't
get into Jerusalem … he will return by the way he came" (verses 33-34). That
was exactly what happened – after a siege of two years (!) and tremendous
losses in their camp (God caused some kind of sickness), they packed up
and left. Jerusalem's gates were opened once again – how they survived,
no one knew. One day, when Sennacherib was worshiping his god in its
temple, his sons came and speared him to death. God's people's enemy is
His enemy too and He, not the enemy, will ultimately be victorious. Hang
on to that truth!

Lord, save me amid these circumstances! Amen.

Even during the most desperate conditions,
we do not have to lose hope. Things can change. Keep praying,
because God promises that He hears your prayers.

Saved, but Not Because of You

"I will defend this city to save it, for My own sake and for the sake of My servant David."

Isaiah 37:35 ESV

God's message to Hezekiah was that He would save the city, but He added that it wouldn't be because of the faithfulness of the people. On the contrary, Isaiah had warned them all along about their sin and godlessness. In fact, they deserved to be captured. However, God saved them, for His own sake. What does this mean? God was referring to His covenant. God kept the covenant, even when they broke it day after day. He remained true, in spite of their indifference.

God Himself provided for their rescue – and for ours, for in Jesus Christ God took the responsibility for us. He took the punishment; we take the forgiveness. How wonderful! And for David's sake! Now that's interesting – David lived 400 years prior to this, but was so loved by God that He was still taking care of David's progeny (Hezekiah) so many centuries later. It was about God's covenant with David – which He still honored, all those years later. Our New Testament perspective is this: for the sake of Jesus Christ, God is on our side. Because of Him, He saves us!

Thank You, Lord, for Your grace;
thank You, Jesus, for the cross. Amen.

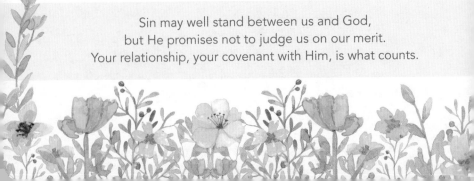

Sin may well stand between us and God,
but He promises not to judge us on our merit.
Your relationship, your covenant with Him, is what counts.

Against the Wall

Then Hezekiah turned his face to the wall and prayed to the LORD.
Isaiah 38:2 ESV

Isaiah told us another story about Hezekiah. During the time that Jerusalem was besieged, he fell very ill. Isaiah's initial response from God was chilling: "Set your house in order, for you shall die" (verse 1). Stricken with grief, Hezekiah turned to the wall and prayed. When you're literally and figuratively against the wall, the only way is to look up, not so? He pleaded for his life – he reminded God of his sincerity and God's promises. He persevered like a true man of prayer. Then suddenly Isaiah was back with a new message: "Thus says the Lord, the God of David your father: I have heard your prayer; I have seen your tears. Behold, I will add fifteen years to your life" (verse 5).

Here is the lesson: God changed His mind, because a man of God prayed! That is the power of prayer. The rest of the chapter is a song of praise to God: "My dwelling is plucked up and removed from me like a shepherd's tent … He cuts me off from the loom … The Lord will save me, and we will play my music on stringed instruments" (verses 12, 20). It's so beautiful, but where is *our* song of gratitude, *our* praise?

Thank You, Lord, thank You – for everything! Amen.

God promises that your relationship with Him is a dynamic one.
It functions in the reality of your everyday life –
He actively lives with you through your circumstances.

God's Time and Your Time

"Comfort, comfort My people, says your God."

Isaiah 40:1 ESV

We now begin with the second part of the book of Isaiah. According to scholars, it was written during the Babylonian captivity by a successor of the prophet Isaiah. Many, many years went by and everything that Isaiah had said came to pass: Jerusalem fell eventually to the Babylonians and the Jews were deported into captivity, which lasted 70 years. The older generation died there, in the foreign land, and a whole new generation was born: a generation who had only heard about the motherland. They spoke a different language (Aramean), thought in new ways and even developed a new script for writing.

Then the message suddenly came – they were returning! Significant political moves had made it possible. Here is the lesson: everything happens within God's specific timing. The season of captivity that the prophet Jeremiah had fixed at 70 years was now reaching its end. A new season was at hand. God's timing is what it's all about. There are also seasons in our lives – and yes, this season you are in will also come to an end, at exactly the right time!

Lord, I pray that my times
and Your times will coincide. Amen.

God promises deliverance, but His time is not always your time.
If you remain close to God, your time
and His time will overlap more and more.

A Voice to You

Someone is shouting: "Clear a path in the desert! Make a straight road for the LORD our God. Fill in the valleys; flatten every hill and mountain."

Isaiah 40:3-4 CEV

The captives in Babylon received the message that they were to return to their land, and to Jerusalem. The news was conveyed in the style of a pronouncement that would accompany a king of old: "make way, make way for the king!" The "way" is a metaphorical way, of course, but it's a powerful image. It prepares the scene: the king is not there as yet, but his coming is imminent. Everyone should be ready!

In the Bible this is a well-known image used by John the Baptist (see Mark 1:3), who prepared the way for Jesus – and it's also how we think of Jesus' return. Still, the king's arrival *did* follow such an announcement, the people *did* return to their land and Jesus *did* come after John's proclamation. So, it's no mere figure of speech, no idle promise. Rather, it is a real and true announcement. Today, I proclaim to you with confidence the following: prepare, for God is on His way to you.

I will prepare as best I can – come, Lord Jesus! Amen.

God promises that He is on His way. His arrival should not surprise you, because He let you know ahead of time that He would be coming so that you can prepare yourself.

If God Has Decided

The grass withers, the flower fades, but the word of our God will stand forever.

Isaiah 40:8 ESV

The prophet was instructed to announce to the Jews that their release was imminent. However, it's as if there was doubt about the possibility of it really happening. Were the Jews so long in captivity that they had forgotten their own country? Indeed, the new generation knew nothing else – they even spoke the language and followed the habits of their captors. We read that the prophet pleaded for his Jewish kinsmen, saying they were merely like grass – ephemeral – and only a small nation. Their experience was one of constant oppression and subjugation, always exposed to the big empires of the world. It could be that the prophet was quoting from Psalm 90:5-6: "They are like grass that is renewed in the morning: in the morning it flourishes and is renewed; in the evening it fades and withers."

God's answer to this objection is important: yes, He says, people are like grass, but His word stands forever! In other words, He has made His decision, regardless of whom and what you are. Listen, it's not as much about you as you may think; it's more about God's decision to bless. Who will stop Him from fulfilling His promises?

Thank You, Lord, that Your decision is said and done! Amen.

If God has said something is going to happen,
He promises that it will. Nobody can stop Him –
not even your fallible human nature.

In His Arms

He will tend His flock like a shepherd; He will gather the lambs in His arms; He will carry them in His bosom, and gently lead those that are with young.

Isaiah 40:11 ESV

The prophet said that the people had to start believing in their return; in fact, they should have made it widely known and shouted it from the hilltops! It was as if they were struggling to accept it. They had to take hold of it then, because it was going to happen. They should have left their inferiority, their beggar's mentality, behind. God still loved them, even after all those years. He would gather up His lambs again – carry them in His arms and cuddle them. What a beautiful image! It brings to mind Jesus' words that He is the Good Shepherd, that He loves His sheep and would leave the whole herd to look for one that is lost.

The people needed these encouraging words after everything they had been through: the war, the death of many family members, being uprooted from their homes and having to find their feet again in a foreign country. They really felt rejected by God! That was not true, of course – they were still His people. Likewise, you are still God's child, still His beloved! Believe it and say it!

I believe it, Lord – that You love me. Amen.

You cannot rate your standing as a child of God based on circumstances. God promises that you are His child, regardless of your circumstances – because He says so!

You Were Made by Hand

> Who has measured the waters in the hollow of His hand and marked off the heavens with a span, enclosed the dust of the earth in a measure and weighed the mountains in scales and the hills in a balance?
>
> *Isaiah 40:12 ESV*

The Lord wanted His people to believe that the unthinkable was possible: that a nation that was uprooted 70 years ago would be completely repatriated. Still, it happened! The prophet motivated this possibility by referring to the wonder of creation. He described – in human terms – how God scooped up the earth's water with His hand, how He measured the sky as precisely as a handbreadth wide (an interesting take on God's size!), how He brought in soil in a container and how He weighed the mountains on a scale – beautiful images!

If that was easy for God, how easy would it be for Him to move a nation back to their homeland? Or how easy would it be for Him to help you and me? Didn't He also make us by hand? Didn't He finish off our bodies perfectly, install our delicate souls expertly and blow into us His own life-giving Spirit? Yes, He did! Our whole making is a costly work of art, and the Artist stood back after creating us (as artists do), smiled and said that it was beautiful, blessed! Yes, He said that of you!

How wonderful is Your handiwork, Lord! Amen.

God promises today that He regards you
as His special handiwork – something precious and valuable.
He thinks He has done a great job with you!

Speak Less

*Has anyone told the L*ORD *what He must do or given Him advice?*
*Did the L*ORD *ask anyone to teach Him wisdom and justice?*

Isaiah 40:13-14 CEV

In this part of Isaiah, the prophet was encouraging his people – the Jews in captivity. It contains some of the most beautiful passages in the Bible, and is the part that is quoted most in the New Testament. At this stage the prophet described how great God is. He referred to the Holy Spirit and emphasized that the Spirit doesn't need anyone's input – as God, He is completely self-sufficient.

In practice that means that we can stop telling God what to do! Our prayers are often so full of instructions for God – it's as if we think He doesn't really understand our needs! Did He forget, or is He perhaps too busy? Is it the one who prays the loudest that receives His attention? No, of course not! God already knows everything about you, especially your genuine needs – that which is best for you. Let's try something else in our prayers: let's stop talking. Let's just come to be with Him and to listen: listen intently to His Word and listen to His Spirit. That is enough for now.

Lord, I want to speak less and listen more –
help me to do this! Amen.

Sometimes we feel that we have to give God instructions
regarding our needs. God's promise is that He knows about
your every need. If you spend time in His presence
and listen to Him intently, you will hear what He has to say.

The Image of God

An idol! A craftsman casts it and a goldsmith overlays it with gold and casts for it silver chains.

Isaiah 40:19 ESV

The prophet was telling his discouraged people that their suffering was over. Their God was a reality and was still involved in their lives. He was not like the idols of the heathens that they made for themselves. It is interesting how he described how they manufactured such an idol – there was one for every budget!

We too have a specific "image" of God – our personal idea of who and what He is. Each of us has such an image, based on our personality, background and needs. It's who God is "for you." For one person He is a strict Master and for another He's a loving Dad. One individual may believe that God is really not interested in every minor trespass and another may not want to drive somewhere without praying to Him first. This process is very natural, but we should be aware of limiting God. He is always bigger than our perception of Him! We should at least acknowledge that our personal grasp of who God is, is restricted and subjective, that our minds are too small to comprehend Him. Let's not worship the small God we have made, but the *big* God that He is! That includes accommodating other believers' understanding of Him as well.

Lord, I know that You're bigger than I
can ever think or imagine. Amen.

Although it is natural for you to create an image of God in your mind, God promises that He is far greater than you can think or believe. Don't limit Him to your understanding.

Greater Than You Think

It is He who sits above the circle of the earth, and its inhabitants are like grasshoppers; who stretches out the heavens like a curtain, and spreads them like a tent to dwell in.

Isaiah 40:22 ESV

The prophet had to convince his people in captivity of God's greatness and power, because they reasoned that God deserted them and that the gods of Babylonia had "won." He referred them to the heavens. In those days the people distinguished between three heavens: the blue sky was the "first heaven," which they thought was spread out over the earth like a tent. There is a beautiful connotation in the text to this "firmament" as having been made of a delicate material, like gauze. The "second heaven" was probably the realm of the gods or spirits, at the same time referring to the sun, moon and stars. These were, after all, the heathens' gods. Then there was the "third heaven," where God lived – above everything else.

The lesson of such a view was that God was enthroned high above every possible idol, power or authority. This is our lesson as well: no man-made god, devil, evil spirit or worldly system can separate you from God – nor can any situation, accident or obstacle, or even death itself! That's the clear Bible message. Your God is greater than you think.

Thank You, Lord, for being greater than this situation. Amen.

We have our perceptions about the powerful forces in our lives, but God promises that He towers above all the principalities and powers in our lives. It's all under His control.

God Creates, and God Cares

Look at the evening sky! Who created the stars? Who gave them each a name? Who leads them like an army? The LORD is so powerful that none of the stars are ever missing.

Isaiah 40:26 CEV

To demonstrate God's greatness, the prophet pointed the people to the stars. Ancient humankind knew much more about the stars than their average modern counterpart! Not having had electric light (and television!), they had time to view the starry sky in its full splendor night after night. In biblical times, society measured people's eyesight by which smaller or bigger stars they could see, but even those with the keenest eyesight saw that there was an infinite multitude of stars.

To think that God rules over such a host is a remarkable thought. What we want to notice in this verse, however, is the following: (1) God creates the stars in their awe-inspiring number and then (2) He takes care of them. God knows the condition of each (the verse says that He has a name for every one) and allows things to happen to each star as it should. Wow! In the same way, God also created you perfectly, knows your name and makes sure that everything happens to you according to His will. You must trust Him for that.

Thank You, Lord, that I am safe in Your hands. Amen.

God made you and He promises that He will take care of you. Taking care of you is not difficult or complicated for Him – He has it completely under control!

Do You Need Wings?

They who wait for the LORD shall renew their strength; they shall mount up with wings like eagles; they shall run and not be weary; they shall walk and not faint.

Isaiah 40:31 ESV

The message that they would return to Israel sounded good to the Jewish people, but they wondered if they were up to it. Remember, they were violently taken from their land and had to re-establish themselves with tremendous effort. The prophet Jeremiah told them not to think of returning soon – he said they should build houses, plant fields and raise children. So that's what they did, while trying to maintain their Jewish identity. Later, it became easier and with the new generation it was even better, since they only knew Babylon. Should they all simply have packed up everything and returned? Did they have the strength?

Yes, said the prophet, God would give them strength! If they trusted in Him, their journey would be uneventful. And when they looked again, they would have traveled all those miles and across all those borders – as if an eagle had gathered them up and put them down again – and be refreshed, not even weary. Do you have a daunting task before you? Do you feel apprehensive or anxious? Trust God for strength – ask Him to lift you up and carry you through it! He will.

Thank You, Lord. I need Your strength today! Amen.

God promises that He will enable you to overcome
that difficult time or daunting task. In retrospect,
you will see that He carried you through it all.

Keep Your Eyes on Him

"Who makes these things happen? Who controls human events? I do! I am the LORD."

Isaiah 41:4 CEV

The reason that the Jews could return to Israel was political. While they were in Babylon, a new power from the north, the Persians, rose up. The king of Persia, Cyrus the Great, attacked the New Babylonian Empire and conquered it. He had a different view on all the foreign people who lived there, like the Jews. Suddenly there was light at the end of the tunnel!

We will return to the details, but let's just confirm the following for today: clearly the prophet ascribed all these events to God. One person may say it is politics and another might refer to economic or social factors, or perhaps natural occurrences. However, for us – as believers – there is something, or someone, behind all these events. Yes, behind these things we see the Lord. Our eyes are on Him, not on the "factors."

Look beyond your circumstances and trust God.

Yes, Lord, in these circumstances my eyes are on You. Amen.

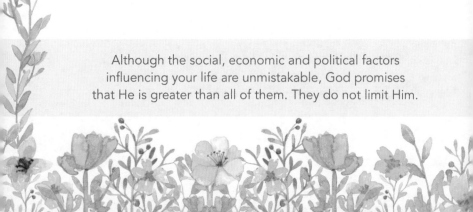

Although the social, economic and political factors influencing your life are unmistakable, God promises that He is greater than all of them. They do not limit Him.

A Wonderful Tomorrow

"Who controls human events? I do! I am the LORD. I was there at the beginning; I will be there at the end."

Isaiah 41:4 CEV

It is the year 540 B.C., Cyrus, the ruler of the Persian Empire, defeated the great city of Babylon by partly diverting the river Euphrates that flowed through it. As the water level receded, his soldiers sneaked into the city by night through the opening through which the river entered into the city. He took Babylon without casualty by capturing the Babylonian king. It was one of the iconic victories of history.

Eventually Cyrus built the biggest empire ever – from Turkey to India. This victory caused a great commotion: the Babylonians themselves were apprehensive of course, while the captives that had been brought to Babylon (like the Jews) were hopeful for change. The prophet mocked the heathen nations by saying that they had gone to consult their idols, but first had to nail down the statue so that it didn't fall over! His words to the Jews were clear – God was at work! He is the Lord of history. So, don't become anxious when you hear bad news, and don't participate in pessimism about the future. It's unnecessary. With God there is every hope for a wonderful future!

Thank You, Lord, for a wonderful tomorrow. Amen.

People often have negative feelings about their country or the future, but they don't consider God. God promises that He will give a good future to everyone who believes – that's you, too.

Rejoice Despite Your Circumstances

"But you, Israel, My servant, Jacob, whom I have chosen, the offspring of Abraham, My friend."

Isaiah 41:8 ESV

There was a new regime and new soldiers in Babylon. The Jewish people, who were moved there many decades before, didn't know how to react – much like the other foreign nations that were similarly displaced. The prophet encouraged the people in today's verse by taking them back to the God of their fathers, to Abraham and Jacob. He confirmed that God was still the same God. They were still His chosen people. God's covenant with them was not annulled. They merely *felt* lost and left behind, although they were not.

Remember, circumstances can make us feel this way. Our doubt in God often comes because we want things to only go well. When circumstances become unpleasant, we complain: God is not there, God has forgotten us, and so on. That is wrong. The truth is that God is trustworthy and loyal in spite of whatever circumstances you might experience. You remain His beloved! Look away from your circumstances, look away from your empty stalls or failed harvest – and rejoice nevertheless in the God of your salvation. That changes things!

Lord, I praise You in spite of everything. Amen.

Although our emotions go up and down, God's reliability remains the same. He promises that He will stay with you, that He won't forget you and will help you – no matter how you feel!

I Am with You

"Fear not, for I am with you; be not dismayed, for I am your God; I will strengthen you, I will help you, I will uphold you with My righteous right hand."

Isaiah 41:10 ESV

What a beautiful verse – one that has encouraged thousands of people in difficult times, a typical Scripture promise that people can identify with personally. Let's today share a very simple, but one of the most important truths of our faith – and it's this: God is with you. If we could only really grab hold of that fact, if we could only really feel or know it – that He is actually with us, around us, in us! Then we would also experience what is further claimed in this verse: we would not fear or be dismayed.

Let's spell it out: God is truly, truly in you by His Spirit. The day you committed your life to Him, He took up residence in your spirit in a special way. Because of that, you are able to feel His presence more, you can keep a conversation going with Him, and you may live boldly today in the knowledge that your God is with you. You may trust unwaveringly in His support and presence in whatever situation you find yourself. You may, and you must, because that's what a life of faith is.

Lord, help me to grow in a practical life with You. Amen.

God promises that He is with you – at this very moment, in the very place where you are. He's right next to you and in you – allow yourself to experience Him more.

Keep Trusting God

"I am the LORD your God. I am holding your hand, so don't be afraid. I am here to help you."

Isaiah 41:13 CEV

In this part of Isaiah, where God was comforting His people, He often used this type of language: I am your God, I am taking your hand, I say don't fear, I will help you, etc. God was speaking here and He was pouring His encouragement and affirmation over them. After a long while in which they felt His absence, they were now experiencing His wonderful closeness.

This is much like our own experience of God. The emphasis was on Him – that He would do all these things. What was expected of the people? God expected them to trust Him. The significance here was not so much on Israel's holiness or righteous living, but on the season that was passing and on God's decisions. Of course God wanted them to continue steadfastly in His will, but He wasn't waiting on them to attain a certain level before He would intervene. No, He would intervene when He decided to. So, carry on doing the right things – this is indeed important – but also trust God today, and keep on trusting.

Lord, I'm waiting on You. Amen.

God promises that He is at work in your life.
He takes initiative and intervenes. He asks that you
trust Him in this. The least you can do is to work with Him.

An Oasis in Your Desert

"I will fill the desert with all kinds of trees – cedars, acacias, and myrtles; olive and cypress trees; fir trees and pines."

Isaiah 41:19 CEV

The people would return from captivity and that was a fact. A new time was lying ahead. In flowery language – like a poet writing a poem, or a seer describing his vision – the prophet sketched a picture of abundance. The barren Judean landscape would change: fountains would burst out of the hills and streams would flow in the valleys. Everything would turn green with all sorts of trees: cedar, acacia, olive, cypress, fir – the desert would turn into a woodland.

Remember, the Jews *did* return to their land and are living there today, although this transition was accompanied with much hardship. Today Israelis quote this verse when they show visitors the productive farms they have established in the desert (using irrigation). For us, the symbolism is this: people can find themselves in a desert far away from God, in the captivity of sin, but God invites them to return to where they belong. Our true home is with Him! He promises to you and me a new life of living water and fruitful trees – an abundant life! That's God's heart: abundance, joy, love and peace.

Yes, Lord, I so desire such a life –
I return to You. Amen.

If you are experiencing a desert in your life at the moment, God promises that He can make an oasis out of any desert. Wherever there is a desert in your life, God can change it.

May

Powerless Idols

"You idols are nothing, and you are powerless."

Isaiah 41:24 CEV

The prophet was rejoicing over the return of his people to their country, because it was a tremendous event. Remember, the older generation had long before lost the hope of returning and the younger generation had already adapted to their land of birth. God was now ridiculing the gods of Babylon. He said they are worthless against Jehovah, that they were nothing and their power was zero. The great king of Babylon had been removed by a still greater king, Cyrus of Persia, and they should have realized that even he was a mere pawn in God's hand!

In this way, God was turning the tables: what was raised up would be rendered low, and what was low would be exalted. That is the way God works! Remember, the principles of the kingdom of God are often directly opposed to the principles of this world. That which is worshiped here and now (and we participate to an extent, don't we?), such as money, possessions, power, position, honor and status, is wiped off the table and replaced with love, compassion, servanthood, faithfulness, hope, joy, faith and peace … Now those are becoming the important things!

Lord, teach me the principles of Your kingdom. Amen.

Even if we think that money, honor and status can bring happiness, they are often just idols and only important in the eyes of this secular world. God promises that He can offer you much more than that.

The Joy of Serving

"Behold My servant, whom I uphold, my chosen, in whom My soul delights."

Isaiah 42:1 ESV

In Isaiah in various places, the prophet referred to a mysterious "servant." Who was this? Well, firstly it referred to Israel in captivity – the small nation, despised by others but chosen by God, yet destined to be saved and returned. Moreover, the promise was that God would exalt them and make them a light unto the nations. That happened exactly so!

The second meaning of "servant" was Jesus Christ. Many Jews came to read these verses about the "Suffering Servant" as a reference to the coming Messiah. By New Testament times, the term was specifically applied to Jesus, especially the parts that referred so clearly to the cross.

Let's stop here for today. What is the lesson in all of this? Firstly, God promised, and God did! Secondly, the Servant that God sent became – incredible as it is – our Servant, your Servant! In life and death, Jesus only served. What a lesson! Let's forget the power games, the vying for control. The meaning – and the joy – of life is to serve.

Lord, teach me to serve. Amen.

God promises that it is better to serve than to be served, since there are blessings and joy in serving. He proved it personally by sending a Servant to earth. By all means, serve.

God's Servants in the World

"Here is My servant! I have made Him strong. He is my Chosen
One; I am pleased with Him. I have given Him My Spirit."

Isaiah 42:1 CEV

The prophet referred a couple of times to someone he just calls the
"servant" – whom we also call the "Suffering Servant." By that he primarily
meant Israel, who is God's servant in the world. However, Jews and
Christians later on also saw the servant as the Messiah. The New Testament
applies these passages directly to Jesus Christ.

There is also a third meaning: you and I are also in the world to be servants! We are called to make His will known to the nations, and we are
anointed by the Holy Spirit to minister. We also share in Christ's rejection
and His cross. Don't think it's humiliating to serve. No, if we represent Christ
the Servant in the world, it's an honor – even if we have to suffer for our
Christian faith. Blessed are you, Jesus said, if you suffer rejection or insults
when you stand up for Him, or when you want to do what is right (see
Matthew 5:10-11).

Lord, teach me to serve with gladness! Amen.

We think that life is all about us – our needs and our desires.
However, it's really about other people and about God, and He
promises that that path holds more meaning. You are there for others.

The Spirit and the Nations

"Behold My servant whom I uphold ... I have put my Spirit upon Him; He will bring forth justice to the nations."

Isaiah 42:1 ESV

The "Suffering Servant" that Isaiah refers to so mysteriously was Jesus Christ, the Messiah, through whom the whole Messianic Era was ushered in. Jesus calls it the "kingdom of God" and it's an era of serving. *What?* Do you say you're indeed a child of the King, but no person's servant? Then remember that in the kingdom of God the leaders shall be as servants, just like their Master was, the ultimate Servant King. No, in the Kingdom we don't mind washing others' feet! Moving on, we see two other characteristics of the Messianic Era in this verse:

1. The Era of the Spirit. The Holy Spirit was poured out on Pentecost to equip the church to be effective ministers and servants (which is the same word!) in the world;
2. The Era of the Nations. By the power of the Spirit, the church goes into the whole world and makes God's will known to every tongue and nation.

In the book of Acts, we see how these two aspects come together: the gospel is proclaimed by the power of the Holy Spirit. Both are essential! Let's put it the other way around: you and I need today to be filled with the Spirit and to live as witnesses for Jesus. Here is a tip: life works best when we serve.

Lord, fill me with Your Spirit of grace,
and make me a servant today. Amen.

God sees your heart. By loving and serving others,
you show your love for Him. Even if others forget what you've done,
God promises that He will never forget.

Always a Gentleman

"He will not cry aloud or lift up His voice, or make it heard in the street."

Isaiah 42:2 ESV

God, through Isaiah, talks about the "servant of God" – a personalization of Israel, but also the coming Messiah. The Messiah is described here as humble and kind, someone who talks softly, who doesn't shout in the streets. Quietly He does His work – from person to person; encouraging, comforting, healing. That's how Jesus was! He never shouted at sinners, even when they were clearly guilty or wrong. No, He accepted them, spent time with them and showed them the right way. This was His attitude with the tax collectors Levi and Zacchaeus, with the Samaritan woman, the woman caught in adultery and the sinful woman who wept at His feet.

Do you see His heart – so different from ours, not so? He kept His harsh words for the hypocrites, especially the religious leaders. For us, the Holy Spirit works in our hearts in exactly the same way – always as a gentleman. Have you lost your way? Did you fall morally? Do you realize your need, your dependence on God? The Spirit will quietly and lovingly help you up.

Holy Spirit, thank You for working with me so graciously. Amen.

If you are on the wrong path but have a need for God's deliverance, He promises that you will find Him. He will not scold or blame you, but will gently show you the right path.

He Won't Break You Down

"A bruised reed He will not break, and a faintly burning wick He will not quench."

Isaiah 42:3 ESV

The "servant" that Isaiah referred to is identified in the New Testament as Jesus Christ. The description in this verse fits Him like a glove: He came to restore, not to break; lost sheep should be searched for and brought back, He said; lost sons should be welcomed back into the Father's house. How different from us, who angrily react when someone strays off the path! Tax collectors were befriended and converted by Jesus and even adulterers were not condemned but saved from the punishment of the law. "Sin no more," He merely said.

No, when Christ sees a broken reed, He doesn't break it further; instead, He binds it up. A faintly burning lamp is not quenched, but patiently trimmed and fixed so it can burn again brightly. He is only interested in healing, restoring, renewing – that's His heart! So: are you broken? Lost? Is your light flickering? Are you in despair and feeling tearful? Jesus will never break you down further. No, He will restore you completely.

Do it today, Lord: heal me! Amen.

If you are disheartened and broken,
God will never break you down further.
He promises to pick you up, restore you and heal you!

He Will Hold You

"I am the LORD; I have called You in righteousness; I will take You by the hand and keep You."

Isaiah 42:6 ESV

God is not a man that He can disappoint us. He is the "Lord" – *Yahweh* (Jehovah), who is what He is, and who will be what He will be. In other words, He does not change. God often referred His people back to His covenant with them – an enduring covenant that's still valid.

Remember, in Christ (to whom these words were aimed) we are part of God's people and God's covenant. That's a fact. The "covenant" is God's contract with His people, sealed with His own blood. He cannot and will not go back on His promises! Even though we don't keep our part of the covenant, He will keep His! He remains true, even if we don't. That's what the Bible says.

The covenant promise is that He will be our God and we will be His children. That includes taking us by the hand, holding us, carrying us through safely until the end, whatever the cost. Yes, that's His promise!

Thank You, Lord, that Your signature
underlines this promise. Amen.

You don't have to worry that God will forsake you.
Despite our unfaithfulness, He promises to be faithful –
to His own promises and character.

Healing to the World

"… To open the eyes that are blind, to bring out the prisoners from the dungeon, from the prison those who sit in darkness."

Isaiah 42:7 ESV

God spelled out the task of the Messiah in these verses. Jesus Christ took these words on Himself as He started His ministry in the synagogue in Nazareth: "The Spirit of the Lord is upon Me … to proclaim liberty to the captives and recovering of sight to the blind" (Luke 4:18).

Indeed, no one brought sight to so many blind and freedom to so many captives as He did! However, I want us to focus a bit further down the line: you and I are continuing in the work of Christ. His command to us was similarly to heal the sick, cleanse the lepers, proclaim freedom, and so forth. As God gives us the gifts in this regard, we can be obedient in this task. See above all God's heart behind this – we are here, as He was, to have a healing and restoring influence in the world. You, fellow believer, have the task today to fix, to restore, to build, to heal, to encourage, to liberate, and to let God's light shine in the darkness. Do this today!

Lord, make me a healer today. Amen.

God promises that He will use you as a healing
and restoring influence in the world. Much healing
will flow through you if you open yourself up to be used by Him.

You'll Sing His Praise

Sing to the LORD a new song, His praise from the end of the earth.

Isaiah 42:10 ESV

To sing "a new song" is a theme that we find from time to time in the Bible. Here the reader is called up to rejoice because God has announced that He'll send an anointed Servant, the Messiah. What He promised came true, as it always does.

From the New Testament, we know that this Servant was Jesus Christ. Let's underline something else here: the people – actually the whole world – should rejoice on account of this promise, not the fulfillment! Remember, God's promise of salvation is as good as His salvation – both are equally true and factual. For God, it's the same thing, although for us the one happens after the other.

The lesson is this: if God promises His salvation to you (and I proclaim it to you today), it's as good as already being saved. Accept it! On account of that alone, you can now rejoice. Sing His praise! Play praise and worship music, write a prayer praising God, and tell people that you know for sure that God will deliver you. He will!

Thank You, Lord! I trust You –
and I sing Your praise! Amen.

We often first want to wait for the fulfillment
of the promise before we give thanks and rejoice,
but the promise in itself is already cause for thanks and praise!
He indeed promises to do what He says. Thus, rejoice!

God Will Birth Something New

"For a long time I have held My peace; I have kept still and restrained Myself; now I will cry out like a woman in labor; I will gasp and pant."

Isaiah 42:14 ESV

Remember we said that God is sometimes described in the Bible in female terms? Here we find another example. God was speaking here, He was promising a new season for the Jews in captivity. Had He forgotten about them in Babylon? No, He hadn't! He merely restrained Himself, waiting for the set time to go by. Now He could not wait any longer – the time had come!

The prophet conveyed this message in dramatic language, using the images of pregnancy and birth. After nine months, the season of waiting was over and the birth had come. It was inevitable. He painted the picture of God in the pangs of labor with all the intensity that it entailed. This is graphic imagery indeed! At last the birth took place – the new time was at hand! The lesson is this: the current season is merely a season, a set period. Then it will pass. God will usher in a new time, even for you. And yes – it might involve some pain, but that is inevitable with all new beginnings.

Yes, Lord, usher in a new time in my life! Amen.

The pain that you may be experiencing could be the birth pains of something new that God is planning for you. He promises that He will bring something new, and the pain is just part of that.

Your Path Will Become Clearer

"I will lead the blind on roads they have never known; I will guide them on paths they have never traveled. Their road is dark and rough, but I will give light to keep them from stumbling. This is My solemn promise."

Isaiah 42:16 CEV

What a beautiful verse! God promised a new season to His people. Their captivity was almost at an end – they were going home! In verse 18, however, the prophet described them as "blind" – they still didn't realize their ignorance, their sin – and they didn't comprehend what was happening or what to do. They just could not see it. However, that didn't matter. As they returned, the unknown road would become clearer, the difficulties would be resolved and the darkness would lift. What they thought of as impossible would be possible, after all!

Friend, do you struggle to see the way? Does the future seem uncertain, unsure and dark – even dangerous? That's no problem for God. As you walk, He will show you the way. As you follow, things will fall into place. Before you know it, you will be on an even road, with the future clear ahead. Remember, it's not about your perfect vision; it's about following Him who knows where He's going!

Lord, lead the way – I'll follow! Amen.

You do not have to see or understand the whole future.
You only have to follow God every day.
He promises to take you to where you need to go.

God Will Change Your Heart

The LORD was pleased, for His righteousness' sake, to magnify His law and make it glorious.

Isaiah 42:21 ESV

This verse contains the wonderful suggestion that it pleases God to be righteous and true. He delights in it! That's the way it should be, not so? The Lord is really not so interested in obedience for the sake of obedience – although it *is* better than no obedience at all.

Someone may come to you and ask precisely how much they are permitted to drink; how far they may make out or do whatever they surmise may be wrong. Then they take their behavior to exactly that point. Surely God must be happy with that? Unfortunately such an attitude is the wrong way round: external obedience is only half the obedience God is looking for. That goes for any obedience that is done for the sake of acceptance by a group. It's worth little, because it's not done out of love but out of fear. Oh, God is so longing for a heart that truly wants to please Him, that truly delights in doing His will! A heart that genuinely loves Him with everything it has – *that* is the great commandment! God loves loving us – He really does, and that's a promise. But do we love loving Him?

Lord, change my heart, I pray! Amen.

God promises that He loves being in a relationship with you.
He truly delights in it. It would be wonderful
if your heart beat just as fast for Him!

God Will Honor It

Was it not the LORD, against whom we have sinned, in whose ways they would not walk, and whose law they would not obey?

Isaiah 42:24 ESV

The prophet wanted the people to have the right perspective on their captivity. He asked them: "Who brought you into this situation?" He didn't want them to think that it was merely the Babylonians. No, behind the enemy's actions was God, who allowed them to do it. Then the prophet added the confession of this verse. He included himself – "we have sinned" – not so much because he had personally sinned, but because he identified with his people. That is true intercession.

The lesson for us is that we should take everything to God. Not everything that happens is the result of sin, but we should realize that sin has a definite consequence in our lives. Regardless of that, we need to keep our whole life – including our failure – on the agenda between God and us. We cannot and should not hide anything. Let's rather acknowledge our failures and disappointments to Him, so that we can turn away from them. It's important that we learn our lessons, write our tests and move on. If you're honest and keep things in the open between you and God, He will honor that.

Lord, You know about … [name your failure or disappointment]. Amen.

If you are honest about what's wrong in your life,
and keep talking to God about it, He promises
to forgive you and to help you to overcome them.

Listen; God Will Speak

Now thus says the LORD, He who created you, O Jacob, He who formed you, O Israel.

Isaiah 43:1 ESV

We now come to one of the most beautiful chapters in the Bible. So many people have found encouragement from these words! In many Bibles, these verses are underlined and annotated with notes and dates. The prophet started off in a typical way by drawing the hearer's attention to a new message from God, along the lines of: "Listen up, people! God is saying …" They had to pay attention, because God was about to speak.

This applies to us as well. How can we ever hear His voice, guidance or comfort when we don't pay attention? Often we are so caught up in our problems that we cannot listen at all. Let's make it clear: God wants to speak to you – in fact, He is speaking to you at this very moment! His message comes to us in different ways throughout our day: perhaps in something we read (especially His Word), in something we hear, in the occurrences of the day … messages, messages, messages! Unfortunately, we're seldom in listening mode. Perhaps we should pay more attention!

Speak, Lord, Your servant is listening. Amen.

If you start paying attention to God's messages all around you,
you will perceive them everywhere.
The signs will be all around you. He promises it!

He Knows You So Well

"Fear not, for I have redeemed you; I have called you by name, you are Mine."

Isaiah 43:1 ESV

Do not fear, said God. That's always His first instruction to us in our need. We should trust Him – He *will* save us! How and when He does so is His business and it's part of our faith that we leave that up to Him. God motivates His instruction (not to fear) by adding that He knows us well, that He has called us by name. These verses were written to "Israel," the name God Himself gave to Jacob, the Jewish patriarch. God was intensely involved with His people since He called Abram, Jacob's grandfather, to follow Him.

God knows you just as well – He knew your name long before your parents thought of it! Perhaps – who knows – He gave your parents your name through their thoughts? Perhaps He has His own name for you? God says, "You are Mine" because He personally made you and He remains involved with you, personally and intensely. Do you now better understand why you shouldn't be afraid?

Thank You, Lord, for knowing me
personally and intimately! Amen.

God promises today that He knows you better than you know yourself and that He is intensely involved in your life. With God being so involved with you in your life, you no longer have to fear.

He Will Be with You

"When you cross deep rivers, I will be with you, and you won't drown. When you walk through fire, you won't be burned or scorched by the flames."

Isaiah 43:2 CEV

The most common mistake of the spiritual life is to expect never to go through difficulties. Isn't God with me? We have the naive idea (we are actually taught that way) that God's blessing includes preventing us from enduring hardships. When difficulties come our way, we are dismayed and ask: "Where is God? Why did He allow it? What did I do wrong? Where is my blessing?"

Unfortunately, that is a misunderstanding. Look at this verse – it's not about avoiding the water or the fire; it's about being preserved despite them. We will experience adversity – as did Christ, Paul, Peter and all the faith heroes of the Bible – but He will be with us in our hardship. As this verse promises, we will not perish: not in the water, nor in the fire. That is His promise!

Lord, thank You for Your protection. Amen.

If you are going through difficult circumstances –
deep waters or fire – God promises to protect and preserve you.
He'll go through it with you.

You Are So, So Precious

"Because you are precious in My eyes, and honored, and I love you,
I give men in return for you, peoples in exchange for your life."

Isaiah 43:4 ESV

What a wonderful verse! The prophet assured the people that God loved them. The words He used were intimate and warm – the sort of words that lovers share, words that are best whispered. Reading such words as coming from God may cause some to feel embarrassed. It is no wonder that the spiritual life has been described through the centuries in terms of an intimate love affair – think of the Song of Solomon. There are no better words to describe it!

Let's rephrase what we have read: you are precious and valuable to God, you are beautiful and unique! You are a handmade piece of art, fashioned by God personally at a price that cannot be measured. God is more than satisfied with you – He is proud of you and loves you deeply! His total commitment to you has been proven through Jesus Christ, who died so that you wouldn't have to. There is no greater love than that! Now two things are needed:

- You may never again deem yourself inferior – you are not bad, ugly or worthless. No!
- God desires that you love Him back – with your whole heart, soul and mind. Will you?

Thank You, Lord. I love You too! Amen.

God promises that He harbors an intense love for you –
that His heart bursts with care for you.
Don't be embarrassed about it – it's what He says in His Word!

You Will Be Gathered In

"Fear not, for I am with you; I will bring your offspring from the east, and from the west I will gather you."

Isaiah 43:5 ESV

The prophet was overwhelmed by God's love for His people. His Spirit-inspired words flowed like a stream. He assured the people that God would gather them together and bring them back to their land. He didn't only mean the group of Jews in Babylon – no, his thoughts went much wider. He was thinking of *all* Israelites in all countries, as they were dispersed over the centuries – the "lost tribes" and everyone who had been displaced by persecution or whatever.

From the east, west, north and south they would be gathered and come before God as one nation. We're not sure where the prophet draws the line – it could be that he is just speaking in general terms. But remember, we also consider ourselves among that number of God's people. Yes, we do! And we are! I believe that *you* will be there, sincere believer. You *and* I!

Yes, Lord, I do want to serve You,
and I do want to be there,
as part of those who will gather before You. Amen.

If you sincerely want to serve the Lord,
He promises that you form part of His people. In fact,
He went to great lengths and made an intrepid journey to include you!

Chosen to Know

"My people, you are My witnesses and My chosen servant. I want you to know Me, to trust Me, and understand that I alone am God."

Isaiah 43:10 CEV

In some circles, a lot is made of the doctrine of "election" – in other communities less so. The fact is that God "elects" or chooses people with whom to work. It can be a difficult topic to discuss in a daily devotional! Think of Israel, God's chosen nation: what we see is that individuals could enter Israel's covenant or leave it. Think of the Moabite Ruth, who was included with God's people because of her faith, and of genuine Israelites (like some kings) who were rejected because of their sin.

Yes, humankind's responsibility and God's selection are equally true in the Bible – in fact, in a way they are precisely the same thing. The person who truly believes is also elected. Elected for what? Our verse states the answer beautifully: elected to know and trust God. Isn't that a wonderful privilege? We may truly get to know God – God Almighty, Creator of everything. Yes, we may know Him personally! Perhaps our whole life goal should be to know God more and more. In fact, that is precisely the goal to which we're called.

Lord, I have such a need to know You more. Amen.

God promises that a person – like you – may get to know the almighty and eternal God. To get to know Him better is in fact the greatest adventure there is.

He Alone Remains God

"I, I am the LORD, and besides Me there is no savior."

Isaiah 43:11 ESV

The Lord confirms to His people that He alone is God, their Savior. In their captivity the Jews were exposed to the different gods of Babylon and other nations came to live there. In the primitive thought of their time, the gods of Babylon, especially Marduk, "beat" the gods of the other nations, including the God of Israel, since these gods couldn't prevent their worshipers from being taken captive.

It was a real problem for the Jews to hang on to their religion and identity in Him under such circumstances. They literally felt like the *"children of a lesser god."* Even though their faith underwent changes during that time, the Jews faithfully kept to their belief in Jehovah, their covenant God. Their priests, prophets and rabbis had a big part to play, of course. Let's apply this to ourselves: we also live in a world filled with idols, of which money is probably the biggest. One may at times wonder who is really in control in this world. Let today's verse confirm to you today that there is only one God and His name is Jehovah. Do not turn away from Him.

Thank You, Lord, that You are God
and that You will always remain the same. Amen.

There is only one Creator and Keeper of all that exists –
not many, only one! Even our various idols can never replace Him.

No One Can Stop Him

"I work, and who can turn it back?"

Isaiah 43:13 ESV

God, in His sovereignty, declared the captivity of His people over. Then a lot of things happened in Babylon: Cyrus and the Persian kings after him issued decrees that liberated all the foreign nations residing there. Families had to sell their possessions and transport what was left across several country borders – an enormous journey!

A large proportion of the Jewish people merely stayed behind and Babylon remained an important Jewish center of learning for at least a thousand years! Miracles happened surrounding the return; for example, Nehemiah getting the state's full support for the restoration of Jerusalem's walls and the temple. Over several years and in many groups, the people returned to their homeland.

The lesson is this: if God has decided something, nothing will stop Him. He makes things happen! Friend, you and I can relax in God's hands. Whatever happens, the Almighty is right beside you. Nothing can happen if He doesn't allow it! Everything works together for good and brings us nearer to the goal. It might be difficult to understand, but that's the Bible's message. What a comfort!

Lord, thank You for Your might and Your love. Amen.

If God has decided that something is going to happen,
He promises that nothing will be able to stop Him.
He allows things to work out in such a way that it achieves His plan.
Everything is in His hands – including your situation.

Unbelievable, but Believe It

"For your sake, I will send an army against Babylon to drag its people away."

Isaiah 43:14 CEV

What we read here is almost unbelievable. The prophet was referring to a major world event. The mighty Babylonian Empire, which brought the Jewish nation into captivity, was overrun by the Persians. International news! One could say that it was the news of the decade. The incredible thing is that the prophet said it was all for the benefit of Israel! Remember that the Jews in those times (as in ours) were only a tiny nation – a small group of people tucked away in a corner of the known world. No one really took notice of them. But God did! As unbelievable as it seemed, He chose to work through them – and yes, He changed history for their sake.

The same applies to us – God is interested in you and me, who are really unimportant people, not so? He even changes circumstances for our benefit. Don't even try to understand it – it's almost impossible. Just believe it – it's true by faith. God is working: in you, and around you!

Thank You, Lord, for working in my life. Amen.

God promises that you are significant in His world, no matter how unimportant you may feel. Hold firmly to His promises and believe that God has a purpose only you can fulfill.

Look Back and Believe

Thus says the LORD, who makes a way in the sea, a path in the mighty waters.

Isaiah 43:16 ESV

God said those who doubted whether He could return the Jews to their country should look at the past. He referred them to Israel's passage through the Red Sea. By a miracle the Israelites passed through the sea and eventually came to the Promised Land. When the Egyptians tried to follow, they all drowned. The same God could bring His people home again.

This also teaches us that we should look back when we struggle to trust God. It makes us realize that God has carried us though safely to today. When we look back through our old prayer journals, we realize with joy that most of the problems prayed for in the past have been resolved. Many concerns never materialized and sometimes there was a surprising turn of events. Mostly the future turns out quite differently than we anticipated! Think of your own life: has God been with you this whole time? Yes, of course He has – and in the future He will faithfully remain with you as well.

Thank You, Lord, for always being faithful. Amen.

God asks that you look at the past
and see how faithfully He has carried you until now.
He promises to faithfully deliver you in the future as well.

Look Ahead and Believe

"Behold, I am doing a new thing; now it springs forth, do you not perceive it?"

Isaiah 43:19 ESV

The Lord reminded the Jews of their past and all the miracles of His provision. Then He said that they shouldn't just think of their history, but also of their future. He would create something brand new! This verse was a quintessential one that has encouraged thousands of Christians through the ages: "Behold, I am doing a new thing; now it springs forth …" Many people have a date written next to this verse in their Bibles!

Listen, the future is unknown to all of us. We don't know what tomorrow may bring. Most often things work out differently than anticipated – most of our fears never materialize. Also, the future isn't fixed, but is still being created today by our decisions and actions. However, God knows what the future holds! He knows, because He holds the future! He promises His people that their future will hold something new, something beautiful. Take this promise for you, my friend! Also in your own future God will do something new – something good! He will, He will!

Thank You, Lord, for the new things that You are doing. Amen.

God asks that you trust Him with your future.
He promises that He is in control and that He is planning
something beautiful. You just need to work with Him in certain ways.

He'll Make a New Way

"I will make a way in the wilderness and rivers in the desert."

Isaiah 43:19 ESV

God promised to do something new and He wanted His people to expect it soon. He said He would make a way in the wilderness, rivers in the desert. Why does God use these images? Well, He just reminded them of the time when He brought Israel out of Egypt into Canaan – through the wilderness! He now promised to do it again, through similar surroundings.

There's also a spiritual meaning: in biblical times, the deserts were barely traversable – there were no roads, yet God would provide a road. Also, deserts are very arid places, yet God would supply streams of water. So – let's not say that there's no way forward, that the road ahead is impossible or that the future holds no provision.

There *will* be provision and there *will* be a way – everything you need will be there! Continue on your journey with more confidence – with trust, and with faith.

I trust You, Lord, for today and tomorrow. Amen.

You do not have to see what path your future will take.
God promises that He already knows the way.
You just need to follow Him.

He Forgives and Forgets

"I, I am He who blots out your transgressions for My own sake, and I will not remember your sins."

Isaiah 43:25 ESV

In the Old Testament, people counted much more on God's grace than we might think. They simply believed that God knew we were human and fallible and that He wouldn't remain angry at us forever – even when we do wrong. That's how they understood grace. It's beautiful in its simplicity, isn't it? Of course the New Testament teaches us that God's grace through Jesus Christ is infinitely more abundant. Here God tells the Jews that they're forgiven. We read something profound: "I will not remember your sins."

Take note that God cannot forget in the way we forget. He is omniscient and knows everything! God decides not to think of the past; He resolves not to think about the sins that He's forgiven. Isn't that wonderful? Remember this, because it is the definition of forgiveness: to resolve to no longer think about someone's trespasses. If it comes up in your mind, just reconfirm your decision not to dwell on it, to move beyond it. That's forgiveness! There's more: what happens when we don't think of something after a while? It gradually fades, not so? That's the way we "forgive and forget!"

Friend, do you need to forgive? Decide to stop thinking about that hurtful event and those hurtful words. Give it to God.

Lord, thank You for Your forgiveness. Amen.

If you have asked God to forgive your sins,
He promises that He will totally and completely forgive you –
and that He will never think about it again.

Feel His Comforting Hands

Thus says the LORD who made you, who formed you from the womb and will help you.

Isaiah 44:2 ESV

In this verse, the image of God making and forming us is striking. The clear message is that we were made, that we didn't just "become." God was an integral part of our creation. His Spirit was there in the womb from the very beginning! He was involved in all the stages of conception, multiplication, differentiation and growth of that human being who now carries your name! Even before conception, God was involved in our lives – yes, indeed – which makes us view life differently from non-believers.

The word "form" makes me think of God's hands. We can say that God's hands were on you right from the start, fashioning you into the thing of beauty that you are today: precious and costly! What is more, God's hands were on you, or around you, all the years of your life, protecting you and guiding you, helping you as this verse confirms. Perhaps you should close your eyes and feel His comforting hands on your shoulders today.

I praise You, Lord, for Your hands on my life today! Amen.

God promises that He – as your Maker – personally formed you and made you, and knows every part of your body and soul. He knows you and continually helps you.

You Have a Special Name

"Fear not, O Jacob My servant, Jeshurun whom I have chosen."

Isaiah 44:2 ESV

This verse is extraordinary, for we find here an unusual name that God used for His people – *Jeshurun*. It appears only four times in the Bible. It seems like an ancient title of honor for Israel. Some rabbis say there was an inscription on the breastplate of the high priest (the *kohen gadol*), with the twelve jewels, that read: "The Tribes of Jeshurun."

Out of the origin of the word (meaning "upright one"), we assume that when God used this name He was thinking of His people's best qualities, not their worst. It is used with fondness. There is tenderness and warmth to it – like God's personal name for His beloved and chosen people.

God has a special name for you as well! When you meet Him, He will call you by that name.

Thank You, Father!
Thank You for Your love. Amen.

God promises that He knows and loves you intimately.
One day He will give you a "new name" –
His very own special name for you!

You Have a Future

"I will pour My Spirit upon your offspring, and My blessing on your descendants."

Isaiah 44:3 ESV

God promised His people a future. Not a future there in Babylon, although He was with them during their captivity, but a future in their own land! Yes, we may feel that this confusing and foreign world is our land. It's not! We are still on our way to our true land, the eternal Canaan. God is with us in this world's Babylon in which we sojourn.

Like the Jews of old, we may settle, build our houses, rear our children and live our lives to the fullest. We may enjoy what this land offers us – we may and we must. But in our hearts we know that this isn't our final destination. Some day the call will come and we'll be going home! Our true destiny is with Him, forever. That is the future that awaits us! But now, back to this world, and this verse: the prophet foresaw that the future in Canaan would be wonderful, with the Spirit of God upon them and their children. Yes, even the children would serve God! Pray for this for your own children also.

Lord, I really pray that my children would serve You.
That's my heart's desire. Amen.

If you trust God for your children's future,
He promises to look after them. He will also pour out
His Spirit on them – although not against their will.

You Are the Lord's

"This one will say, 'I am the LORD's,' another will call on the name of Jacob, and another will write on his hand, 'The LORD's.'"

Isaiah 44:5 ESV

In this verse the prophet was describing the future. He said God would pour out His Spirit on His people's children. Even their descendants would testify that they served God. They would take encouragement from the fact that they belonged to Him. How beautiful it is that he predicts that they would write "the Lord's" on their hands. In ancient times, some people were marked in this way on the hand, wrist or arm: soldiers with the name of their regiment, slaves with the name of their owner, idol worshipers with the name of their god. Those were tattoos, but in this verse we're thinking more of someone writing God's name (in the usual way) on their hand – in order to be reminded of Him.

Writing "I belong to the Lord" is a moving and personal confession of faith! God had also written His people's names on His palm, according to Isaiah. Pray that your children will serve God and then set them an example of how it's done. That's the most important thing you can do for them! Then trust God for His promise that He will draw them to Him.

Yes, Lord, my children are for You! Amen.

If you trust God for your children, He will answer your prayers for them. He promises to draw them to Him. You can also trust that they will grow to serve Him with joy, like you do.

Come to Him

"They will worship Me and become My people."

Isaiah 44:5 CEV

The prophet was promising that the Jews' descendants would also serve God. That's wonderful, because we really want our children to serve God, don't we? However, let's focus on the following, more general question: when can you say that you belong to the Lord? Some churches emphasize God's selection and others an individual conversion, which are two approaches that actually complement each other (and also have a lot to do with our cultural or historical context).

Let's cut through the theology and make it simple: you belong to God when you (merely) come to Him. No person who genuinely wants to belong to Jesus will ever be turned away by Him. Oh no, His invitation is for all who are burdened and heavily laden to come to Him (see Matthew 11:28). Let's repeat His invitation to everyone: come to Jesus! His arms are open wide – when you come to Him, you'll walk into His embrace, His acceptance and His love. You will become His child and be truly able to say: "I am His; I belong to the Lord."

Lord, yes, I want to belong to You – and I come ... Amen.

God promises that those who come to Him will never be turned away. He accepts them with open arms and they become His children forever! Will you also come to Him today?

June

He Is God

Thus says the LORD … "I am the first and I am the last; besides Me there is no god."

Isaiah 44:6 ESV

God made Himself known as the only God. The Jews shouldn't have thought that He disappeared from the scene because they had a hard time in captivity. No, He was still involved and would take them out of that season and into the next.

What is the meaning of the striking words in this verse, which are also repeated in Revelation: "I am the Alpha and the Omega, the first and the last, the beginning and the end"? Well, for the Jews it meant that God would stay their God forever – wherever they may find themselves and in whatever situation they may be, good or bad. That's an important lesson: God remains God despite your particular circumstances and despite your personal experience of Him being far or near. That has nothing to do with it! It doesn't change who He is. He remains God and will always act as God – from your birth to your death, from the morning to the evening. He remains almighty and exalted, always bigger than what we think, always more than our attempts to understand and predict Him. Let's stop doing that! Let's accept God as God and serve Him … and love Him, which is the first commandment.

Lord, You'll forever remain God.
I do not understand all about You,
but I do love You. Amen.

God promises that He is forever God and will forever remain God.
He especially emphasizes that your personal experiences
or circumstances have no influence on this.

No One like God

"Who is like Me? Let him proclaim it ... Let them declare what is to come, and what will happen."

Isaiah 44:7 ESV

God said He alone is God – there is no God but Him. The Jews should have known that the so-called "gods" of Babylon were not real gods but simply man-made idols. Of course we don't bow before literal idols anymore, but that doesn't mean we don't have false gods in our world – we do! Most prominent today is Mammon (money), who is truly the god of our materialistic culture. Don't forget the god of pleasure, who also has millions of devotees. Another major idol of our day is man himself.

Our humanistic culture teaches us that we should be our own god, "the captain of my own soul, the master of my own destiny." God should be pushed from the throne, so that humankind can rule!

In today's verse, God wished good luck to such people. He invited them here to come and say what their share was in creation, how they hold the future, how they supply purpose, direction, love and meaning to life. No, there are no contenders: God alone is God. He belongs on the throne of every life.

Yes, Lord, rule as King in my life! Amen.

God promises that He alone is God and that no one should even think of comparing Him to an idol. You and I should also not think we can just be our own god.

He Is Your Rock

"Is there a God besides Me? There is no Rock; I know not any."
Isaiah 44:8 ESV

There is a beautiful gospel song with the words: *There is no other rock but You* – and yes, it's rock music! The Lord declared to His people that He is their only God, or, as He puts it, the only Rock. In the Bible, God is often called a rock, many times in this same formulation: "there is no other rock but Him." Another instance in which we often find this image is when the psalmist prays: "The Lord is my rock and my fortress and my deliverer, my God, my rock, in whom I take refuge" (Psalm 18:2).

In the New Testament, Christ is also called a rock, or even the rock of the Old Testament. What does it mean that God is our only rock? It means that we cannot trust in anyone else for support or help in the way we trust in Him. As wonderful as your friends may be, or as loyal as your family is, they can never be like God in our life. Also, don't expect too much from your appearance, talents or monetary resources – they may all be well and good, but they're fleeting, limited or even deceptive in promising what they cannot deliver. None of these can ever be a rock. God is the only true Rock.

Yes, Lord, You are my rock, my refuge,
my hope, my expectation. Amen.

God promises that He is the only Rock you can rely on.
It is senseless to put your trust in money or people,
because in your day of need they cannot truly help.

Only One True God

… The rest of it he makes into a god, his idol, and falls down to it and worships it. He prays to it and says, "Deliver me, for you are my god!"

Isaiah 44:17 ESV

The prophet mocked the heathens who bowed before idols. He described how they made such an idol, to prove how ridiculous it was. The blacksmith had a hard time working the iron in the fire, forming an image. It was tiring work! Or a woodworker shaped a tree with his chisels, forming it into the figure of a man. The irony for the prophet was that the person used the offcuts to stoke a fire and cook his meal on it. The part that had become an idol figure, however, was bowed down and prayed to: "Save us, because You are my god"! No, it's clearly nonsensical to worship something you have made yourself. Who would be the god? Who would be the creator and who the creation?

An idol is any human-made construct that is overly trusted in our lives, taking the place of God. In that sense our world abounds with false gods: money, health, certain people – or perhaps we trust in blind luck. We do need resources, good health and so on, but they should never become our gods. There is only one God and only He can really help you. Bow before nothing but Him!

Yes, Lord, I trust in You alone! Amen.

God promises that He will help you – you can rely on Him in all circumstances. He stresses that human-made constructs can never serve as a god.

You'll See the Truth

He cannot deliver himself or say, "Is there not a lie in my right hand?"

Isaiah 44:20 ESV

Idol worshipers made their own gods. They formed an image out of metal or wood, plated it with gold or silver, or painted it, and then bowed before it and prayed to it. Such prayers were much like ours: help us, merciful lord; save us today, etc. We must be fair by adding that the heathen people didn't really think that the physical image would do something for them. They saw the image as an effigy of a real, unseen god to whom they prayed – a symbol, a point of contact. However, the invisible gods and the visible idols were all part of the same lie (and in folk religion, they become mixed up). The prophet accused the people of not realizing this. They never asked: "Is this a lie?"

Let's pose that question to ourselves, though – about our own false gods. "Is my money or my health going to save me?" "Can I trust in a person to make me happy or in myself for salvation?" No, those are lies that slip in unheeded. Let's detect the falseness in our thinking and every time return to the truth. His name is Jesus.

Lord, You are the way, the truth and the life! Amen.

We should recognize and examine that which we as humans put our trust into. We need to ask ourselves, "Can we rely on this?" God promises that we can indeed rely on Him.

You Have Been Redeemed, So Come

"Return to Me, for I have redeemed you."

Isaiah 44:22 ESV

It's fantastic how God's initiative works. He doesn't just wait for humans to do something, and then to react to it. No, God's not passive, He's proactive – He takes initiative and leads us toward His goals like a true leader. We are the ones who react – and so often in the wrong way! In these verses of the past few weeks, God sought to remind His people that: 1. He made them, 2. He never left them, 3. He forgave their transgressions and, 4. He redeemed them – all by His own initiative! Because of this, He expected them to return to Him. The message was simple.

God also made us, guided us and helped us. Many centuries ago, God provided us with a Redeemer. Christ opened the way to God for everyone and His invitation to a life with Him is offered to all – also to you and me. God has been busy with you for such a long time – will you come to Him now? Accept His offer in faith!

I come, Lord! I return to You. Amen.

If you have wandered far from the Father, like the Prodigal Son, you need only return. You know the way! He promises that He will receive you with open arms.

Earth Rejoices
and So Must You

*Sing, O heavens, for the L*ORD *has done it; shout, O depths of the earth; break forth into singing, O mountains, O forest, and every tree in it!*

Isaiah 44:23 ESV

The Bible often states that all of creation should praise God. In the Psalms, it is often phrased that "everything that has breath" should praise Him, meaning all living things. Think of the angels (who live, but do not breathe!), all men and all animals. Every little bird and cricket joins in! More than just the living things, the physical creation also praises God: the stars, planets, the earth, mountains, woods and rivers – every molecule and atomic particle. Yes, the whole moving and whirling universe – with its enormous forces – testifies to God's power and glory!

Our own songs add only a tiny bit to that immense chorus. The tremendous testimony of nature is an all-encompassing and rousing song of God's goodness and greatness. Still, it's vital for us to praise God. If we don't praise Him because things are perhaps not going our way, or because we don't feel like it, we should be ashamed. Do we really believe that praise for God is dependent on our circumstances? Never! The universe does not revolve around us. It's all about Him! Even our own life is not about simply us.

Lord, You're worthy to be praised and I praise You! Amen.

If you add your voice to the songs of praise raised to God by the whole universe, He promises that you will find your rightful place: as an integral part of His great creation and as God's beloved child!

His Word Will Be Confirmed

"… Who confirms the word of His servant and fulfills the counsel of His messengers."

Isaiah 44:26 ESV

The prophet shot down the predictions of the fortune tellers. In ancient times, science was still primitive and magic was often a part of life. Learned men studied astrology and healers used rituals and incantations to heal their patients. Heathen priests made predictions based on the analyses of the livers of sacrificed animals or the flight patterns of birds. The Lord, however, forbade His people to have anything to do with soothsaying or conjuring. We should take note! Some see it as a joke, but many people today pay attention to horoscopes or put value on something a psychic once predicted over them.

By trusting on things like this, we create false gods or even open ourselves to evil. Let's rather trust God only, and consult Him alone about our lives. Let's stay with what trusted teachers and prophets tell us about God's Word. His Word will be confirmed in our lives – nothing else!

Thank You for Your Word, Lord –
I stand on Your promises! Amen.

God does not want you to have anything to do with the occult. It will only disappoint you, but He promises that His own Word will be confirmed in our lives.

Everything Can Turn Around

"… Who says of Jerusalem, 'She shall be inhabited' … Who says to the deep, 'Be dry; I will dry up your rivers.'"

Isaiah 44:26-27 ESV

It's amazing how things can change. Some who once were very rich have lost it all; others who once had nothing ended up wealthy. The rulers of a previous regime can become the refugees under a new one. Someone who as a child was sickly or poor can become a huge success in adulthood; an "ugly duckling" can turn into a beautiful swan. A pauper can hit the jackpot, only to lose everything afterwards.

We see something similar in this verse. Jerusalem had been in ruins for decades – the temple completely demolished – while Babylon was the capital city of the world. On God's command, things changed around – and see now how it did: today Jerusalem is a beautiful city and the spiritual center for millions of people, while Babylon is a mere ruin, a detail on an Iraqi tourist map. Let's therefore never be shortsighted or only see the immediate circumstances. See the long-term vision – the big picture! Understand that with God, everything can change.

*Thank You, Lord, that everything
can still change in my life. Amen.*

God promises that everything can change for you.
Your current situation is not a predictor for the rest of your life.
With His power, your dreams are attainable.

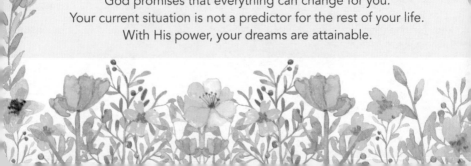

God Will Use Unbelievers

"I am also the one who says, 'Cyrus will lead My people and obey My orders. Jerusalem and the temple will be rebuilt.'"

Isaiah 44:28 CEV

God announced a great thing to the Jews. They had been in exile for two generations, their land was taken from them and their families had been killed. Now, however, the time to return had come! The miracle was so great that most of them weren't ready. The older generation had already passed away and the new generation had only heard about the Jewish motherland. The wonder of it all was that it was happening because of an unbeliever: Cyrus of Persia. He never served the Jewish God – his decisions were purely political. Still, Scripture is clear that God was using him for exactly that purpose.

Today, this happens in the same way: an unbelieving benefactor helps us; a manager makes a decision to our advantage; a law is passed that creates new opportunities. The question is not whether the people involved are Christians (and sometimes we put misplaced trust in believers), but whether God is using them. He uses whomever He wants! Tonight, when you look back on the day, ask yourself whom God sent across your path.

Lord, help me to see Your hand in my life every day. Amen.

God promises to work in your life. For this purpose,
He uses different people – believers or non-believers –
and all kinds of circumstances.

God Can Anoint Unbelievers

Thus says the LORD to His anointed, to Cyrus, whose right hand I have grasped, to subdue nations before him.

Isaiah 45:1 ESV

The Lord used a gentile king, Cyrus of Persia, to enable His people to return to their land. Cyrus "the Great" issued the decree in 539 B.C., which allowed all foreign nations that were brought there by the Babylonians to return. He was a wise ruler who brought peace and prosperity to the empire and was honored and loved by his subjects. His grave can still be visited in Iran.

It remains surprising, though, that in this verse God literally calls Cyrus His "anointed" (the word used is "messiah"). Other people in the Bible were also called God's anointed (apart from Christ), but they were kings and prophets of Israel – this man was a heathen! Cyrus can even be seen as a prototype of Jesus – a deliverer of God's people. The lesson here is to realize that God also works by using unbelievers. Sometimes it is they who carry out God's will – sometimes more so than some believers! So, when unbelievers do what is right or show love, we should praise God. His will remains His will – it is meant for all.

Lord, use me to do Your will! Amen.

God promises that He works with all people. Through His Spirit,
He knocks on hearts, leading people and allowing His will
to be done – whether they believe or not. He also works with you.

The Goal Will Be Achieved

"Shower, O heavens, from above, and let the clouds rain down righteousness."

Isaiah 45:8 ESV

God was silent for seventy years. Here and there a minor prophet spoke for Him, but during this period of captivity the priests and rabbis mostly just continued to teach the law and the traditions. Now God was speaking again through a great prophet. The people had been exiled for utterly turning away from God, but that period was now drawing to an end. Ironically, the exile was beneficial for them, however painful it was.

During their isolation they were forced to preserve and cherish their Jewish heritage. Jewish schools and butcheries (for kosher eating) were established and their religion was reformulated and revalidated. It grew into the belief system that Jesus knew, which grew into the Judaism of today. Now the goal of the captivity was achieved and they could move on. That's how seasons work – even the unpleasant ones have a purpose. May we also achieve the goals of our current season, so that God can speak the word and we can move on into the next!

Lord, what is the purpose of this season? Amen.

God promises that every season in your life has a purpose. Everything contributes to your formation and your growth in character. You simply have to trust Him and work with Him on each step of your journey through life.

God Will Work the Clay as He Wants To

"Does the clay say to him who forms it, 'What are you making?'"
Isaiah 45:9 ESV

The Jewish people were in captivity for seventy years because they totally strayed from God. From the kings to the common person, they worshiped idols and participated in the indecent acts that went with it. The judges were corrupt and the priests bent on their own benefit. The people didn't know the Law of Moses at all and upheld almost none of its precepts. The many warnings by the prophets were not heeded. Here and there a good king brought reforms, only for these to be reversed again by a successor.

In Jerusalem, every street had a pagan altar and at times idol statues were even erected in the temple. *That* is why there was an exile! Could the people complain to God about this? No! The clay cannot prescribe to the potter how they should work with it. The Potter knows what He is doing. In today's world He uses everything in our lives to make something beautiful, something good. For that you have to trust Him.

Lord, I do not understand everything,
but I trust You! Amen.

God works in our lives and we cannot always understand what He is doing. You are like clay in the hands of the Potter. However, He promises that He will make something beautiful out of you.

No One Will Prescribe to God

"Do you dare question Me about My own nation or about what I have done?"

Isaiah 45:11 CEV

God was in a debate with His people. It was as if complaints had been made: why did You bring us here? Why did we have to go through so much? Why do we need to return now? Why didn't You rather do this – or that …?

Now remember, as the people of the Old Testament did, so we do today. They represent us! We also sometimes feel that God is not fair in His decisions: why did this thing happen to me? Where was God when I needed Him? Why did Christ have to die on the cross – wasn't there another way? Take note how God answered them. He didn't patiently explain His actions so that they could understand. He didn't supply a logical answer at all! Like elsewhere in the Bible, He merely directed them to the fact that He is God. He must be trusted as God – and He won't be prescribed to! That's what it means to have a God in your life! Stop with the questioning and start with the trusting!

Lord, You are God of my life.
I trust You completely. Amen.

God wants to be God in your life. This means that He
is more than simply a friend or even a father. He is the Almighty,
the Creator, the Lord. He promises that you can trust Him.

He Makes the Stars to Shine

"I made the earth and created man on it; it was My hands that stretched out the heavens, and I commanded all their host."

Isaiah 45:12 ESV

Science teaches us wonderful things – and the more we discover, the more wonderful it becomes. Quantum physics, astrophysics and cosmology lead us into an ever-increasing, but dazzling complexity. Although we can accept all good science, we as believers also accept another truth: that God is behind all these things! The whole of creation is His will and intention; He called into being all matter and all the energy that moves; everything is His power. He is the Creator! Science tells us about the what and the how of creation, but the Bible tells us about the why and the Who.

Even at this moment, God is still involved with every atom and every star in His creation; He knows about everything and cares about everything. The lesson is this: if God is so involved with the physical world, how much more is He involved with you, whom He made so carefully and beautifully – whom He so loves? Much, much more! He is intensely involved in your life.

Thank You, Lord, that You are busy working in my life. Amen.

The universe is incredibly complex in its design – the more science discovers, the more complex it becomes. God promises that He is the principle, the power, the Person behind it all. Radically believe it!

God Can Bless Unbelievers

"I have stirred him up in righteousness, and I will make all his ways level."

Isaiah 45:13 ESV

It remains wonderful to see how God blessed Cyrus. Remember, Cyrus, the king of Persia, was a heathen. Still, God declared him blessed and anointed. God gave him prosperity and favor to become king and removed all the hindrances in his way. The purpose was so that he could use his position to release the Jews and allow them to return to their land – which he did.

Don't think that God only blesses His children or only works through believers. No, Jesus clearly says that God in His goodness sends His rain and sunshine on everyone. Unbelievers and even evil people receive blessings: they become rich, enjoy good health and experience love. That's true. But the rest of the truth is that they receive blessing in order to honor God for it, and to serve Him in return. Blessing leads to a responsibility toward God – to not acknowledge God for it and to not use it for His glory would be unbelievably ungrateful.

Yes, I praise You, Lord!
Thank You for Your blessings. Amen.

The Bible says that God pours His blessings on everyone. He promises a special blessing, however, to those who recognize Him for that blessing – as it should be. Acknowledge your blessings from God.

Unbelievers Will See Your Blessing

"They will plead with you, saying: 'Surely God is in you, and there is no other, no god besides Him.'"

Isaiah 45:14 ESV

The prophet encouraged the Jews who were in captivity and now faced an arduous journey back to their homeland. He kept their eyes on the goal – Judea! He said that times of victory were ahead: the Gentiles would come to Jerusalem to worship their God and celebrate His feasts with them. They would acknowledge that God blessed His people and that He is the only God.

We see the fulfillment of this prophecy partly in the church – representing all nations, peoples and tongues – worshiping the God of Israel, coming to Jerusalem, joining in the feasts of Israel. The final fulfillment of this prophecy is still ahead, though. In the meanwhile, you can take this promise for yourself: unbelievers will see your blessing and they'll acknowledge that your God is good. How can that be? Well, by moving into the blessing of God! This means starting to live as God's beloved, as God's blessed – in victory, joy, love, peace, faith and a firm hope for the future. It's a fact that people will notice these things in you!

Yes, Lord, help me to live out Your blessings. Amen.

God promises that your relationship with Him is something that other people also need … by all means let them see what a blessing it is for you!

God Will Emerge Again

Truly, You are a God who hides Himself, O God of Israel, the Savior.
Isaiah 45:15 ESV

It is surprising that God was sometimes described as someone who "hides" Himself. Earlier in this book, Isaiah said: "I will wait for the Lord, who is hiding His face from the house of Jacob" (8:17). Moses described God as hidden in darkness, or as having darkness under His feet. Paul says: "How unsearchable are His judgments and how inscrutable His ways! For who has known the mind of the Lord?" (Romans 11:33-34). What does this mean? It means that we cannot completely understand God – what we don't know about Him is far more than what we do know! He is hidden in mystery. He acts in ways we cannot comprehend. For example, the Jews didn't understand God during their captivity: to them He was absent, out of sight.

We also experience God the same way – and we also struggle to explain or predict Him. We can do something of the sort, but then He surprises us again by acting in a different way. Sometimes God feels so far, far away! Here's the prophet's promise: God will emerge again – as the sun rises in the morning, so will He shine over you; on that day you will understand.

Lord, I am mystified by Your greatness –
but I do love You! Amen.

God is too great for our minds to comprehend.
We can only understand Him in part – that which He reveals to us.
He promises that this is enough for us.

You Shall Not Be Ashamed

Israel is saved by the Lord with everlasting salvation; you shall not be put to shame or confounded to all eternity.

Isaiah 45:17 ESV

Isaiah described God as a God who hides Himself. In a sense that makes spiritual life difficult, doesn't it? We sometimes experience God as absent – especially when we need Him so! Where is He? If He is hidden in mystery, what can we expect from Him? Will He act consistently? The prophet assured the people that God was indeed trustworthy – 100% so! Those who depend on idols will stand ashamed, because those things cannot help them. Those who trust in God, however, will not be ashamed, because *He* is God, and He makes good on His promises.

Sometimes, though, we get the timescales all wrong. That fact that God doesn't immediately do what we ask is just part of having a relationship with Him: *He* is God, not us! He decides the what, when and how! That shouldn't be thought of as inconsistent. Not at all! We should simply keep on trusting, because we have surrendered our lives to Him. Ultimately, He will do what is good for us – and we *will* be saved, satisfied, secure. That remains the promise.

Lord, You are God, not me. I do trust You. Amen.

The fact that you do not understand God – or His actions, or His timing – does not mean that you cannot trust Him. He promises to remain faithful to you.

He'll Help You Here

(… He did not create it [the earth] empty, He formed it to be inhabited!): "I am the LORD, and there is no other."

Isaiah 45:18 ESV

The Lord says He made the earth for us – and us for the earth, correct? We're perfectly fitted to living here. We cannot live under the sea, nor in outer space or on another planet. That is highly unlikely! No, earth is our place – the Bible says so beautifully that it's the house that God built for us. Sometimes – when things go awry – we long for heaven, but the Bible teaches that eternity will play out on earth. The Lord *will* come and make everything new. He will bring a new heaven (the sky) and a new earth. It will become "heaven" here, because God will be here with us.

Let's therefore understand our deep connection to the earth. Let's find our place as human beings and live our lives to the fullest, to God's glory, because that's our purpose as His creation! We were made for this, we belong here and God wants to help us with our lives here. Eventually we'll live in God's presence forever (by the grace of Christ), but here on earth. That's the purpose of humankind since Paradise.

Yes, Lord, help me to find my place on earth –
and thank You that one day You will come
and make everything perfect! Amen.

Sometimes we just want to escape our earthly life,
but we were made for the earth. God promises however
that He is coming to join you on earth and will make it all worthwhile!

His Words Create the Possibility

"I the LORD speak the truth; I declare what is right."

Isaiah 45:19 ESV

God was bringing His people home. After seven decades – as previously determined – He was going to fetch them, as it were, from Babylon. Now a long expedition lay ahead – like an emigration, since they had to move with all their belongings to another country. And, yes, they had to walk! Many weren't up to it – a number of groups returned over several years, but many simply never attempted the journey. Still the door was open, because God opened it. He spoke the word and now it could happen.

God's words have power; they create new possibilities, new potential! We should see things the same way: if God says we should do something, we can do it. If He says something is going to happen, it will happen. His words create life, as of old: it makes things happen! Our own words do not have the same creative power, but our words should correspond with God's. That's faith! Therefore always say: "I can …" and "God will …"

Lord, I agree with what You say.
May my words never contradict Yours! Amen.

God promises that His words and promises are powerful realities that can change the world. He asks that you allow your words to correspond with His – that's the sound of faith!

God Will Be Fair

"I am the only God! There are no others. I bring about justice, and have the power to save."

Isaiah 45:21 CEV

Sometimes we're worried that God won't be fair. What about those who have never heard about salvation? What about those who can't properly understand the message? What about those who testify about a conversion, but whose life hardly reflects any evidence of it? What about those whose lives are so beautiful, but they don't have a "testimony" of salvation? What about me? How will God judge my faults and sins? Did I resist sin enough in my life? Did I show enough love and compassion to those who were hungry, thirsty or without clothing?

Do you know that our salvation includes being saved from all such thoughts? Faith means leaving the difficult things to Him. But let's emphasize the following nevertheless: yes, God *will* be fair in His judgment. He is the most just Judge that we can think of – the epitome of justice! He demands justice from us, not the other way round! This verse confirms that God is a God of justice and salvation. The Israelites did nothing that deserved salvation – but by His love and mercy God saved them anyway. Remember, included in God's justice is His love and His grace!

Thank You, Lord, that You are just,
loving and merciful. Amen.

You don't have to worry about whether God will judge fairly.
God promises that He is the Righteous One –
the measure of all fairness and justice! Just leave it to Him.

God Is the God of All

"I invite the whole world to turn to Me and be saved. I alone am God! No others are real."

Isaiah 45:22 CEV

God chose for Himself a people – the covenant nation of Israel. They had no special distinction that made them stand out from the other nations – God's choice was based purely on grace. He could just as well have chosen any nation in India or Japan. In a sense, Israel stands for any nation. The purpose of their election was to be the "model nation" of the world. They were to exemplify to the world the blessings of serving God, inspiring other nations to also turn to the only true God. They were to be a light unto the world. With this responsibility also rested a tremendous blessing for Israel, because being involved with God always results in a blessing.

Here is our lesson: God isn't only interested in Israel as a nation; He is interested in the whole world. God's heart is with all nations! He is the God of *all*.

In our verse for today, the prophet reiterates the invitation to everyone to come to the God of Israel and be saved. Everyone can be saved, friend. Alas, not all are, according to the Word – many simply won't come to Him.

Lord, as a non-Jew, I also come to You,
the God of Israel. I bow before You. Amen.

God promises that His heart is with all people on the earth –
He loves everyone equally and died on the cross for everyone.
He began with Israel, yes, but His final goal is for all the nations.
You, too, can show love to everyone.

Everyone's Knee Will Bow

"By Myself I have sworn; from My mouth has gone out in righteousness a word that shall not return: 'To Me every knee shall bow, every tongue shall swear allegiance.'"

Isaiah 45:23 ESV

God is the God of the whole earth – not just the God of the Israelites. Israel is indeed His "covenant people," but others were also welcome to join the covenant and to serve the God of Israel. The purpose was for Israel to become the "model nation," to inspire others to come to God. Even the Old Testament vision was that all nations would know God and come to Jerusalem to worship Him.

In this verse God makes this a solemn pledge, namely that one day all knees shall bow before Him. In their captivity the Jews might have felt intimidated by the Babylonian gods – could it be that these gods were perhaps more powerful than their God? Isaiah wanted to rectify any such misconception. There exists only one God and eventually everyone would agree to that fact. This also remains our truth, and our knees will bow on that day. Let's bow even now, today! To bow now to Him leads to a life with God – the best life possible!

I bow my knee before You, Lord. Amen.

God promises in His Word that every knee will bow
and acknowledge that He is God. The real blessing, however,
lies in bowing your knee to Him even now and serving Him as Lord.
You, too, can bow your knee before God.

Everyone Will Confess

"Everyone will bow down and worship Me."

Isaiah 45:23 CEV

The Jewish prophets looked forward to the day when their God would be acknowledged all over the earth. In that day all the nations of the world would come to Jerusalem to worship God in His temple. This is still a definite Jewish expectation, set in a coming Messianic Era. As Christians who see Jesus as the promised Messiah, we consider the worldwide church as the (partial) fulfillment of this prophecy. Remember, we do worship the God of Israel! Still, there are parts that are unfulfilled, because the prophet says *every* knee shall bow and *every* tongue confess …

We do believe that one day every person on earth will confess Christ (the New Testament applies this to Him), but only after the separation that God will bring at the end of time. According to Scripture, at the end God will separate the good from the bad, the sheep from the goats and the wheat from the tares and chaff (see Matthew 13:40-41; 25:32-33). Let's confess Jesus as Savior now already, and be part of eternity with Him!

*I confess You as Lord – and I believe in my heart
that You're my Savior. Amen.*

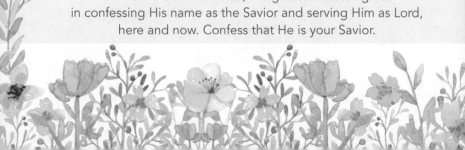

God promises in His Word that every tongue will confess
that He is God. However, the greatest blessing lies
in confessing His name as the Savior and serving Him as Lord,
here and now. Confess that He is your Savior.

You Will Come before Him

> "To Him shall come and be ashamed all who were incensed against Him."
>
> *Isaiah 45:24 ESV*

The prophet foresaw that one day everyone would have to come before God. At the end of time a new dispensation will commence and peace will reign forever in His kingdom. First, however, God will judge the nations. Everyone will stand before Him. Exactly what this means we don't know, but Scripture is clear that our conduct is subject to God's judgment. God already knows everyone and sees what they do. For those who live far from Him, this is a reason for concern, because they know God will know their sins and their transgressions – yes, all the secrets they want to hide.

For God's children, however, it is a comfort. He as our Father knows our heart and our intentions! He knows what we can do and what we cannot do. He of course knows our sins, but then again, He took those upon Himself long ago: the sins of our past, present and future! Our whole sinfulness is already dealt with! We don't need to hide our sins from God. We will be forgiven and when we get to Him – His arms will be wide open to us! For us, Judgment Day is Salvation Day.

Lord, I cannot wait for that day! Amen.

One day all people will face judgment. However, God promises that His children have already passed over from this. The judgment that Jesus took on the cross was also meant for you.

You Are a Child of Abraham

"In the LORD all the offspring of Israel shall be justified and shall glory."

Isaiah 45:25 ESV

Did Abraham realize how true God's promise to him was – that one day his offspring would be as numerous as the sand of the sea or the stars in the sky? Millions of Jews count themselves as his physical descendants, as do millions of Muslims (through his son Ishmael). After them, hundreds of millions of Christians join the queue, claiming to also be Abraham's children by faith! Everyone wants to be a child of Abraham!

According to the Bible, those who are his physical progeny are not necessarily his "children," but those who do God's will as Abraham did. What's more, those who accept Christ can count themselves as his children, according to the New Testament. Yes, by faith we are children of Abraham, because he is the father of our faith – we believe as Abraham believed, according to Paul. How wonderful to be a child of the King, according to the prophet in this verse, because all those are justified by God – saved, in other words! Salvation means God's acceptance, relationship, protection, healing and blessing – now and always!

Thank You, Lord, for saving me through Christ Jesus. Amen.

Being a child of Abraham means you are included in the covenant of blessing that God made with him. God promises that by faith you are also a child of Abraham!

You Will Glory

"In the LORD all the offspring of Israel shall be justified and shall glory."

Isaiah 45:25 ESV

The prophet said that all the children of Israel will be saved, by which we understand true children, not merely physical descendants. God will distinguish between them on the last day. We include ourselves as God's children, because He promised this to us in His Word and we have accepted Christ as Savior. For us it's an undeniable fact. We'll not only be saved *one day*; we are already saved *today*. We already belong to Him through Christ Jesus and already experience His work in our lives.

We "glory" in Him – which means praise, celebrate. Joy is even now a part of our lives, because God made us beautiful and wonderful, because He loves us so, because He forgave our sins and trespasses, because He takes care of us in all our circumstances, because everything is going to be OK with Him, because we will experience peace and joy forever … It's more joy than any unbeliever can experience! Sometimes we lose our joy when we focus on the circumstances, on the small picture, on the ego. Don't! Get your focus straight and glory in Him!

Lord, I am indeed so thankful and joyful in You.
Thank You for Your love! Amen.

"Not all who are descended from Israel belong to Israel" (Romans 9:6).
We must act like children of God. If you trust Him with your life,
He promises that you are included, and saved.

Earthly Glory Will Pass

The gods Bel and Nebo are down on their knees, as wooden images of them are carried away on weary animals.

Isaiah 46:1 CEV

The capital city of Babylon (*bab-ili*, meaning "gates of god") was beautifully designed on both sides of the Euphrates River. On either side of the river were two huge circles. One contained the impressive royal palace; the other surrounded the temple of Bel, the Babylonians' main god. It was built as a high tower, with a walkway on the outside going up and around it. At the top there was a chapel containing a statue of Bel in a sitting position, which was located behind an altar. Parts of the altar and throne were made of solid gold and right at the top there was an astrological observatory. Imposing feasts and ceremonies were held at the temple. Nebo was Bel's assistant and messenger.

The Jews who were in captivity were very conscious of the "glory" of the foreign gods – and the fact that their God hadn't kept them from being taken captive. Perhaps they were jealous? Eventually, however, those idols were captured by other enemies, packed up on animals and carried off … how ironic! Don't let the world's glitz and glamour blind you – the glamour is superficial and the glory is very temporary. Only God has enduring worth – faithfully stay with Him.

Lord, I see many things,
but my eyes are fixed only on You. Amen.

We shouldn't let the world's glitz and glamour blind us.
These are things that have little lasting value.
God promises that you will find eternal value in Him.

Earthly Gods Will Not Help

They stoop; they bow down together; they cannot save the burden, but themselves go into captivity.

Isaiah 46:2 ESV

The prophet ridiculed the gods of the Babylonians. Bel (in names such as *Belshazzar*) and Nebo (as in *Nebuchadnezzar*) were for decades shrouded in the glory of the empire, but now their end had come. It is unclear precisely what the prophet meant in this verse, but it seems as if the gods, the spiritual powers the people worshiped, couldn't prevent their images – these idol statues that represented them – from being packed up and shipped out. The gods were powerless, in other words.

That makes us think about the idols of our day e.g. Mammon, the god of money. The quest for riches is the drive behind most activities of our time! Many people really live as if money is the solution to all problems. Although we need money, of course, it is not everything. It cannot buy happiness, health, relationships, fulfillment or peace! Don't expect these things from money – it cannot carry such a weight, we are told in today's verse. Only God can give these things – that's a promise!

Lord, You alone make me happy. Amen.

To some extent we need to rely on things like money, health and education. God, however, promises that these things will disappoint you if they become idols in your life.

July

He Carries You Still

"Listen to Me, O house of Jacob, all the remnant of the house of Israel, who have been borne by Me from before your birth, carried from the womb."

Isaiah 46:3 ESV

There is something sad in this phrase "the remnant of the house of Israel." Of God's covenant people, not many were left. Of the northern ten tribes, most were gone, and those who remained of Judah and Benjamin had suffered great losses over the years, in Judea and also in Babylon. The point that God makes in this verse, however, is that He carried Israel from its birth. This statement is in stark contrast to the false gods, who couldn't carry their worshipers, but had to be carried themselves!

Who carries whom – that is the question! Idols are human-made things and we must make sure not to carry around such notions about God as if they came from Him. We all have notions about God, but we should remember that part and parcel of the true God is His mystery. Also, we can never carry Him; He carries us!

Take this, faithful believer: God carries you. You are still in His hands. He hugs you warmly. If you're facing difficulties, He will see you through them, He will protect you. Be acutely aware of God's love today! Yes, you so need it – we all do.

Lord, just hold me today. Amen.

God promises that you are safe in His hands today.
He is still carrying you. He will never let you go.

He Carries You Always

"Even to your old age I am He, and to gray hairs I will carry you. I have made, and I will bear; I will carry and will save."

Isaiah 46:4 ESV

God says He carried His people since their birth as a nation. They are His people and that is their salvation. Friend, our obedience and good living is only a part of the picture. We are not saved by that, because what we offer is simply too little and too flawed. We are saved by the fact that we belong to God – that we've become part of His family – a child – in Christ Jesus. That is the grace that saved us!

In this verse, God says that He will keep on carrying His people even in their old age. How beautiful! The senior years are often a time of more vulnerability, insecurity and dependence. Sickness, loss and loneliness are often a daily reality. Still, God is present and our old age is a time to grow nearer to Him and to grow spiritually (although some older people sadly become hardened).

This is God's message for all who are challenged by old age and all it brings: *I have made you and I will bear you; I will carry you and will save you.* Accept God's word!

Thank You, Lord, for Your encouragement. Amen.

God promises each person who is growing older
that He is keeping their future safely in His hands.
Until the last day, the last minute,
He will hold their – and your – hand.

You'll Do Better with God

> "To whom will you liken Me and make Me equal, and compare Me, that we may be alike?"
>
> *Isaiah 46:5 ESV*

Nowadays many people answer these questions posed by God rather easily. Yes, modern humankind often feel quite capable of being the god of their own life. They create their own "faith" – and live according to a certain frame of reference, a worldview, towards chosen purposes, in compliance with their own assumptions and ethics.

Some people are deeply spiritual in their own way, some find themselves exploring other religions and some accept the otherworldly influence of the "transcendent," or "the universe," as they might call it. Often it is a reaction to their Christian upbringing.

The fact is that we struggle to live without faith (and without God), since we have such an inherent need for a meaningful life. Science can only describe an empty and cold universe, and cannot prescribe a way of life or explain the purpose of it all. For that we need God! A lot of the things we chase after, such as money, pleasure, honor and power, are merely ways of trying to fill the void. But only He can fill it! No, we'll do better with God in our lives.

Lord, thank You that I could find You! Amen.

Many people are searching for something or someone, for the purpose of everything. The God of the Bible promises that He is what they seek. Search for Him and find Him!

You'll Be Carried Through

They lift it to their shoulders, they carry it, they set it in its place,
and it stands there; it cannot move from its place.

Isaiah 46:7 ESV

The prophet refers in this passage a few times to the idea of "carrying."
He finds it ironic that *people* could carry their gods, not the other way
round. The wording of this Scripture verse brings to mind the legend of
Reprobus, a tall, strong man who served Christ by helping travelers through
a dangerous river.

According to the story, one stormy night he carried a child on his shoulders and almost drowned, because the child became heavier than any
person he ever carried. On the other side the child revealed Himself as
Christ, who carried the whole world on His shoulders. After that, Reprobus
was known as Christophorus ("Christ-bearer"), also known as St. Christopher
(later, the patron saint of travelers).

It is true that we carry Christ in our hearts, but the greater truth is that
He carries us. This is not just a charming idea, but an everyday reality. When
the waters rise around us and we feel we're sinking, we find that we are
wonderfully carried. If you must get through a difficult situation today, you
can trust God for just that, because that's the promise: He will carry you!

Thank You, Lord, for carrying me through this situation. Amen.

When you are going through deep waters, God promises today
that He will see you through. You can rely on His strength
every day to do what you have to do. He will be there.

Not Salvation, but Grace

"Listen to Me, you stubborn of heart, you who are far from righteousness: I bring near My righteousness; it is not far off."

Isaiah 46:12-13 ESV

There are two extremes in this verse: 1. the people are stubborn and do not deserve to be saved, and 2. God saves them in Babylon and brings them back to Israel. Remember that these are topics that are rich with meaning and symbolism the whole Bible through. The people stand for us; Babylon stands for the world that is far from God; and the Promised Land, Israel, stands for life and eternity with God.

The people did not deserve salvation; they were in captivity because of their disobedience. Nevertheless, God fetched them from there. If a sheep has strayed from the herd, it's because it has left the group, not so? Nevertheless, the Shepherd leaves the herd to fetch the one that is lost!

It is the same with us. What is the motive behind God's moving toward us? What compels Him to save us? It is grace – God's grace working through His love for us! Yes, God's heart burns with love! That's why He doesn't leave us where we are – and that's why He'll never leave you.

Thank You, Lord, for Your love! Amen.

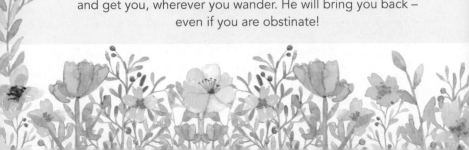

God assures you of His love and promises that He will come and get you, wherever you wander. He will bring you back – even if you are obstinate!

Salvation Is on the Way

"I will soon come to save you. I am not far away and will waste no time."

Isaiah 46:13 CEV

The Lord promised salvation to the Jews and it happened exactly as He said. It's not just a historical fact; this verse also speaks to us. Its words touch us deeply, so many centuries later. Read it again, it's such a wonderful and direct promise from God: *I will soon come … I am not far away …* Don't we, as modern readers, also have our troubles, worries and pains? Yes, of course! Can we also take this promise for ourselves, as if God is promising this to us, today? The answer is yes, but let's formulate carefully now.

Objectively and literally speaking, this verse wasn't meant to promise anything to us, so many centuries later. However, because the Holy Spirit inspired these words, and we can apply God's Word subjectively and individually to our lives, we can take it in faith.

Read this verse again and ask yourself: do these words work faith in your heart, hope, a feeling of being answered, of promise, of joy? Then the Spirit has shown you in this verse God's heart of love, His goodness and His faithfulness! May you now, based on that knowledge and faith, also trust God to quickly come to your salvation. Of course you may! Take your promise, friend.

Lord, I also trust, here in my situation,
that Your salvation is near. Amen.

The Lord promises that He is a Keeper of His word.
He will do what He has promised.
He is with you in your situation –
and He will always save you.

God Is Where God Lives

"I will put salvation in Zion, for Israel My glory."

Isaiah 46:13 ESV

The Jews were in Babylon, far from Judea and Jerusalem, their city where God's temple stood. Of course the temple at that stage was a mere ruin after the Babylonians had torn it down and carried its contents away. Therefore it's surprising that God calls it *Zion* – the beautiful old name for Jerusalem as God's abode. We can see it as the "spiritual" name for Jerusalem, emphasizing God's presence and glory there.

Zion also referred to the temple itself or to the mountain on which the city was built, but always emphasized the fact that it was God's city, God's temple, God's holy mountain. *Zion* was where God lived. Now He would bring back His people to Jerusalem, and Jerusalem back to its status as God's dwelling.

Ponder the following question: am I where God is, or am I far from His presence in a foreign land? Metaphorically speaking, of course. Do I long for God's presence and glory in my life – for the mountaintop where I once met with Him? Yes? Then ask Him to return you to that Zion. He will!

Lord, bring me to You – where I belong. Amen.

If your heart is far from the Lord and feels like a deserted temple, you can return. God promises that He will welcome you back and fill your life with His glory.

They Won't Get Away

"Come down and sit in the dust, O virgin daughter of Babylon; sit on the ground without a throne, O daughter of the Chaldeans!"

Isaiah 47:1 ESV

According to the prophet, the city of Babylon was like a spoilt and rich girl who was not used to hard work. She spent all her time on her appearance, and pleasure. She always got what she wanted. Hard times lay ahead for her – she would have to work like an ordinary girl, dressed in working clothes with bare arms and legs. Bystanders would laugh at her nakedness, which the prophet blatantly describes.

That's the way it was for Babylon, the capital of the empire. The city was only used to the best – the treasures of the world. However, many nations, including God's people, and thousands of others were downtrodden in the process. Thousands were murdered for the glory of the empire.

God would not let that pass. Babylon would get what Babylon deserved. Today's world will also receive what it deserves. The seer John described in Revelation how the worldly system (which he also called Babylon) would fall: "Fallen is Babylon the great!" (Revelation 18:2). The point is that God will judge everything. Bad people will not get away with their misdeeds. They will assume responsibility before Him. Have you experienced injustice? Those people will stand before God as well.

Thank You, Lord, for being just. Amen.

If you have been wronged or unfairly treated, God promises that you can leave your pain with Him. He will take care of the perpetrators. Their punishment or pardon is totally in His hands.

Angels at the Ready

Our Redeemer – the LORD of hosts is His name – is the Holy One of Israel.

Isaiah 47:4 ESV

The prophets loved to intersperse their oracles with utterances about God like: *Holy is His name!* or *His name is Lord!* It confirmed that God was speaking through them and stamped their prophecies with authenticity.

Here the prophet refers to *Jehovah Sabaoth* – "the Lord of Hosts." This is a military term referring to God as the general of the armies, which conveys His power. The armies of the Lord included the soldiers of Israel, but also referred to the hosts of heaven, the angels.

The Bible accepts and testifies to the fact of "ten thousand times ten thousand" angels, indicating an enormous number. All these angels stand at the ready to exercise God's orders – i.e. to watch over humans.

What a great comfort! You and I can rest assured in the fact that angels are watching over us today, keeping us from harm. Listen carefully: do you hear the rustling of wings?

Thank You, Lord, for angels that are with me even now. Amen.

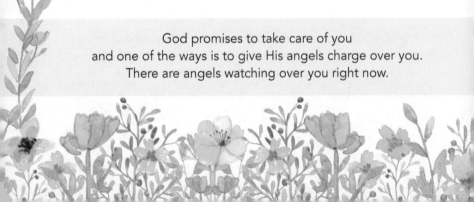

God promises to take care of you
and one of the ways is to give His angels charge over you.
There are angels watching over you right now.

Consequences Will Follow

"You didn't care what you did; it never entered your mind that you might get caught."

Isaiah 47:7 CEV

The prophet delivered God's bitter judgment on Babylon, the enemy who had captured His people and taken them from their country. He said that Babylon's sins would catch up with them. The Babylonians were hard on the Jews – even the elderly – and now God's retribution would follow.

We must remember that sin always has consequences, just as all decisions have their effects. Sin isn't just bad behavior; it is also the transgression of God's will. If you harm the created, the Creator also becomes involved.

The "curse" of sin is therefore a debt against God and also sin's inbuilt consequences. We cannot escape the consequences of sin, because it follows sin like a shadow. Even if you receive God's forgiveness, you still need to deal with whatever results follow. It is better to make good choices now – then you can expect a good result!

Lord, help me with this choice ... [name the difficulty you face]. Amen.

If you make the wrong choices, you will have to deal with the bad consequences. However, if you make good choices, God promises that you will experience the blessings of those choices.

Temptation Leads to Nowhere

"Now therefore hear this, you lover of pleasures …"

Isaiah 47:8 ESV

The prophet says that Babylon is like a temptress. The theme of spiritual adultery is a big one in the Bible. It refers to people turning away from God in a spiritual sense. Remember, God sees Himself as a "husband." To turn to idols, as happened so frequently, was tantamount to unfaithfulness, to adultery. It was about the seduction and allure of the world.

Nahum described the great city of Nineveh – long before that – as a "great harlot" and then Isaiah used the same language for Babylon. The city's greatness and wealth tempted people away from God. The book of Revelation used exactly the same description – *centuries* later – for Rome which John also called "Babylon, the great harlot."

The "shameless prostitute," as one translation has it, is the world system that flashes her smile and whispers promises of pleasure and riches. However, if we love the world, we lose God. Today's promise is an upside down one: the world can never, ever offer you what God does!

Lord, I choose only You. Amen.

To choose the world – to accept the standards of money
and joy of this world – does not bring satisfaction.
God promises to give you true peace.

Pride Leads to a Fall

> "I am, and there is no one besides Me; I shall not sit as a widow or know the loss of children."
>
> *Isaiah 47:8* ESV

Babylon was like a proud woman who was so prosperous that she couldn't imagine that she would ever be anything else. She would never lose her independence or status. Affluence can do that to some people – make them feel independent, untouchable and even arrogant.

People can believe that they're more important than others or that their wealth is solely their own doing. That is wrong of course, because success usually has to do with the privilege of having been able to study; parents who could share resources, skills or knowledge; the right contacts; or simply good luck.

Never forget God's favor, His blessing! However, when one rides the wave of earthly success, pride can be the end result. Scripture is clear that the proud will fall. Babylon had to fall and so everyone who has not learned humility from God. Humility is not an inferiority; it is submission and obedience to God.

Lord, I look to You alone.
Please remove all pride from my life. Amen.

Wealth can make you feel independent and powerful, untouchable and haughty. God promises that this is a lie. Modesty is what leads you to true humility.

Magic Leads to Regret

"These two things shall come to you in a moment ... in spite of your many sorceries and the great power of your enchantments. You felt secure in your wickedness."

Isaiah 47:9-10 ESV

Babylon was a great center for the occult and magic. The idol priests of that time were trained in sorcery, and their aim was to control the physical world and its events. For example, outcomes of wars and harvests had to be influenced.

One way that magic was performed was by incantations. The people believed that certain secret words had power when they were spoken out loud – that it would force the gods or spirits to act in a certain way. The priest was then paid to come and pronounce such spells, curses and enchantments. In Babylon, they believed that they had perfected the craft, since they had overrun the whole known world!

God said in today's verse that the people had no enchantment that could prevent the doom that was coming to them. The other way of doing magic of course was by mixing potions – secret mixtures that could be swallowed, worn or buried. These things still happen in many places in the world, even in our own country. Many believe in the occult and strange things happen, it is true. However, all these things are forbidden by God. Do not put your trust in evil things – you will live to regret it.

Lord, I turn away from all evil – I turn to You! Amen.

Some people try to improve their lives through sorcery.
God, however, forbids these things. He alone is in charge of your life –
He promises that you can trust Him.

The Occult Leads to Isolation

You felt secure in your wickedness; you said, "No one sees me"; your wisdom and your knowledge led you astray.

Isaiah 47:10 ESV

When the prophet blamed the people for their "wisdom and knowledge," it sounded peculiar because we see knowledge and wisdom as something positive. Knowledge is facts that we learn from books or the Internet, and wisdom has to do with insights that experience brings. Isn't that good?

What the prophet meant, however, was knowledge of the occult. Babylon was the chief center of alchemy, magic, astrology and other similar "sciences." Even their medicine and mathematics were filled with occult symbols and purposes. Nonetheless, all their occult knowledge wasn't sufficient enough to prevent the Persians from overrunning the Babylonians, dethroning their king and introducing new gods and beliefs.

Today we live in a scientific world and we really have fantastic knowledge, yet many still are interested in the occult. Up to a point that is seemingly only curiosity, but it can also turn into experimentation and practicing. Remember that God forbids these things! It isolates us from Him. No, let's rather seek the knowledge and wisdom of the Holy Spirit.

Lord, be my only source of wisdom and insight! Amen.

Some people try to gain knowledge from the occult, which God forbids. He is the only One who has that knowledge – but He promises to give you His Spirit.

Enchantment Leads
to Entanglement

"Stand fast in your enchantments and your many sorceries, with which you have labored from your youth."

Isaiah 47:12 ESV

We discussed Babylon being the center of the occult. All the ancient "sciences" were completely intertwined with magic knowledge, secret symbols and attempts to alter physical reality.

Idol temples were particularly evil places: the statue of the idol stood in the light of torches and the altar fire, attended to by priests who worshiped and sacrificed to it. They would also go into a trance and "communicate" with their god. All types of occult activities were performed there: sorcery, divination and conversing with spirits.

The Jewish people in Babylon had to make sure that they weren't drawn into these things. The Lord forbids these things for us as His people, because communion with evil rubs off on us. It pulls us away from God and binds us spiritually. It's important to steer clear of the whole occult realm – it's not for Christians.

Lord, deliver us from evil. Amen.

Some people get involved in sorceries that God forbids. You must confess all these things to God – He promises to forgive you and to free you from such evil.

Horoscopes Lead to Lies

"You have worn yourself out, asking for advice from those who study the stars and tell the future month after month."

Isaiah 47:13 CEV

Babylon was the origin of the "zodiac" that we still know today. The Babylonians divided the whole sky into 12 segments on a plane with the sun's orbit. In each segment they connected the stars to form a "sign": Leo, Taurus, Aries, etc. Against the backdrop of these signs – which were assigned certain characteristics – the movements of the planets were studied. As the planets went through these signs, certain conclusions or predictions could allegedly be made, as is done in tabloids today.

It is amazing that astrology is still popular in our time, since it's factually false on every level: the old divisions of the signs are no longer the current position of the stars, the signs are made up of stars that have absolutely no relation to each other and it is scientifically proven that there's no relation in the least between the stars and anything that happens on earth. It's all a lie! Why is it still read?

Well, people only see in it what they want to see and later it becomes a habit – even a belief. Some people trust in their "lucky stars." However, as Christians we have nothing to do with astrology. We trust God for our future.

Lord, You alone are in control of my future.
I thank You for that. Amen.

Some people read their weekly horoscopes "for the fun of it,"
but still give credit to what they read. Rather confess these things to
God – He promises that you can trust Him with your future.

Idol Worship Leads to Failure

"… lest you should say, 'My idol did them, my carved image and my metal image commanded them.'"

Isaiah 48:5 ESV

The prophet announces God's redemption beforehand, so that no one can say that it was the work of the Babylonian gods. We've said enough about the idols and false gods of our own day: money, health, pleasure, honor, status, power, food, drink, addictions, etc.

Remember, an idol is anything for which we erect an altar in our life: a "high place" (a place of importance) on which we offer sacrifices of time, money and energy. *What do we sacrifice to? – that* is the relevant question.

The lesson here is that God allows these idols to fail us. Yes, as the Babylonians' idols failed them in the end (they were loaded up and carted away by the new regime), so our own false gods will fail us – that's for sure!

God will allow money, power, status and the like to fall away if these take up our whole sacrifice and effort. Let's rather realize that the Lord is the only trustworthy God.

Lord, I do trust You with my life! Amen.

If we put too much trust in our money, appearance or status,
it may lead to us losing it. God, however, promises
that He will always stay loyal – forever!

New Things Will Be Heard

"From this time forth I announce to you new things, hidden things that you have not known."

Isaiah 48:6 ESV

The Lord said the salvation of the Jews would be something new and surprising – something unexpected. This is typical of the way God works! We are forever trying to understand, explain or predict God. Most probably we're just trying to make sense of things – which is the way our brain works – or trying to gain some control in difficult situations.

God, however, cannot be boxed in, in any such way. The moment you have figured Him out, or have made up a 1-2-3 scheme or spiritual "law" of how He should behave, He does something else. He breaks our schemes and rules with such ease! Yes, God typically does new things.

Let's not try to work with God in this way – He's really too big for our understanding. God cannot be figured out or understood in this way – He can only be trusted and loved. And that's all He asks! Plainly trust in the fact that He will do a new thing for you!

Yes, Lord, thank You for the new thing in my life! Amen.

Although it is difficult to predict or understand God,
He promises that His deeds in our lives are always for our own good.
He only means well. You must believe it!

God Will Do It

"For My own sake, for My own sake, I do it."

Isaiah 48:11 ESV

The Old Testament has such a beautiful perspective on God's grace. The Lord commanded a certain good and fulfilling life to His people – the Law of Moses – and He expected them to keep it. He said that they would surely experience blessing if they followed it. But then the people didn't keep the law – they kept some of it, some of the time, but not all of it, all the time. They wanted to, but they couldn't.

As with all bad choices, the consequences of their disobedience followed (their captivity), but God came to their rescue. This was not because of their merit; it was because of His grace! He did it for His own honor's sake.

In the New Testament this topic of grace is put in the context of Christ Jesus. Grace is multiplied! Here is the good news: everything doesn't rest on your shoulders. It's not about your personal merit. You don't have to make it as a Christian, let alone be perfect. He will do it on your behalf. Accept it and honor Him for that!

Thank You, Lord, for Your grace toward me! Amen.

So often we want to be perfect in everything to obtain God's approval. However, God's grace is bestowed upon us and He promises to accept us just as we are.

Everything Is Under Control

> "My hand laid the foundation of the earth, and My right hand spread out the heavens."
>
> *Isaiah 48:13 ESV*

In several places in Isaiah, the Lord reminded His people that He had everything under control. With His own hand, God laid the earth's foundation and over that (with His "right hand" or right palm) He spread out the heavens – the blue and the black night sky. It refers of course to the ancient view the people had of the physical world. That doesn't matter to us, because they had no scientific knowledge to believe anything else.

God works with any person in His specific context and thinking – how else? It merely means that God made everything: the heavens and the earth. Everything is under His control – from the smallest atom particle to the biggest galaxy. The universe declares the majesty of God, according to Scripture (see Psalm 19:1)!

Understand this today: your life may seem to spiral out of control, but it can never fall out of God's hand. He is still intensely involved, intensely in control. He knows exactly what is happening and He knows that the end will be good. Yes, your situation will end well, friend.

Thank You, Lord, that my life is under Your control. Amen.

God promises that He has complete control of your life –
He made you and subsequently has never let you slip out of His hand.

God Will Send Someone

And now the Lord GOD has sent me, and His Spirit.

Isaiah 48:16 ESV

God's relationship with Cyrus, the king of Persia, was remarkable. Cyrus was a complete heathen (although a very good king), but God declared that He loved him. He had a plan for him and wanted to use him. We can see Cyrus as a prototype of Christ: a beloved and anointed savior (which is literally what God called him) sent by God to save his people.

In this verse, the savior/Cyrus is speaking out poetically to confirm that he is coming to save the people by the power of the Spirit. The one is a human forerunner of the other.

The point for today is that God calls someone to do His work. He works through someone whom He sends. It doesn't matter if that person is a Christian or not – they will be used by God for His purpose. You can believe that God still sends someone to His people – even to you – to help and save them. God will send someone!

Lord, send someone to me as well! Amen.

God promises to be with you and to help you.
He can use anybody for this purpose.
Don't keep your eyes on people, but on God.

Here Is Your Promise

Thus says the LORD, your Redeemer, the Holy One of Israel: "I am the LORD your God, who teaches you to profit, who leads you in the way you should go."

Isaiah 48:17 ESV

Today we'll take this verse phrase for phrase. The "Holy One of Israel" is speaking and He calls Himself "your Redeemer." To start off, let's highlight the importance of knowing God as a Redeemer. Personally and purposefully trust Him for this life and for eternity – confirm it again!

Then God says that He is the Lord, "your God." Of course He's speaking to His people as a nation, but today God's "people" include you and me. It's wonderful to know that God is your God, that He's on your side, that He's with you and that He cares for you!

Lastly, He says that He teaches the people to their "profit," which means to their benefit. Remember, God's "teaching" doesn't only refer to His words, but especially to His deeds – for example the fact that the Jews had to be in Babylon taught them some important lessons. They had to accept that this would work to their benefit. So, too, we must learn to read the circumstances. What do they tell us?

When we pay attention, we will see His guidance: through His Word, through others, through our circumstances, in our heart! He'll lead us "in the way we should go."

Lord, lead me today! Amen.

God promises He will be your God –
in all circumstances by your side –
if indeed you accept and serve Him as God and Savior.

Your Peace like a River

> "Oh that you had paid attention to My commandments! Then your peace would have been like a river."
>
> *Isaiah 48:18* ESV

The Jews (as with us) had to learn their lessons the hard way – in captivity. They did in fact learn a lot in Babylon: the Law of Moses was reinterpreted and dutifully taught, their doctrines and beliefs were expanded – the whole of Judaism took the form that we still find today!

From their side, the people (more or less) stayed faithful to the synagogue meetings, the feasts and their ritual purity. On the whole it was a pivotal time for the Jewish people and they came away stronger. Now they could enjoy the benefits of obedience. Their peace would be "like a river" – what a beautiful image!

Divine peace (*shalom*) is a broad and inclusive concept: it included peace of the heart, but also peace in our lives, in our relationships, in our work and income – peace with God. It's the comprehensive favor of God. *Shalom* is like a strong and silent river flowing in our lives, taking away our worry, bringing us rest, rejuvenation and new life! Seek God's will and experience that peace.

Lord, grant me that peace! Amen.

God promises that peace will flow through your life like a river if you dedicate your life to Him.

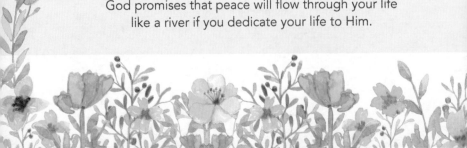

There Will Be Provision

They did not thirst when He led them through the deserts; He made water flow for them from the rock.

Isaiah 48:21 ESV

The Lord reminded His people of the miracles of the past. The previous time they had to travel through the desert was when they came out of Egypt. Now a new journey was ahead, but the miracles of the past could build their confidence. God reminded them that when the water ran out in the desert, it only *seemed* like the end of the road.

Who could foresee that Moses would strike a rock and that an abundance of water would gush out? No, they "did not thirst," says God. Of course we all would be worried to be without water in a hot and dry desert, but let's see it from God's viewpoint: they had no real need, because He was there with them!

As individuals we are also traveling through our own particular desert on the way to our Promised Land. Certain difficulties and problems will be a given – it's part of the journey. Listen up: you will not suffer a lack of the essentials. Ultimately and essentially you "shall not want." That's a great comfort!

Lord, thank You that You'll provide for everything I need. Amen.

God promises that you will eventually have enough of everything. From His point of view, you are completely equipped for your specific journey.

The Wicked Will Not Have Peace

"There is no peace," says the LORD, "for the wicked."

Isaiah 48:22 ESV

Accept the truth of this verse as an absolute fact. Since biblical times, believers have been disconcerted about the apparent success of unbelievers. Let's first just repeat the word "apparent," because it's simply not true that unbelievers only prosper and believers only struggle. Nonsense!

Let's also define the word "success." What does it mean? According to whose standards is anyone successful? Do we mean affluence, health, pleasure? With these things it's not so that unbelievers do any better than believers.

Let's return now to the truth of this verse. The "wicked" can never have the peace that believers have – since it's faith in God that brings us peace! Unbelievers remain looking for something – the sense, the purpose, the meaning of life. They will look for it in money, in health or in pleasure, but those things (on their own) cannot bring meaning or peace. Only after they find God – whom they are in reality looking for – will they have peace. But we found Him – and it!

Thank You, Lord, for the peace
that surpasses understanding. Amen.

The Word says that non-believers don't have true peace
within their soul – it's impossible. However,
God promises you peace of mind beyond this world.

He Knows You So Well

The LORD called me from the womb, from the body of my mother He named my name.

Isaiah 49:1 ESV

In this part of Isaiah we read of a certain "Servant of the Lord," who is also called the "Suffering Servant." There are several "servant songs" in Isaiah and here we have another one. The "servant" refers to Israel personified, poetically speaking – but also to the Messiah. In the New Testament, the "servant" is clearly Jesus Christ. In a certain sense we can also see ourselves in the "servant."

Here the "servant" says that the Lord called him "from the womb." The Bible confirms in more than one place that God knows our names from before our birth – which makes us very protective of pre-natal life, although we know the topic is fraught with ethical questions.

The fact remains that God knows us from the very beginning, that He's intimately involved in our growth on every level and that He has a dream for every one of us. Such a God wouldn't leave you in the lurch now, would He?

Thank You, Lord, that You are so involved with my life! Amen.

God promises that He was with you when you were still being formed in your mother's womb. He had already held His hand over you, and still does today. Such a God must be served with joy and gratitude.

He Will Look After My Rights

I have spent my strength for nothing … yet surely my right is with the LORD, and my recompense with my God.

Isaiah 49:4 ESV

How wonderful is the faith of this "servant of the Lord," who is speaking in this verse! The enigmatic "servant"-figure in Isaiah is Israel personified or the Messiah, or both. The "servant" shows us the way spiritually.

There is confidence in this verse, which the translators emphasized by the word "surely." Although the servant feels they have worked in vain, they are *sure* that God will be just, see their efforts and reward them accordingly. That's what faith is: a deep knowledge of who God is, a firm conviction and trust in Him, and finally a complete surrender to the fact that God will intervene.

Do you also live with such an expectation, with such faith? If so, it's wonderful! Sometimes radical faith is the only option left! At other times, though, we find faith difficult – sometimes it's hard to look away from the circumstances and emotions involved and to trust God unconditionally. Then we need to exercise our faith. Learn to say: God *will* supply in my need! God *will* provide a way! When we continue to confess our trust in God like this, faith will build up in our hearts.

Lord, I know You will help. I place my trust in You. Amen.

You need to believe (and say) with assurance
that God will help you – He promised
that He would. Truly believe it!

You Will Receive Strength

I am honored in the eyes of the LORD, and my God has become my strength.

Isaiah 49:5 ESV

Sometimes we just haven't got the capacity for spiritual living – our schedule is too tight to fit in prayer time, Bible reading, spiritual books and so on. We also find it difficult to witness, give a tithe and do all the other wonderful things that one can do to grow spiritually. Things like these often seem like luxuries that we just can't afford. They are for others who have the time and the inclination. They only serve to make us feel even guiltier than we do! Do you identify with this? Then take note of the following:

The spiritual life is not meant to make you feel guilty or judged. That's not God's intention! Scripture does not prescribe specific spiritual forms, since the spiritual life is as unique to every person as they are to their particular personalities and rhythms. No, the spiritual life is only meant to bless and build us up.

The Lord will give us the strength for everything He asks of us. He won't ask what we cannot do. When we ask Him to help us to grow spiritually – in particular ways – He will make it possible.

Ask God's help and take small steps. Integrate your spiritual life with your everyday life.

Thank You, Lord, for Your empowerment. Amen.

God will not ask something of you that you cannot do.
He promises that if He asks you to do something,
He will provide you with the strength and ability to accomplish it.
This means you can do what He asks.

You Will Be a Light

"I will make you as a light for the nations, that My salvation may reach to the end of the earth."

Isaiah 49:6 ESV

The "Servant of the Lord" is talking in this verse about their calling – and let's distinguish three levels to this call:

1. God's call to Israel was to be a light for all nations. The whole world was to see the glory and blessing of a nation serving God, so that they would be drawn to Him as well. That's the purpose of Israel's election.

2. Jesus Christ – also identified as the "Servant" in the Bible – said that He is the light of the world, which means that the world would see the glory and grace of God in Him.

3. Finally, Jesus commands us to shine our light before the world, so that people can see our good works and praise God for it. Don't think that you can't shine some light! You *can* shine for God and you do every time you help, comfort or encourage someone with a smile, a touch or a word.

Today, look at others with the "soft eyes" of kindness, not the "hard eyes" of condescension or judgment. Whisper to someone: *I'll pray for you.* Then, God will be praised!

Lord, let Your light shine through me today. Amen.

God promises that you are a light to the world around you if you live out your Christian faith. People see when you show love and they will associate it with the fact that you serve Him.

The Tables Will Be Turned

"You are slaves of rulers and of a nation who despises you. Now this is what I promise: Kings and rulers will honor you by kneeling at your feet."

Isaiah 49:7 CEV

It's wonderful that in the kingdom of God – of which we already read in the Old Testament – the tables are turned so completely. The values of God's kingdom and the world's empire are completely different, even opposite.

In the world it's all about personal honor and success, about individual power and glory. In the Kingdom, it's more about caring and serving others; about love, joy and peace. Also, in the Kingdom, those considered significant are different from those who are thought of as important in this world – often they are exactly the opposite!

Jesus emphasized this in His parables and daily life. He paid attention to those who were regarded as unimportant in their day, like children, women, lepers, Samaritans and sinners. Are you important in this world? If you are, it's not wrong – congratulations on being successful – but now also grow in God's kingdom. However, if you're not too particularly important in this world, like most of us, that's also good – we are important to God! All of us need to grow in humility and love, though. God will honor this!

Lord, I live for Your glory! Amen.

God promises that you are valuable and important to Him.
Whether you are important in the world's eyes is not
as important as you might think – it really doesn't matter to Him.

It Will Be as He Decides

This is what the LORD says: "I will answer your prayers because I have set a time when I will help by coming to save you."

Isaiah 49:8 CEV

We are often desperate for God to intervene. We feel that change *must* come! For this to happen we often look for the "right way" of praying, for "effective" prayer: perhaps by feeling more faith, by adding "in Jesus' name" or by first binding the evil powers.

Perhaps we should confess that the miracle is already there and not ask for it again? Shall we get someone to pray for us – someone with more faith or who has the gift of intercession? Remember that there's a certain merit in all these things. Our purpose is surely not to take away what faith we have, but perhaps to take away our faith in our faith, or in our prayers!

Remember, no particular method or "right words" or worked-up faith or weeping or confessing will save you. In that sense, not even your faith will save you – God alone will save you, and faith is merely trusting that He will. Trusting Him includes accepting that He decides on the "set time," as the verse says, and on the method of intervention. Ask God and trust God – and keep on asking and trusting. That's faith!

Lord, I still trust You for this ... [name the problem or issue] Amen.

We are in a relationship with a living Person – not a method or a power. God promises to always remain in dialogue with you, but reminds you that you cannot twist His arm.

August

You Will Be Set Free

"You will set prisoners free from dark dungeons to see the light of day."

Isaiah 49:9 CEV

The theme in the Bible of God setting captives free refers first and foremost to the Jewish people who were literally held captive – in Egypt and also in Babylon. God intervened miraculously on both occasions and returned them to their Promised Land.

The topic, however, also has a strong spiritual meaning. People find themselves far from God and their true purpose, but then He comes into the picture and brings them back. The Bible described this as the bondage of sin, as the evil one that had authority over us. Then Christ came as God's powerful Redeemer and delivered us from the dominion of sin and death.

If you're a believer, you've been set free from the darkest dungeon of all – the darkness of God's absence. Love has shone on you and you've been made a child of God! How wonderful is that? Your liberation continues – for the rest of your life. God is still setting you free from all the remaining ties and hindrances that stand between you and Him. Remember that He is your Promised Land! You *will* overcome and you *will* inherit life with Him, eternally.

Lord, please help me with the following areas
from which I need deliverance … [name them]. Amen.

God promises to loosen you from the ties that bind you –
the ties of sin, death and evil. This presumes of course
that you ask Him for deliverance.

You'll Find the Way

"I will make all My mountains a road, and My highways shall be raised up."

Isaiah 49:11 ESV

It's a well-known image in the Bible that God levels the hills and fills up the valleys – in order to make a way for His people. God is the spiritual road builder *par excellence!*

The message is meant spiritually, of course: the highway that God builds is for men and women to return to Him. Isaiah is especially thinking of the return of God's people during the Messianic Era, when the Anointed One will come and restore everything.

As Christians we believe that that happened when Jesus Christ came ("Christ" being the word for *Messiah* in Greek). Jesus declared that He is the Way (and the Truth and the Life) that God built to us.

If you're with Christ on that way to God, there's a wonderful consequence: He will level out our lives more and more, remove the obstacles, fill up the voids, and help us to overcome the challenges. He creates ways for us to grow, to flourish, to serve Him better! He is still the Way Maker – that's a promise.

Lord, make a way for me today! Amen.

As we walk on God's path so we see it appear before us. We don't see the path too far ahead, but we see Him walking ahead of us. He promises that is all you need.

Everything Will Come Together

"Behold, these will come from afar; and lo, these will come from the north and from the west, and these from the land of Sinim."

Isaiah 49:12 NASB

The prophets of the Old Testament expected God's people to be restored completely in the Messianic Era. All the lost tribes and children of Israel would return from the *Diaspora* to their homeland and be one nation again.

In today's verse, the prophet rejoiced at the idea of the Israelites returning from the north, the west, they themselves from the east and others from the land of "Sinim" (a region to the south, possibly Arabia or Egypt). The reference to Sinim is actually a mystery – it could literally refer to the Chinese, who were known to the ancients as Sinites, but most commentators find it unlikely. Modern translations render it as "the city of Syene."

Paul sees the "whole of Israel" not as the physically restored Israel, but as the spiritual Israel: all Jewish and other people who have accepted Jesus as Messiah – which includes millions of Chinese believers! Perhaps we should just realize again today that God is finishing His plan like a puzzle – piece by piece. A beautiful picture is emerging, made up of all the nations of the world. You and I are also in that picture!

Lord, thank You for including me in Your grand plan. Amen.

God promises that you are also a puzzle piece in His big picture.
Without you, His picture would be incomplete.
You must be there, where you belong!

The Lord Cannot Forget You

"Could a mother forget a child who nurses at her breast? Even if a mother could forget, I will never forget you."

Isaiah 49:15 CEV

The Jews thought that God had forsaken them in Babylon. Yes, they sinned and they suffered the consequences, but what now? Would they just be forgotten, left there to disappear from among the nations? Had God abandoned His covenant with them?

No, of course not! The prophet stressed that God hadn't forgotten them – in fact, God could never forgotten them! As impossible as it would be for a mother to forget her own baby, so it would be impossible for the heavenly Father to forget His children. He had brought them to life – they were His!

You and I are also part of God's people, also part of His children. Didn't John say that by faith in Jesus we have received the right to be called children of God? Yes, He is also our Father, our *Abba* – our heavenly Dad.

Will He forget us – He, who created us so beautifully and cared for us so faithfully? Just because we don't always get 100% what we want – do we doubt His love? No, He will never forget you! His covenant with you is still in place; His plan for you still on target.

Thank You, Lord, for Your great love for me. Amen.

God adopted us as His children and promises
that this process can never be overturned. He does not
dispose of His children – with love He draws them (and you) closer!

Your Name Is in His Hand

"Behold, I have engraved you on the palms of My hands; your walls are continually before Me."

Isaiah 49:16 ESV

What a beautiful verse! The word "engraved" is correctly translated – it doesn't say *write* or *draw*, it says etched, carved, tattooed. The verse doesn't say that our names have been engraved in God's *hand*, but that we have been engraved in God's *hands* (plural). The conclusion of some translations is that our names are in God's hands.

In ancient times, the slave's hand was tattooed with his master's name, but it would be unthinkable for a master to tattoo his slave's name on his hand! Why does God do it? Because we are His children – not slaves – and He never wants to forget us. It's like a father showing off the pictures of his children that he carries with him.

Similarly, Jerusalem – His Holy City – is always on His mind. It displeased Him that the city's walls were in such ruins. That's the way God also thinks about us! Your name is written in His hands, to always remind Him of you! It also bothers Him – so to speak – that you still struggle.

Thank You, Lord, for wanting to be reminded of me. Amen.

God promises that He cannot and does not want to forget you.
He thinks about you all the time: your needs, your fears,
your dreams and your ambitions. He knows these very well!

You'll See if You Look

"Lift up your eyes around and see; they all gather, they come to you."

Isaiah 49:18 ESV

The prophet rejoiced over the tribes and children of Israel who had returned from all over the world. They had been subjected to a lot of oppression over the centuries and were scattered across the nations. The prophet expected their return. He could already see it in his mind's eye and he drew the people's attention to it by saying: "Look around, it's already starting!" Shortly after that, the Jews started to return from Babylon.

Perhaps we too should look around us and take notice of what God is doing. He is doing huge things in the world today! As the church is losing ground in Europe, it is growing sharply in South America, Africa and the East. Millions of Chinese, Koreans and others are coming to faith in Christ.

All around the world, revival is taking place – thousands are turning anew to God and are eager to grow spiritually. Local churches all over the world are making a difference in the needs around them. If you're prepared to look, you'll see that God is working. He is also working in your own life, even in the difficult circumstances that you experience. Can you see it? What is God doing? What is God saying?

Lord, what are You busy doing in my life?
Give me eyes to see. Amen.

God promises that He is building His church throughout the world. No one will stop it! He is doing a great work so that hundreds of thousands of people can be included in His kingdom.

You'll Have Joy

"Your city with its people will be as lovely as a bride wearing her jewelry."

Isaiah 49:18 CEV

It's interesting how the Lord refers here to a bride's jewelry and adornments. A woman naturally wants to look and feel attractive – "lovely" as the Bible says here, which is not wrong. Elsewhere the Bible also refers to a woman's jewelry in positive terms when it says that the church is like a bride adorned for her bridegroom. In those times, brides were lavishly adorned and practically covered with gold and jewelry.

When the New Testament says that women shouldn't seek their beauty on the outside, it doesn't mean that jewelry is completely disallowed. No, it means that our focus should be on inner beauty – aside from having good taste in our appearance, be it men or women.

The outward appearance is temporary and less important; rather, our values and morals should be right. It's interesting that people who have gone through a crisis often say that their values have turned around, that earthly things do not hold much importance anymore.

But let's return to the verse at hand, of which the topic is gladness and joy: not joy about a beautiful necklace or any earthly things, but gladness about God, about the beauty of a life with Him! Now *that* has true value!

Lord, help me to find joy in the right things. Amen.

God promises that you will have reason again for true joy, for real, deep peace. In fact, you already have a reason for it if you simply take a closer look.

You'll Wonder How It Happened

"Who raised these children? Where have they come from?"

Isaiah 49:21 CEV

Israel would soon be many again, said the prophet. The Jews would return from captivity and then – when the Messiah comes – God would call the "lost children" of Israel from out of all the nations of the world.

As Christians we see the fulfillment of these messianic prophesies in Jesus Christ, the Messiah. In Christ we also belong to the same covenant, and new believers – once lost – are streaming into God's kingdom, the spiritual Israel. Many Christians believe that God still has a great plan for the physical Israel as well – we'll have to see! However it plays out, we can be assured that God fulfils His promises. Remember that His promise to the patriarchs included two things: 1. descendants, and 2. land.

Do these promises still stand? The prophet guided the people to the future, back in their own land, when these people would come streaming in. The "lost children" would return in such masses that people would ask where all the people were coming from. Astonishment would become joy when they realized that God's promises came true! When God fulfills His promise to you, faithful believer, you'll be similarly astonished and overwhelmed.

Thank You, Lord, that Your promises are true! Amen.

The Word of God is often gradually fulfilled –
if you look back you will realize that what you have experienced
is exactly what you have asked for! He indeed promises fulfillment.

You'll Win This Struggle

"Behold, I will lift up My hand to the nations, and raise My signal to the peoples."

Isaiah 49:22 ESV

God promised to honor His covenant promises to Israel: they would become a big nation and inherit their own land. Here He says that all the scattered children of Israel will return. The image that He used here was of a war. God would defeat the other nations and then demand His children back. Then the kings of the nations would have to bring out the children of Israel.

Isaiah loved to describe God as "lifting His hand" or "raising His standard." In biblical times, the "standard" – a particular flag – was the sign or signal that the king, general or regiment was on the battlefield. It also acted as a rallying point for the troops.

What the prophet said is that God's banner was already waving on the battlefield, that the victory was already assured! In our own lives the victory is also certain. Yes, we will experience struggle and strife, but God is with us on the battlefield! Your own struggle will be won. Can you hear God's flag fluttering in the wind?

Thank You, Lord, for my victory. Amen.

God promises you victory. There's no way the Lord can lose a battle. Just stay close to Him and you will celebrate the victory into eternity.

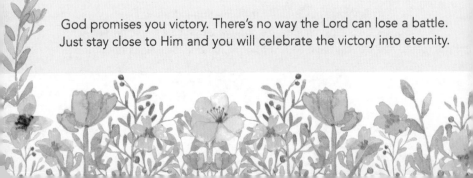

You Won't Be Disappointed

"You won't be disappointed if you trust Me."

Isaiah 49:23 CEV

What a radical promise! In the most direct terms, God promises us that we will not be disappointed. Sometimes we do feel a little disappointed in Him, not so? When He doesn't do what we ask – or how and when we asked for it? Didn't we spell it out in sufficient detail? God doesn't work like that, remember. God is God. He decides and He does as He wants.

We do not always understand why some things happen (or don't happen) – and He doesn't feel obliged to explain it to us. Still, we can keep on trusting Him. God remains a loving and faithful Father. We cannot be "disappointed" by God – just as the clay cannot be "disappointed" in what the potter makes with it or as a dog cannot be "disappointed" by his master for not playing with him. He might not realize that his master also runs a whole company – and we also know little about God's business, although He surely has time for us.

The fact remains that ultimately you will not be disappointed, ultimately you will understand, ultimately you will receive everything and more – because God is faithful.

Thank You, Lord, for this amazing promise. Amen.

God promises to never disappoint you. You can accept that 100%. However, you cannot dictate to God how to be God.

He Will Bind the Strong Man

"Even the captives of the mighty shall be taken, and the prey of the tyrant be rescued."

Isaiah 49:25 ESV

God said it didn't matter that the Babylonians were so mighty or that they had strong spiritual powers in the form of their demonic gods. Any soldier's captive could be taken from him by an even stronger soldier. God is definitely not afraid of any earthly or demonic power!

He was probably referring to this verse when He said that a "strong man" must first be bound before his house can be raided. By that He meant that He had come to bind the "strong man" (the devil) and take away his treasures (which are the people he holds captive).

For me and you it means that God will protect and save us from any onslaught of the enemy. We are engaged in a continuing struggle against the evil one, but his power is no match for God's power. Jesus Christ has already defeated him on the cross and limited his reach. Jesus also gave us the authority to expel the enemy from our lives, in His name. Do so in the name of Jesus!

Lord, thank You for giving me authority over the evil one. Amen.

Whatever authority or power – demonic or earthly – there might be, God promises His power is infinitely greater. He wipes all opposition out of the way. You can rely on His strength.

God Is on Your Side

"I will contend with those who contend with you, and I will save your children."

Isaiah 49:25 ESV

Right at the start, God was the God of only one man: Abraham. God made a personal covenant with him. Yes, it was only between the two of them! God asked of Abraham that he "walk before Him" and be "blameless." From His side, God would bless him with descendents and his own land. He would also make Abraham a blessing to others. How wonderful is that?

In a real sense, God was Abraham's personal God. Only centuries later God gave His law to Moses, when the Jewish religion was officially instituted. At the start, however, Abraham just lived his life with the knowledge that his God was with him. He prayed to his God and served Him by doing what he felt God wanted and from time to time he built altars to Him.

One thing remains the same: God still wants to be your personal God. You can still live with the knowledge that your God is with you, that He is so on your side! No power is stronger than that knowledge!

Thank You, Lord, that I can walk with You
and know You personally. Amen.

God promises that He also desires a personal covenant with you.
God can be your personal God too,
as He was to Abraham, Moses and David.

God Will Save You

"Behold, for your iniquities you were sold, and for your transgressions your mother was sent away."

Isaiah 50:1 ESV

In biblical times, a man could easily divorce his wife (but never the other way round!) or even sell his children, if he became indebted.

In Babylon, it was as if the Jews blamed God for selling them out, for "divorcing" and abandoning them. God said no, it was never like that – He wouldn't do such a thing! On the contrary, He was the One who remained faithful – they were the unfaithful ones! Their situation was their own doing – they sold themselves. Even so, God promised to save them from their actions.

Let's learn not to blame God when things don't go our way. It's not Him! It's usually other people who do bad things to us. Sometimes it's the consequence of our own choices and the sin and brokenness of the world.

But it's not God. No, He would never abandon you. In fact, He's with you in your current situation and He'll save you. Stop with the blaming and start working with God to make your life – and the world – a better place!

Lord, I need You. Thank You for being with me. Amen.

God promises that He does not bring bad things your way.
The cause lies elsewhere. Rather, He wants to help you through them.

God Is in the Good and the Bad

"Is My hand shortened, that it cannot redeem? Or have I no power to deliver?"

Isaiah 50:2 ESV

God said that He didn't forget or abandon the Jews in Babylon – they needed to take responsibility for their situation themselves. They were not to think that He was powerless to help them. No, His arm was not too short to deliver them.

If things are not going well with you, it's not because He is weak. No, God is almighty. In this world good and bad things happen. Sometimes life is wonderful, but we also go through deep waters. That's life.

Of course we would like for only good things to happen to us, but that will only be the case in the next life. Until then, we have the sweet with the sour. So, enjoy the good things as gifts from God and also live through the bad times with Him – the best way of handling adversity! Eventually God will bring you out of all that too. That's a fact – believe it!

Thank You, Lord, for never leaving me.
You have the power to deliver me from adversity. Amen.

Bad times are not a sign that God is far from you, or that He has become powerless. He promises He is still the same God. However, God does not bring about the bad things – it's simply part of life.

God Encourages You Today

The LORD God gives me the right words to encourage the weary.
Each morning He awakens me eager to learn His teaching.

Isaiah 50:4 CEV

Do you remember the figure of the "Servant of the Lord" that features in this part of Isaiah? Here we have another "servant song." The "Servant" is Israel personified, but was also seen by the Jews as the coming Messiah.

The New Testament clearly sees Him as Jesus Christ. It is Christ – the Anointed One – who declares that He's called to encourage the weary, to give strength to the weak. He said: "Come to Me, all who are weary and heavy-laden, and I will give you rest" (Matthew 11:28).

Are you weary today – discouraged perhaps? Then the Lord is speaking to you through these words, encouraging you not to give up. He'll be with you and He'll help you! These things have a solution, friend. He is the solution! The end will be for the better, not for the worse, because at the end of this matter Jesus is waiting. Yes, there is all hope! There now, get up. Wipe your tears. Smile again!

Thank You, Lord, for wiping my tears away.
Thank You for the peace I experience in You. Amen.

God promises you today specifically that the end
of the situation is good, because it ends with Him.
He encourages you and wants to wipe away your tears.

God Will Speak
if You Will Listen

He made me willing to listen and not rebel or run away.

Isaiah 50:5 CEV

The "Servant of the Lord" – known in the New Testament as Jesus Christ – is speaking: "He made me willing to listen …" Jesus Himself said that He listens to the Father; that He does nothing if the Father didn't command Him to do so. We see Jesus often praying and seeking God – early in the morning, right through the night, on the mountain, in the desert. Now remember that praying is only one half talking, the other half is listening to God – as with all conversation!

We can accept that Jesus' nights of prayer didn't involve Him just talking and talking – no, such nights spent in God's presence would involve talking, listening and just being with God.

The point is this: we must relearn how to listen, to be aware, to attend, and to become conscious of God and of His voice. Don't say that He's not speaking – oh no, we're not listening! Open your eyes, your ears, your heart … Find His voice: in the Word, in the silence, in the conversation, in the situation. Shh – simply listen …

Thank You, Lord, for talking to me.
I want to learn to listen. Amen.

God promises that He is always talking in your life – though you're not always listening. We need to be more attentive.

He Does It for You

> "I let them beat My back and pull out My beard. I didn't turn aside when they insulted Me and spit in My face."
>
> *Isaiah 50:6 CEV*

These are the words of the Anointed One, the "Suffering Servant," which we know from the New Testament is Jesus Christ. Such sad words, which were literally fulfilled.

When the Anointed One came, His people rejected Him. Only a small group received Him – thereby becoming children of God. The rest turned their backs, condemned and delivered Him to the heathen authorities. He was mocked by having to put on a purple robe and a crown of thorns, and by being spat on. His beard was pulled out, a terrible humiliation for any Jewish man. Then He was whipped until He couldn't stand anymore.

The surprising and hard-hitting irony in this verse is that Jesus held His back, held His cheek, took the robe, took the crown! It was voluntary! Christ understood that His death would be a "ransom for many" and that's why He did it willingly and lovingly – for me and for you. Such a love will not turn its back on you now, will it? Never!

Thank You, Lord Jesus, that You loved me so much – and that Your love will carry me always. Amen.

God promises that He gave Himself willingly to the cross – because He really loves you.

You Will Not Give Up

"The LORD God keeps Me from being disgraced. So I refuse to give up, because I know God will never let Me down."

Isaiah 50:7 CEV

Interestingly, it's the "Servant of the Lord" that is speaking here about giving up. Remember, Christ (whom the New Testament identifies as the "Servant") was as human as He was God. We see His humanity vividly in His anguish in Gethsemane, where He sweated blood. It shows up in His emotions and temptations – and where He said that He didn't know when the end time would be, but only the Father.

We can believe that Jesus struggled a lot with God about His call, His ministry, His people – much the same way we do. In this verse we see the Anointed One confirming His conviction that God would be with Him, that He wouldn't disappoint Him.

Faith is the ability to see God in situations where others only see the negative. Faith brings hope where others have become downhearted, faith can laugh where others cry, faith can forgive where others seek vengeance, and faith can persevere where others have given up. Faith can start again, and again … May you have this faith – and refuse to give up! God will not let you down.

Thank You, Lord, for being with me – I will not give up! Amen.

God promises that He is with you and will stand by you every moment. Truly believe it, and look away from the crisis. Look at Him instead!

You Are Exonerated

"My protector is nearby; no one can stand here to accuse Me of wrong."

Isaiah 50:8 CEV

The so-called "Servant of the Lord," whom we identify as Jesus Christ, is speaking here. Yes, He was rejected and humiliated, delivered to the heathen and then executed. Still, the Servant was innocent. He didn't sin and never hurt anyone. He demonstrated love and restored people's dignity. *His law is love and His gospel is peace,* goes the song (*O Holy Night*).

Above all, He died so that others could live. He died in our place, so that we would go unpunished. Even though we are sinful and wrong in so many ways, we are now free before God, guiltless and blameless – because by faith in Christ we have been reconciled with God. In fact, God doesn't even recognize our sin anymore, because it has been dealt with – once and for all – by the Suffering Servant. You already know these things – it's the gospel message!

But perhaps we should embrace it more, live more in its reality. How? Banish all feelings of guilt and inadequacy! Yes, you're human and you'll sin. Of course you will – but Jesus dealt with that and God completely accepts you. Enough said!

Lord, thank You for my total exoneration
and total acceptance in Christ. Amen.

Even though we still sin and fail in many areas,
God promises that we are and will remain His children.
No one can accuse you – He will not allow it.

If You Listen,
You Will Be Saved

"Who among you fears the LORD and obeys the voice of His servant?"

Isaiah 50:10 ESV

Do you see the Old and the New Testament here – in one verse? Note that the verse refers to two things: 1. to fear the LORD (*Yahweh*), and 2. to listen to the voice of His "servant," which we accept as Jesus Christ. Both are necessary. The Old Testament teaches us about God and His demand for righteousness and love, but we also learn from it that we are powerless to fulfill those demands. No Old Testament or any other religion is able to save us from that inherent inability we have!

However, the New Testament teaches us that God came to save us – in Christ Jesus – from exactly that sin and failure. The acceptance of that, and of Him, leads to salvation. We see from this that salvation can never be from within ourselves: we need to be saved from without! Don't think that the Bible merely asks us to live with more love or justice. The Bible asks us to accept and follow Christ. Otherwise you'll just end up with yourself again. Do you hear the voice of Christ in your heart? Respond to that and share in His salvation – say "yes" to Him again!

Yes, Lord! I accept You as Savior –
make me loving and righteous. Amen.

Ditch your own efforts to be spiritual or holy
or right with God. Throw yourself totally into His mercy,
like jumping off a cliff, and He promises to lift you up.

You'll See the Light in the Dark

"Let him who walks in darkness and has no light trust in the name of the LORD and rely on his God."

Isaiah 50:10 ESV

Don't think the Old Testament is all about law, and the New Testament is all about faith. The Old Testament is also full of faith. Yes, there's a shift of emphasis, but this verse is one of many that describe a walk of faith. It says that we sometimes experience wonderful times in which life is bright and easy, but then we also have those times when everything seems dark and uncertain. In both situations, God's blessing is present – not just in the good times! God's blessing in both circumstances involves His presence, His strength, His help.

The "Servant of the Lord" says here that the person who experiences darkness should trust in "the name of the Lord" – literally the name of *Yahweh*, the Covenant God.

Are you currently facing darkness? Then cling to the trusted name of God! Call on Him in your sorrow and need – and He will save you, says the Word. This is your truth and your promise for today.

Thank You, trusted God – Your name is my strength. Amen.

If it is dark in your life, you must put in extra effort to rely on God more. He promises that the light will break through as you continue to focus on Him.

You Won't Fear the Fire

"Go ahead and walk in the light of the fires you have set. But with His own hand, the LORD will punish you and make you suffer."

Isaiah 50:11 CEV

The "Servant of the Lord" warns that people shouldn't ignite fires that they cannot control. Literally it says: *you made the fire – now you walk in the fire!* Your own fire will burn you, in other words. It makes us think of James, who said that our words could start a fire right out of the pit of hell (James 3:6). It means we should be very careful about the things we say.

Also, we should be wary to propagate any story that reaches our ears. It might be best to let the fire die out right there with you. Never be known as a gossip or a bearer of tall tales! What should you do if a rumor is circulating about you – truthful or not? Well, tell the truth upfront to the right people and be honest, and apologetic if you were at fault. That robs the story of its power.

Ultimately you haven't got much control over everything people say. Live with integrity and leave the rest to God. The statement in this verse remains true: what people sow, they'll reap!

Lord, help me to act with integrity today. Amen.

What you sow, you will reap. That is a promise from God.
Those who start fires for others will be burned.
However, if you act with integrity others will respect it.

Seek Righteousness, Find God

"Listen to Me, you who pursue righteousness, you who seek the LORD."

Isaiah 51:1 ESV

Many people think that the whole purpose of a relationship with God is only to get them into heaven. To be "saved" means not to go to hell, right? And isn't eternal life far more important than earthly life? Why then would you give people food or an education, or preserve the earth, if everything will eventually collapse anyway? What if well-fed and well-educated people got lost forever? Shouldn't we rather just focus on saving people for eternity?

Such arguments may sound logical, but it's not the emphasis that the Bible puts on matters. The Bible reveals God's will as justice and mercy and faithfulness in this life. The one who serves God is one who lives in this way. To accept Christ is to accept such a lifestyle.

A child of God is a person who cannot just overlook another's hunger or hurt or need. Being "saved" primarily means being saved from our self-centeredness and sin and from a senseless, meaningless life without God! Then, after that – as the bonus, the reward of it all – comes eternity. Remember, God's focus is on love and justice, now.

Lord, I am available – work Your love
and righteousness through me! Amen.

If you show love toward others, and seek righteousness and justice, your heart beats like God's. He promises that this is His will and purpose too. Make sure you search for Him and find Him!

His Blessing Is for You

"Look to Abraham ... for he was but one when I called him, that I might bless him and multiply him."

Isaiah 51:2 ESV

The Lord reminded His people of the wonderful covenant He made to Abraham. God's covenant promise to Abraham was to bless him personally, to bless his descendants and make them a people and finally to bless the whole world through him. Yes, a blessing upon blessing upon blessing!

Now, Abraham wasn't just the father of the Jews, but also of the believers, according to Paul. Paul wrote that we as Christians do receive the covenant's blessing (Ephesians 1:3), because Christ bore the covenant's curse (the guilt of our non-compliance) on the cross. The curse has been removed!

Never think that there isn't a blessing intended for you – oh no, God's purpose is to bless you mightily, to shower you with blessings! Just don't directly equate God's blessing with money alone – that's not what the Bible means. Biblical blessing focuses on God's presence, His protection, love and peace – His *shalom* – as well as His provision.

Lord, bless me and give me peace! Amen.

God promises His blessing in abundance.
Think about all the ways you are blessed right now
and thank God for that.

You'll Find Comfort

For the LORD comforts Zion; He comforts all her waste places and makes her wilderness like Eden.

Isaiah 51:3 ESV

"Zion" is Jerusalem. It is the city's spiritual name. It emphasizes God's presence in the city, its holiness and its temple. The massive temple buildings took up almost a tenth of the ancient capital's size! At this time Jerusalem was in ruins, but then Yahweh spoke words of comfort to it.

The terms "comforts" and "waste places" in this verse stand out and draw our attention to a peculiar fact. We're often unsettled by opposites that are paired – as is happening here. We don't like paradoxes! We would rather put things into more definite categories, for example either a wasteland or a comfort, or first the desolation, then the consolation. Similarly, we like to think of either a curse or blessing, sin or holiness – not both! Unfortunately, life is more complex than that.

What God says here is that in the desolation we'll find comfort – yes, in sorrow we'll find hope, in tribulation there will be strength. Remember, it's over the chaos that the Spirit "broods" in order to create beauty. It's in the blood-sweat of Gethsemane that the surrender to God happens, and from dying on the cross that the resurrection power is born! So, search through the ruins – yes, search – and you'll find encouragement, strength, even joy – and your answers.

Lord, thank You for using everything in my life
for my growth and Your glory. Amen.

God promises that He is in your circumstances today –
that He is present even in the ruins of your life, bringing you comfort.
In time He will also bring you out from the wreckage.

You'll Receive a Vision

He … makes her wilderness like Eden, her desert like the garden of the LORD.

Isaiah 51:3 ESV

The prophet looked at the ruin that once was Jerusalem, but he saw something completely different: beautifully restored buildings, strong city walls and a grand temple. He looked at the desert, but he saw a garden, a paradise! He looked at the dejected Jewish captives in Babylon, but he saw a people rejoicing in the Lord! Yes, the prophet didn't just see the reality; he saw a vision of God's reality, God's dream. That's the duty of a prophet, isn't it – to present God's view of the future?

It's important that you and I also obtain a vision of God's dream for us. It's not enough to just live our own reality – we must also live God's reality! If we could just see God's plan for us – more than that, if it could grab hold of us, overwhelm us, if it could become our own dream – then we would have the faith to attain exactly that. Go to the Lord and ask Him what His dream is for you. Even the slightest glimpse of it will change your life!

Lord, what is Your dream for me? Amen.

God promises that He is nurturing a unique
and beautiful dream for you. It relates to how He created you.
Pray and think about who you are.

Gladness and Joy for You

Joy and gladness will be found in her, thanksgiving and the voice of song.

Isaiah 51:3 ESV

Never think that our faith is super serious or depressing! Life itself is sometimes serious, but other times it's uncomplicated and easygoing. Our relationship with God corresponds to that: sometimes it's full of praise, other times full of pain. In this verse God promises "joy and gladness" – a beautiful promise to a depressed and forlorn people, far from home!

All of us long for joy and laughter, for pleasure and happiness – it's human and not wrong. Fortunately, that's also God's longing for us! Let's distinguish between pleasure and joy, however. The source of pleasure is outside of us, but joy comes from deep within. Pleasure is not wrong in itself – but God wants to give us joy. His joy is the knowledge and peace that we are accepted and loved, that our life has meaning and purpose, that everything will work out and that we are safe for ever. Isn't that wonderful?

Laugh the laugh of faith! God's joy is the impenetrable armor against anything that life may throw at you.

Lord, give me Your peace and Your joy! Amen.

God promises that you can and will experience joy and pleasure. It's human and it's necessary. However, the greatest joy is to be found in a life with Him.

Heaven and Earth Will Disappear, But ...

"The sky will vanish like smoke; the earth will wear out like clothes. Everyone on this earth will die like flies. But My victory will last; My saving power never ends."

Isaiah 51:6 CEV

God says that His salvation will be forever. His "saving power never ends." He puts it even more strongly: the sky above will blow away like smoke and the earth beneath will tear up like a worn-out garment. People will live and die like gnats. What we hold as permanent and secure – the heavens above, the earth below, human life – is not as lasting as we might think. No, they're fragile and fleeting.

Our lives are like grass, says the Bible, like smoke, like mist, like a flame flickering in the wind. We live for about 70 years (since biblical times) and then we move on into eternity. In this scheme of things, God alone is eternal and immovable, as is His word, His promise and His salvation. He is the only security, the only anchor. In our few years on earth we'll experience something of God's faithfulness, but in eternity His faithfulness, salvation and all-encompassing love will be our reality forever and ever! Trust Him for that in Christ Jesus.

Lord, I come to You with my need.
Show me Your faithfulness, now and forever. Amen.

Our earthly life is like a flame that flickers for a moment and then dies. Yet God promises that your salvation will last forever, with Him. That is the true life!

Rahab Will Be Beaten

Was it not you who cut Rahab in pieces, who pierced the dragon?

Isaiah 51:9 ESV

The Lord reminded His people of their deliverance from Egypt. He called Egypt *Rahab*, the mythological sea monster or dragon. They did believe – as did all ancient nations – that a sea monster lived in the depths of the ocean, but the word was especially used metaphorically. It is used here for Egypt as their archenemy, but in the Bible it generally refers to the chaos, disorder or evil that threatens our existence and God's handiwork (as does the so-called "Leviathan").

The New Testament perspective on the "chaos monster" is that it is the devil. Only God can defeat him and Jesus did so, time and time again. Ultimately, the book of Revelation looks forward to the day when God will finally crush the dragon, the beast.

The application is evident: the struggle against the evil one is a reality. Our victory is in the cross of Christ on which Jesus' blood bought our salvation. What can the enemy do to us if we belong to Christ? In every instance of darkness and resistance that you encounter, take charge in Jesus' name and drive the enemy *out*! You've been given the authority – use it!

Lord, thank You for giving me authority
over the enemy and all his works. Amen.

Resisting the devil is a reality in our lives. God, however, promises that He will protect you from evil. Do not fear.

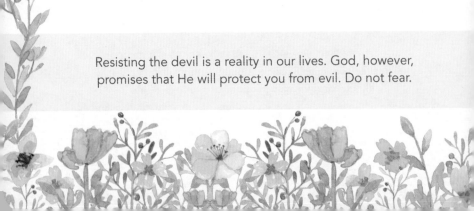

Joy Will Radiate from You

The ransomed of the LORD will return and come with joyful shouting to Zion, and everlasting joy *will* be on their heads.

Isaiah 51:11 NASB

This wording also occurs earlier on in Isaiah, but let's emphasize something else today. The prophet said that "everlasting joy" would be "on the heads" of those ransomed (or delivered) by God. It's a metaphorical, Hebrew way of speaking, translated by some Bible translations as "crowned" or "wreathed" by joy. It's as if their joy is almost visible around their heads. It makes one think of the halo that is depicted around the heads of saints in ecclesiastical art. God is also thought of having a "glory" or *Shekinah* around Him, perceived as a white or fiery light.

Do you agree that some people carry about them a glow or have an energy that's almost bursting from them? Have you seen people whose eyes are always smiling – or people with charisma, presence, a certain *je ne sais quoi*?

Perhaps we should get this "unspeakable joy," as the Bible puts it, and carry it around us like a cloak! It's the fruit of the Spirit, remember: get it from the Spirit and live it through the Spirit. Let your eyes, lips, face and words show your joy!

Lord, give me that ever-present joy
that is so attractive to the world. Amen.

God promises that lasting joy
will be your hallmark one day. It is equally true
that Holy Spirit-joy can already be part of your life now.

If You Wake Up

Wake yourself, wake yourself, stand up, O Jerusalem.

Isaiah 51:17 ESV

It was a common topic among the prophets to encourage their listeners to wake up, to open their eyes, to look and to see. What the prophets did was to shine God's light on situations so that we could become aware of what was happening, of what God was doing. It's as if we're asleep, semi-conscious, in the dark – moving about like robots, without really giving attention.

There's a great truth in this notion, because we live noisy and fast lives full of deadlines and commitments. Our private and spiritual lives are hastily taken care of – often as a formality or duty. In that way we become spiritually more and more unaware.

The answer is to stop, to look, to listen, to focus and to become mindful of God, of what He says and what He does. You don't have to go on a retreat to do that – you can do it every day! Make a point today of seeing God in things or people during your day and asking: *Lord, what are You saying?*

Yes, Lord, where are You working?
What are You saying to me? Amen.

Our lives are so busy that we often become spiritually unaware.
But God promises a spiritual world will open up
before you if you just stop and become more aware of Him.

September

The Celebration Will Begin

Awake, awake; put on thy strength, O Zion; put on thy beautiful garments, O Jerusalem.

Isaiah 52:1 KJV

Jerusalem had been laid to waste, its temple in ruins and its walls torn down, but God said that the people were to get up and prepare for a great feast! In those times, special clothes were put on for festivals or banquets – often white linen robes, which were sometimes supplied by the host. Do you remember Jesus' parable of a guest who turned up for a feast without the proper attire? He was simply turned away. The paradox of course – again – is a celebration right there between the ruins. What a contrast!

The lesson is that we can get up and put on our festive garb, whatever the circumstances. Christ's coming is reason for a celebration if there ever was one! He reconciled us with God amid the ruins of sin in our lives and has clothed us in His righteousness and perfection.

Not our good works, but His good work on the cross covers us like a shining robe! That's the gospel! So – forget the broken walls and the broken everything – lift up your head and prepare for a celebration!

Thank You, Lord, for Your righteousness,
and for the celebration because of that. Amen.

The spiritual life is a faith-filled life. Faith looks beyond the immediate and delights in what's to come. God promises a celebration – so, even now, put on your festive garb in faith!

You'll Break the Bonds

Loose the bonds from your neck, O captive daughter of Zion.

Isaiah 52:2 ESV

In biblical times, rows of prisoners or slaves were transported by tying them one behind the other with a rope, a loop around each person's neck. What God was saying here to the Jews was that their captivity was over and the guards were gone. Yet they were still walking about like slaves, even though they had been set free! They were sitting in their cells, but the prison doors were standing wide open with no wardens in sight! The people simply needed to throw off their restraints!

Sometimes people walk around like that – in bondage or with a hindrance in their lives – without realizing that it's so needless. It's especially ironic when God's children live with bondage, because the enemy himself has been taken captive and is bound, already part of God's victory parade!

Now, let's throw off any bondage or burden and realize that it's unnecessary and unneeded. Let's renounce it once and for all in Jesus' name and then overcome it by persistent new behavior. It might take a while to break down all vestiges of the stronghold's presence in your life by persevering in victory, but it's completely possible, since the power of the evil one over you has been broken!

Lord, thank You for breaking all the bonds in my life.
Help me now to overcome it in my behavior. Amen.

God's purpose for us is true freedom in Him.
He promises that He has broken the evil one's bonds in your life,
but asks that you let go of the bad habits too.

Christ Pays for You

Thus says the LORD: "You were sold for nothing, and you shall be redeemed without money."

Isaiah 52:3 ESV

The enemy came and dragged the Jews off to a foreign country – without compensation, of course. They were plainly hijacked and stolen. God allowed this and in that sense He "sold" them, as the verse tells us. But didn't He warn them against that for so many years? Still, He would redeem them again, and again no money would be exchanged. God would merely come and get His people from where they were. This happened when God's servant Cyrus allowed the Jewish people to leave.

These words remind us of an even greater truth – the price that Jesus paid on the cross. That's when God really ransomed His people, but not with money: Christ, God's true Servant, paid for that with His life. Our salvation is free to us, but it was never cheap. No, it was unbelievably expensive!

Let's show our gratitude and appreciation by utilizing its benefits fully. Let's embrace our pardon and live out our liberty to the fullest, without guilt! Let joy, peace and love overflow in our lives – that is God's purpose for us, the fruit of our pardon, the proof of our forgiveness! That is the biggest "thank You, Lord" we can give Him!

Lord, help me to appreciate fully
what You have done for me – at such an expense! Amen.

God promises that His ransom on the cross was more than sufficient to pardon you of your guilt and punishment of your sins: past, present and future. You just need to take ownership.

This Good News Is for You

How beautiful upon the mountains are the feet of him who brings good news.

Isaiah 52:7 ESV

Good tidings are always welcome, especially in times of adversity or hardship – when we feel fragile or in need. Yes, how welcome, how wonderful – like cool water on a hot day.

Can I share some good news with you today? God loves you more than you can imagine. He, God, is with you now and intensely involved in your life; He has your life completely under control. The end of your particular situation is good, because everything ends well with Him. You can trust God, live with new hope and courage and focus on blessing others. You can ask God about what behavior will honor Him in your current season.

And remember: our earthly lives are temporary, but eternal life awaits in God's love! Now that's good news for you!

Yes, Lord, thank You for … [pray through these statements]. Amen.

God promises the above-mentioned things to you today.
See which of these promises encourage you the most today.

You'll Be Clean

Touch no unclean thing ... purify yourselves, you who bear the vessels of the LORD.

Isaiah 52:11 ESV

The Jews were a people consecrated to God. Accordingly, they had to keep themselves pure, a practice still required of all Jews. Staying ritually "pure" or "clean" meant they had to avoid contact with all prescribed unclean things: certain foods, articles and people.

It would make the person unclean as well, which resulted in being isolated from the people and barred from communion with God. Unclean people couldn't enter the temple grounds, for example. In particular, those who worked with holy things, in the temple or at the altar, had to make sure that they stayed perfectly pure.

Jesus, however, turned the concept around. He didn't hesitate to touch unclean people or spend time with them. These included lepers, Samaritans, tax collectors and heathens. He also said that true purity lies not in external matters, but in the heart: our hearts must be pure!

This is an important lesson, but let's add another biblical truth: in Christ we are already pure before God – yes, we stand in Christ's perfection, sanctified, in full communion with Him! Let's rejoice in that!

Lord, I want to live a holy life – as You are holy! Amen.

God promises that He already considers you as pure in Christ – He ascribes Christ's purity to you. Your gratitude will inevitably lead you to search for purity in your own life as well.

He Already Waits for You

> The LORD will go before you, and the God of Israel will be your rear guard.
>
> *Isaiah 52:12 ESV*

Read this verse again – isn't it beautiful that God is in the front as well as at the back of His people? In our understanding, one is either in front or at the back, not both! God is of course not like that – He is simultaneously in front of us, behind us, to the left and right of us – and yes, also above and below us!

If we struggle with understanding this characteristic of God, we should perhaps think of God as already being where we are still getting to. He is with us today and again tomorrow, but then He's today already in our tomorrow as well and in our whole future – until the last day!

God doesn't live in time as we do, but for us it's a great encouragement that He already knows our whole life – past, present and future! He already knows what we're going to do – good and bad – and He already made provision for all of that! It's already included and dealt with by His love for us. Let tomorrow come – God's already there! He is already waiting for us at the winning post! Run, friend!

Thank You, Lord, for being with me and waiting for me –
today and tomorrow! Amen.

God promises that He already knows your tomorrow, the day after tomorrow, your future and eternity. He is already there as well as being in you today. This must be a tremendous comfort to you!

Believe It and Live It

*Who has believed what he has heard from us? And to whom has
the arm of the Lord been revealed?*

Isaiah 53:1 ESV

We now come to the most beautiful "servant song" in Isaiah. Who can forget these classic words about Christ, the "Suffering Servant": "a Man of Sorrows and acquainted with grief … He was pierced for our transgressions; He was crushed for our iniquities …" (Isaiah 53:3, 5). This is moving and emotional language.

When we read the first verse, we immediately get this rhetorical question: who has believed? The silent expectation is that the reader will believe it – and *must* believe it! The reason why this question is important is because God's salvation, and God's Savior, has been revealed to us in a strange way. It comes to us in the form of a Person who has no stature at all, One from whom we turn our heads, One who is rejected and wounded, and eventually killed.

What Savior is this? What salvation is this? How can we see the strong "arm" of God in this – as the verse says? Still, it's there! In the death and sacrifice of the Innocent Lamb lies our salvation, in the Savior's ransom lies our freedom – in His wounds lie our healing, in His death our life! Yes, that's what God revealed – and we believe it!

*Lord, I see Your might working in Christ Jesus –
and I take it for my own salvation. Amen.*

God's power is manifested in His rejection, in His suffering
on the cross and in His death. If you can accept it,
God promises you His adoption, complete forgiveness and a new life!

The Sacrifice Is for You

He was wounded and crushed because of our sins; by taking our punishment, He made us completely well.

Isaiah 53:5 CEV

The sacrificial system of the Old Testament came to a climax and ended in the cross of Jesus Christ. After this full and final sacrifice, no sheep or goat offered to God could ever please Him again.

There can never again be a physical temple where animals are slaughtered for God's glory – it's unthinkable. In fact, every sacrifice of the Old Testament only had meaning and efficacy because it pointed to the One Sacrifice that was coming. They were symbols, shadows. That's why the temple and altar were destroyed after the cross: the whole system came to an end.

The Bible teaches that Christ was the Man who stood for all people and bore the punishment for all our sins, once and for all. That deed never needs to be repeated, because that sacrifice was perfect – in the form of a faultless, guiltless and godly Lamb. You and I and all our sins and shortcomings, now and forever, are included in that sacrifice. We are in reality rid of the weight and guilt of sin when we take this in faith. We can *really* live free from all guilt and inferiority. Let's live in the greatest freedom ever imagined!

Lord, thank You for the greatest freedom ever –
help me to live it to the full! Amen.

To deny that you are sinful is to claim that you are perfect.
Everyone sins and thus falls short of the Creator.
Nevertheless, He promises that the cross
makes up for these shortcomings.

The Peace Is for You

He was crushed for our iniquities; upon Him was the chastisement that brought us peace.

Isaiah 53:5 ESV

It's unthinkable that Christians should suffer from feelings of guilt and inferiority – but we do! We have accepted Christ and become children of God, and we want to live as followers and believers. We pray, read the Bible, go to church and do spiritual things, but we still experience uncertainty and dissatisfaction. Why do we still have problems and sin; why do we struggle with faith and prayer? Shouldn't we have more victory by now?

Perhaps – but we don't! What we experience is normal for believers. According to the Word, we grow spiritually by surrendering more and more to the Holy Spirit and His guidance. So let's do that and let's grow!

But that doesn't mean that we should live with shame or inferiority about our spiritual life. No, Jesus' sacrifice bought us true and unconditional peace with God – not a provisional peace, dependent on how we perform. The cross made provision for the fact that we're never going to be perfect Christians. God's love is not dependent on our merit. We have peace with Him, regardless of where we are spiritually.

Lord, thank You that I can live in peace with You –
whether I do good or not-so-good. Amen.

You are not a perfect person or Christian.
That's why Christ – the perfect Person – died on the cross.
God promises that through the cross you are 100% acceptable to Him.

The Wounds Are for You

Upon Him was the chastisement that brought us peace, and with His stripes we are healed.

Isaiah 53:5 ESV

It is often asked whether the cross also made provision for our physical healing – above and beyond our salvation. Are we all supposed to be healed and healthy – because Jesus died for that? In Scripture, sin and sickness are often synonymous: sin is the sickness of the spirit, while sickness is the result of sin. Through the cross, God wants to deliver us from sin and all its consequences: sickness, pain, loss, accident and death. And He does exactly that, because one day when God's work is done, only perfect life and peace will remain – forever!

Unfortunately, we're not there yet and therefore a child of God will still suffer sickness, pain, loss, accident and death. In this life, these things remain our reality – it's still part of the world in which we live. Still, together with God we fight sin and all of these things. We can also experience God's miracles in this world, including divine healing. Yes, that's also part of this reality! If you need it, you can trust God for healing today. Ask for it and receive it in faith. Many have been healed in this way.

Thank You, Father, for Your love and might.
Heal me today, in Jesus' name! Amen.

Following the cross we still deal with the consequences of sin, such as sickness, destruction and death. But God promises that He listens to your prayers for healing – and yes, miracles *do* happen!

The Reconciliation Is for You

> By His knowledge shall the righteous one, My Servant, make many to be accounted righteous, and He shall bear their iniquities.
>
> *Isaiah 53:11 ESV*

The "Servant of the Lord" would put people right with God. Remember, humankind's default position is to be at odds with God. It's our nature – since the days of Adam and Eve – to declare independence from God. We turn our backs on Him, ignore His commands and want to be our own master.

Those who do try to be obedient do not succeed: they do it halfheartedly, partially, occasionally. In their hearts, however, even they are like all people: full of ego, bent on personal benefit only, with little love for others. In our hearts, you and I are the same! We cannot help ourselves, because everyone is like that – it's human nature!

Our only hope is Jesus Christ. He is right with God, because He was the perfect, sinless Man. He stood in the place of all people and bore the penalty for the iniquity of everyone, as today's verse says. We can accept this as our personal truth and rely on it. If you have done that, you are right with God, forever! You're justified, righteous and reconciled with God! That's the gospel message.

Thank You, Father, that through Jesus Christ
I am in perfect relationship with You! Amen.

Believe the truth of the cross! God promises you a new life today.

Jesus Is Praying for You

... Yet He bore the sin of many, and makes intercession for the transgressors.

Isaiah 53:12 ESV

This verse about the "Servant of the Lord" refers for us as Christians to the intercessions of Jesus Christ. Remember how He prayed on the cross for His murderers? "Father, forgive them, for they do not know what they are doing" (Luke 23:34). He prayed for many others during His earthly life.

Then the Bible says that Christ is at this moment interceding for us at the right hand of the Father (Romans 8:34). Yes, even after the ascension He is fully involved in His people's lives! There are no words to convey the comfort that this truth holds.

Just think: whose prayers are being heard? Christ's are heard – that's for sure! For whom is Christ praying at this very moment? For you and me! He is standing before the Father and is pleading for you, knowing full well your fears, your tears and your dreams. He presents your case with such conviction! Of course His prayer for you is not the same as your prayer for yourself, because He knows your needs better than you do, but still – He is praying for you!

Thank You, Jesus! Thank You for praying on my behalf. Amen.

What is Jesus Christ doing in the presence of the Father today? What is His task? He promises that He is praying for you there. And His prayer is always heard.

You Can Still Rejoice

"Sing, O barren one, who did not bear; break forth into singing and cry aloud, you who have not been in labor!"

Isaiah 54:1 ESV

In biblical times, women had no "career" other than to marry and raise children. It was their biological and social task – to ensure a progeny. So, if a woman was infertile, she faced a serious crisis, because she had failed in her duty. She was seen as not bringing her side and could be rejected or divorced over this. Remember, in those days they didn't know that infertility could be the man's fault – it was merely seen as the woman's inability.

In this verse, God compares Jerusalem to an infertile woman. She is barren, childless and rejected, but still she's instructed to rejoice. Yes, that's how faith works!

In the lack and the need, faith starts to rejoice, to praise God! We can rejoice because God is there, because He is faithful, because He knows best, because He loves us and because He'll provide – there's always reason to praise God! Praise changes our lives, because it brings us into communion with God. Praise leads to much spiritual fruit.

Yes, Lord, I have reason to praise –
and I do praise You with my whole heart! Amen.

We always need to give thanks and praise –
even if we do not see a "reason" to do it. God is always worthy of
praise. He promises that praise will change you and your reality.

You Can Enlarge Your Space

"Enlarge the place of your tent, and let the curtains of your habitations be stretched out; do not hold back; lengthen your cords and strengthen your stakes."

Isaiah 54:2 ESV

The Lord said that Jerusalem's time had come. He compared the city to an infertile and rejected woman, but said that she'd be whole and have many children. In other words, the city would be built up again and have many inhabitants. Meanwhile, she should prepare and enlarge her living place – the tent of a nomadic family is alluded to – for the wonderful times ahead, and all the children!

What was God saying here? That they should start building new neighborhoods? That would be difficult, since they were in Babylon! No, the "enlarged tent" is firstly a symbol – it's their expectation, their faith. They still reasoned and reacted like captives, not like free people. They needed to radically accept God's message of liberation and start to rejoice in it, trust in it and live in it!

Let's apply this to the here and now: can you accept that God is working in your life and that anything can happen? Does it excite you? Can you persevere in it? Enlarge your expectation! Your tent is too small – God can do much more than you think possible.

Lord, I know You can do it,
and I trust You to do it. Amen.

The tent of expectation and faith in your heart is probably too small. The Almighty promises that He is involved in your life – you must know that anything is possible!

You'll Forget the Shame of Your Youth

"You will forget the shame of your youth, and the reproach of your widowhood you will remember no more."

Isaiah 54:4 ESV

The Lord refers in this verse to two events in the life of Israel, whom He addresses as a woman. The first is the "shame of her youth," meaning her bondage in Egypt. The second is the "reproach [or humiliation] of her widowhood" – her captivity in Babylon. God's people were alienated from both their country and their God, but He would save them from both predicaments. Our focus for today is on the phrase "the shame of your youth." David prayed to God to forgive him for the sins of his younger days.

Does this make you think of the things that *you* did in your youth that you're still embarrassed about? Let's make the following clear: children, teenagers and even young adults are by definition immature and therefore cannot behave in a mature fashion. They can often act foolishly or impulsively. Can you expect maturity of the immature?

So, forgive yourself for your childish or awkward behavior – you were young, after all! Now you've grown up and are wiser (hopefully!). Accept God's forgiveness radically and finally. Deal with your past in a positive and constructive manner.

Lord, thank You that I can leave
my foolish youth in Your hands. Amen.

God promises that the foolish things of your youth have been left in the past. As you asked, He forgave them. He never thinks about it. You should also put it radically behind you.

He'll Remain Committed

"Your Maker is your husband, the LORD of hosts is His name; and the Holy One of Israel is your Redeemer, the God of the whole earth He is called."

Isaiah 54:5 ESV

It's a prominent image in the Bible that God and His people – in the Old and New Testaments – are like a husband and wife, like a bridegroom and bride. The covenant that God made with them is like a marriage covenant.

He expects faithfulness as any husband would from his wife, because He Himself remains faithful. If His people were to worship other gods, it would amount to adultery, infidelity – an occurrence that happened many times in Israel's history.

From His side, however, God remains the perfect Husband. Just think: He cares for us, He provides for us, He loves us – and also feels tenderness, compassion, even pain and sadness. He remains 100% committed. He never leaves us or loses His love for us. He comes to fetch us, forgives us and always takes us back! Yes, God is 100% committed to you.

Thank You, Lord, for Your inexplicable commitment to me! I value it so much. Amen.

God promises that His commitment to you –
and the relationship that exists between you – is absolute.
No matter what happens, He will always love you.

Faithfulness Trumps Weakness

"For a brief moment I deserted you, but with great compassion I will gather you."

Isaiah 54:7 ESV

Today I want to highlight an important and profound biblical truth, which will bless you. Let's call it "the two circles of the covenant." In the Old Testament, God demanded certain things in His covenant with Israel: faithfulness, a sincere heart and obedience to His law. Then the people would experience His blessing. That's the inner, exclusive circle of the covenant. However, Israel couldn't stick to it and therefore couldn't share in God's blessing.

However, it doesn't end there. God is merciful and good and He knows that we're only human and weak. Therefore He comes – as these words attest – to bless us, regardless of our disobedience! His love triumphs over His punishment – that is the outer, inclusive circle of the covenant.

The whole New Testament is part of this second circle of grace. Just take it, God says, take His forgiveness! Grab hold of His pardon! Forget about your guilt and the punishment – Someone already took care of that. With God, grace always wins. His faithfulness overcomes our weakness. That's the good news!

Thank You, Lord, for Your love and grace –
it makes me feel safe. Amen.

God promises that His grace is greater than His law.
His love triumphs over His punishment.
All this is possible through the cross of Jesus.

More Than You Think

"With everlasting love I will have compassion on you," says the LORD, your Redeemer.

Isaiah 54:8 ESV

Here we again see God's heart. His people were disobedient and therefore had to endure punishment – they were banished from the Holy Land to Babylon. However, that didn't lessen God's love for them! See here how He describes His love for Israel as "everlasting." Yes, His love never ceases: in their good and bad behavior, in His will or out of it, in their sin or righteousness, with Him or against Him. Isn't that beautiful?

But wait – there is much more! Follow with me: Jesus Christ is the embodiment, the demonstration of God's love, isn't He? On the cross, Christ carried the punishment for all our sins – so that you and I need no longer be punished. Do you understand? There will be no punishment for you ever again. Never, ever again!

Christ took the whole punishment on Him – all of it! God does not punish you in any way. That's the gospel – take it in faith. Yes, sin has consequences – and we bump into them all the time – but that's a different matter.

Thank You, Lord, for taking my punishment on Your shoulders.
I take it as my personal truth. Amen.

God promises that the punishment for all sin is in the past; there is absolutely no punishment for you in the future, if you belong to Christ. It's over and done.

His Steadfast Love for You

"My steadfast love shall not depart from you, and My covenant of peace shall not be removed," says the LORD, who has compassion on you.

Isaiah 54:10 ESV

Today's verse is so full of promises that it could easily make three devotions! Let's discuss a few points:

God promises His "steadfast love," which is the new translation of the beautiful old word "lovingkindness." It's a good translation of the Hebrew term, because it encapsulates the meaning of unconditional and unwavering love – love that never stops!

God's "steadfast love" is the official benefit of His covenant to His people – signed and sealed! Remember that God's purpose with us is to bless us. Never doubt that, although we should remember that this blessing happens within the reality of this life, with all its ups and downs.

God is described here as the One "who has compassion on you." In some translations this phrase personifies God as "merciful" or "compassionate." It's beautiful because it shows us God's heart. It's exactly and essentially who He is.

Think of these promises today and let them build your faith!

Thank You, compassionate God,
for Your steadfast love! Amen.

God promises you today that the steadfast love
that forms part of His covenant with you is still in place.
You cannot do anything to change that love.

He'll Make You Beautiful

"I will set your stones in antimony, and lay your foundations with sapphires. I will make your pinnacles of agate, your gates of carbuncles ..."

Isaiah 54:11-12 ESV

God said He would rebuild Jerusalem. The city was in shambles, with the city walls and temple completely in ruins. The prophet described the rebuilding in a strange manner: it would be done with gemstones! What was he saying? Well, he used poetic images such as the clay (or cement) used to set the stones would be made from antimony, which the women of the time used as black eyeliner. The stones themselves would be made from blue sapphire. The picture would therefore be of bright blue eyes within black eyeliner – or other jewels like emeralds or rubies. Yes, Jerusalem was described here as a woman, a bride being prepared for her wedding!

Revelation uses these exact images for the "New Jerusalem" as it is described here in Isaiah. Yes, the city should get up and prepare herself, make herself beautiful for her Groom, for He is coming! She would be better in every way and more attractive than ever before. Remember that we as the church are the bride, the New Jerusalem! What an encouragement! Our lives are also in ruins sometimes, but it will turn around – God will intervene! The end of your fears and sorrows will be with Him, in a future far more fantastic than you could ever imagine. Take your promise!

Thank You, Lord, for this wonderful promise –
it gives me strength! Amen.

God is busy working with us, His church.
He has promised to present her perfectly before His Father
on the last day – and He will! You are part of this.

Your Enemies Will Fall

"Whoever stirs up strife with you shall fall because of you."

Isaiah 54:15 ESV

God says that in the future the New Jerusalem will be beautiful, shining like a jewel. It will become the world's capital. God will personally inhabit it and the nations will come to worship Him there. It will be an eternal city, which will never again turn to ruin. No enemy will overpower it – those who might attack it will succumb to it themselves.

Let's focus on this idea for a moment. There is a theme in the Bible that people with evil intentions will suffer from their own schemes – he who digs a hole for another will fall into it himself, for example. Your intentions turn back on you; you reap what you sow! We must therefore always be wary of what we sow into the world or into other's lives – by words or by deeds.

The promise of this verse is that God will stand up for us. If enemies come, don't be alarmed – they will have to face Him!

Thank You, Lord, that I can leave all adversaries
and enemies to You. Amen.

God promises that you can leave all enemies with Him.
He will deal with them.

He Will Act for You

"No weapon that is fashioned against you shall succeed, and you shall refute every tongue that rises against you in judgment. This is the heritage of the servants of the LORD."

Isaiah 54:17 ESV

The Lord encouraged His people in the embarrassing situation in which they found themselves. They were far away from home and stripped of all their securities. But God promised that they would be restored. Jerusalem would not just be strong again; it would be invincible.

Weapons that were made to attack them would be powerless, because God would oppose their enemies – and who can fight against God? Those who wanted to take them to court – perhaps over the possession of the land – would also fail, because they would be arguing against God. No one can argue against Him! He always stands for what is right – and He always stands for His people. The prophet said that God fighting for His people was their heritage, provided for in the covenant.

Are you in a quandary at the moment, in a tight corner, feeling threatened? Let God act for you! Do what you must do – take responsibility and stick to the truth 100% – but leave the rest to the perfect Judge. He will take it further!

Lord, won't You take this matter out of my hands?
[elaborate on your situation] Amen.

It stands to reason that people go to a court of law to obtain justice.
But some things you just have to leave with God.
He promises to deal with it. Rather, put it behind you.

Come if You're Thirsty

"Come, everyone who thirsts, come to the waters; and he who has no money, come, buy and eat! Come, buy wine and milk without money and without price."

Isaiah 55:1 ESV

This verse is about far more than the Jews returning to a new and fertile Canaan. God extended an invitation to the whole world: all who are thirsty could come and quench their thirst. He is the water of life! Jesus Christ called out the same words on the temple grounds: "If anyone thirsts, let him come to Me and drink" (John 7:37). Two things are clear from this passage:

The water is free, *gratis* (a word that originates from the Greek *chariti*, meaning "by grace." You don't have to earn God's love and grace – it comes without any conditions. Just receive it!

You will come when you're thirsty or more specifically, when you know you're thirsty. Everyone is thirsty for God, but not everyone realizes it. Therefore people look for fulfillment in money, power, status, pleasure, possessions and many more – which can never satisfy their need.

This is the bottom line of these thoughts: realize that your thirst is for God – and come, come and receive! Come and receive Him.

Yes, Lord, my need is for You –
give me Your living water! Amen.

If you realize your spiritual thirst and come to Jesus Christ,
He promises to quench it for you.
With Christ you will never lack spiritually again.

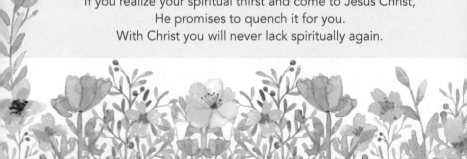

Listen and Live

"Incline your ear, and come to Me; hear, that your soul may live; and I will make with you an everlasting covenant, My steadfast, sure love for David."

Isaiah 55:3 ESV

The text literally says to "bend," "stretch" or "point" your ears, in other words: *pay attention!* It means to "listen up"! It makes us realize again that God's grace doesn't just hit us on the head out of the blue one Thursday afternoon on the way to the library! No, first we become aware of a vague need in our lives, a lack of some sort.

Initially it's not so evident; it's more of a subliminal feeling. Then it becomes more conscious: a longing for something – a sense of yearning. We do not immediately associate this with God, but later realize that our answers can be with Him. Our need then turns into a need to learn more about God.

It's at this stage that we start to take note, to pay attention, to listen up – as this verse says. It's then that our thirsty soul realizes that the water of life is right there – we just need to reach out and take it. Only then do we deliberately receive what God gives – and start to really live, fully and eternally. It all begins when we start to look, and listen.

Lord, I want to come and drink of the water of life! Amen.

Everybody is somewhere on a spiritual spectrum –
either far from or near to God. If you move closer to God out of need
and desire, He promises that you will find the fullness of Him.

He'll Make You like David

"I will make an everlasting covenant with you, according to the faithful mercies shown to David."

Isaiah 55:3 CEV

David was a wonderful person. God loved him so much that He still blessed the Jewish people, five hundred years later, for the sake of David! Why is this so? Let's see … God promised in the Davidic Covenant that a blood-descendant of David would rule Israel in perpetuity.

After their captivity Israel no longer had a literal king, so they saw the promised Messiah as the Davidic king to come. And He came, didn't He? From David's ancestry, Jesus Christ came and lived and died underneath a sign that read "King of the Jews." Now He lives forever as King of kings. The promise held true!

The question remains: why was David such a man after God's heart? Was it because he was so holy, so sinless? Oh no, we all know of David's many sins – even serious sins. So, what was it? It was because he loved God so passionately, lived with Him so intimately and trusted Him so implicitly. Just read the psalms! David was completely sold out to God, and that is the lesson! Be like David and experience God's favor as David did!

Yes, Lord, I also want to live in total commitment to You. Amen.

If you are 100% sold out to God –
totally surrendered to Him –
He promises that your spiritual life
will become a passionate adventure.

He Is Near – Find Him!

"Seek the LORD while He may be found; call upon Him while He is near."

Isaiah 55:6 ESV

The prophets often warned that God might not always be available. He wasn't always "near." How should we understand this? Well, physically God is always near to us, not so? God is all around us. However, we are often not as near to Him as we should be. Our lives are sometimes such that we cannot easily find Him.

As children and teenagers, we are very open to God – as to life in general – and finding God is easier then. In adulthood, we often only seek God when crises come. As we age we often get farther away still and it's unfortunately true that many a senior citizen has become hardened towards God. Yes, being "far" or "near" to God is often a condition of your own heart! That's why God's call is always urgent. It's always a question of reacting now, coming to Him today – while there is still opportunity. Tomorrow it might be more difficult to respond.

Does this message tug at your heart? React immediately! You don't know what tomorrow might bring. Say yes now!

Yes, Lord, I do hear Your call in my heart
and I respond with a resounding YES! Amen.

God promises that He calls to us, but His calls
are not always loud and clear. It depends on where we stand.
If you hear it, you need to respond immediately.

You'll Return, and Return Again

"Let him return to the LORD, that He may have compassion on him, and to our God, for He will abundantly pardon."

Isaiah 55:7 ESV

It's sometimes thought that the God of the Old Testament is strict, but the God of the New Testament is loving and merciful. However, in the Old Testament God is also a loving and compassionate God, like in today's verse. It's beautiful that He's depicted here as the One who pardons "abundantly." The condition, however, is that His people turn (or return) to Him – that they convert to Christianity. Conversion is a thoroughly Old Testament concept and here we see its meaning spelled out: "Let the wicked forsake his way, and the unrighteous man his thoughts" (Isaiah 55:7). Let's never water down the biblical concept of conversion!

In the Old and New Testaments, conversion has to do with new behavior, issuing from a (new) relationship with God. If someone is converted, their conduct will tell! Conversion leads to a life that honors God, period. Let's stop talking about our conversion and rather start living it! A new believer who carries on doing wrong is an anomaly, because conversion is the act of leaving those things behind. Trust God for His help with your issues and then act in faith! Finally, conversion is an ongoing process; we all need to return to God again and again!

Lord, I turn again to You today. Amen.

God promises you immediate grace and forgiveness if you repent. Repentance inherently means that you follow Him with your whole life – in other words by your changed behavior.

You Can Submit and Live

"For as the heavens are higher than the earth, so are My ways higher than your ways and My thoughts than your thoughts."

Isaiah 55:9 ESV

This verse is one of those that one should memorize, or at least put on the fridge! We often try to tie God to certain rules or formulas: *If I do this, God will do that*, etc. However, most of the time God doesn't comply with such expectations – He often acts in other ways than we thought. We cannot figure Him out!

Also, the suggestion is wrong that God is principally there to bless us with health, wealth and possessions, as if the whole thing is about us: our life, our spiritual life, our will … No, a relationship with God is firstly about Him: His honor, His kingdom, His will!

Here is the secret: in His will is the fountain of blessing and joy! So, the lesson is this: forget trying to figure God out. Stop understanding or explaining Him – it's impossible; we cannot! God reveals Himself to us, but He doesn't reveal everything about Himself, because our minds will never grasp it. No, the spiritual life is to submit our personal will to Him, the unknowable but loving God. Die to yourself and find your life again – in Him.

Lord God, You're always different to my perceptions and expectations. My peace is not in understanding, but in trusting You. Amen.

God promises that He loves you and has good plans for you. He also reveals Himself to you in many ways. However, you cannot understand everything about Him. Don't even try.

The Word Will Change You

"As the rain and the snow come down from heaven and do not return there but water the earth, making it bring forth and sprout, giving seed to the sower and bread to the eater."

Isaiah 55:10 ESV

This verse paints a beautiful picture of the fruitfulness and abundance of nature. It draws our attention from the top to the bottom: rain and snow comes down from above – and God is implicated here – until the earth is drenched. Then the trees and the crops flourish and yield their fruit. That gives us an abundance of bread on our table and the seed for our next season. Yes, a picture of blessing and prosperity – and it all starts with the rain from heaven.

God says just like this, His Word always bears fruit and always fulfils its purpose. Let's apply this as follows: the Word of God reaches our ears, and with some that's as far as it goes. It's quickly forgotten again. With others it goes deeper, into the soul, where it evokes some emotion or reflection – but not for long. Nothing changes.

However, with some it goes right to the heart, into a receptive spirit. It changes them deeply and makes them grow and bear fruit. Everything changes! Oh, may God's rain achieve that purpose in your life!

Lord, I open my heart to You.
Do Your work in me! Amen.

God promises that the Word in your life will bear much fruit – fruit in abundance – but adds that it also depends on the fertility and receptiveness of your heart.

The Word Will Permeate Your Soul

"So shall My word be that goes out from My mouth; it shall not return to Me empty, but it shall accomplish that which I purpose, and shall succeed in the thing for which I sent it."

Isaiah 55:11 ESV

God said that His words would not return to Him void or empty-handed. They were not just idle words, meaningless messages – no, God's words are true, powerful, effective, and reach their goal.

The New Testament conveys exactly the same when it says: "The word of God is living and active, sharper than any two-edged sword, piercing to the division of soul and of spirit" (Hebrews 4:12). God's words are living and creative – literally, because He created the world piece for piece, out of nothing, just by speaking. He "calls into existence the things that do not exist" (Romans 4:17) – and then they come into being.

God can also speak something new into *your* life! His Word is more effective than anything you know. It enters deep into the heart, right between the soul and spirit (meaning the place where only God knows you) and starts working. It informs you, evaluates you, convicts you, encourages you and leads you to Him! You and I need more time in God's Word.

Lord, I want to have more exposure to Your Word. Amen.

God promises that His Word can work powerfully in your life. Allow it to settle in your heart and to discern, evaluate, reprimand, encourage and lead.

October

You Can Break Out in Praise Now

"For you shall go out in joy and be led forth in peace; the mountains and the hills before you shall break forth into singing."

Isaiah 55:12 ESV

Years ago we sang a song based on these exact words: *You shall go out with joy and be led forth in peace, and the mountains and the hills will break forth before you.* Is it still sung? What a wonderfully poetic verse this is – full of promise, praise and joy!

The prophet looked ahead as the captives returned to their land. However, he didn't only see the literal Canaan, but also the spiritual Canaan – where the Messiah rules and God's peace envelopes all. Now that will be occasion for praise – joy without end!

Of course we have already entered into that Kingdom and have already started to experience that joy. It's already in us – it's part of the Holy Spirit! We should just live it out by being intentionally joyful. Yes, it's a decision, a discipline! Paul gives it as a command: "Rejoice in the Lord always; again I will say, rejoice" (Philippians 4:4). We have no other choice today than to be exceptionally glad. It's a command: break out in praise!

Yes, Lord, today I am going to rejoice in all things! Amen.

Joy is spiritual discipline. You have to practice it –
through praise and worship – in all circumstances.
God promises that it will change your life.

You'll Find Him There

> "The mountains and the hills before you shall break forth into singing, and all the trees of the field shall clap their hands."
>
> *Isaiah 55:12 ESV*

When we get to the eternal Canaan, nature will be glad with us: *the mountains and the hills will rejoice, and the trees will clap their hands*, figuratively speaking, of course. Paul says that nature is suffering with us the effects of sin, that nature also awaits the coming of the Lord, to be reborn and restored.

Even so, nature is already praising God. Every created thing honors God by fulfilling its creation purpose: the mountains in their majesty, the seas in their shadowy depths, the clouds carrying tons of water elsewhere – as well as every animal clinging to life, beautiful in its own way, procreating and then disappearing forever. Yes, the whole of creation is one big psalm of praise to the Creator! What is the lesson?

First of all, go and find God's praise in nature as often as possible. You'll find it in every flower and leaf if you look for it. Then add your praise to its song. Finally, fulfill your own creation purpose faithfully. It honors the Creator.

Thank You, Lord, for the beauty of nature.
I want to find more of You there. Amen.

God promises that nature's praise for Him is immensely beautiful.
We can learn valuable lessons from each plant and animal
about spirituality – and you should do it deliberately!

The Bad Will Come Out

"Instead of the thorn shall come up the cypress; instead of the brier shall come up the myrtle."

Isaiah 55:13 ESV

Nature will also be changed the day that God intervenes on earth. This verse says that thorn and brier bushes will make space for cypresses and myrtle trees. In Scripture thorns and thorn bushes often stand for unbelievers. The brier bush is a prickly shrub (the word is also translated as a stinging nettle) that stands for wild, uncultivated growth. In God's Canaan these will be removed and replaced by cypress or cedar trees, as signs of the righteous, and myrtle trees that have a beautiful fragrance.

That's not all: these images also take us straight back to the beginning, to the Garden of Eden. There thorns and thistles came up as a result of man's sin. Now God will be removing sin again – for which they stood – and will restore paradise.

This is also of importance in our personal lives: aren't there still "thorns and thistles" growing where it shouldn't? Yes, they do! Further growth is still necessary! A new and God-honoring lifestyle is the "everlasting sign" that the verse mentions further on – the proof of God's work in our lives. Everyone should see that sign, should experience that lovely fragrance of God's presence. Let the Holy Spirit help you with that.

Lord, the following still needs to change in my life … Amen.

God promises transformation in your life. In fact, that is the whole purpose of His involvement. You should not resist change – you have to collaborate with His work.

Salvation Comes, Therefore ...

Thus says the LORD: "Keep justice, and do righteousness, for soon My salvation will come."

Isaiah 56:1 ESV

The prophet said everyone had to sit up and listen: the Jews' salvation – out of their captivity in Babylon – was at hand. They had to sit up and prepare themselves! Why were they acting all apathetic, as though they were not taking it seriously? They had to accept the message and act on it by making right with God, doing his commandments, keeping the Sabbath, etc. God was working, but they were not reacting to it!

This concern of the prophet is interesting, because it tells us that we have a certain responsibility to God's work in us. He takes the initiative, but we can responsibly react to what He's doing. We should be open to His work, submit to it, add our full will to it and be obedient as far as we possibly can.

Would a person lost in the wilderness be casual when his rescuer arrives? Would he pretend as though it were nothing? Would he refuse to cooperate? Of course not! His relief and gratitude and cooperation will be evident in every action! God saves you, friend, from a terrible outcome. Now act accordingly – do what He says!

Thank You, Lord, for salvation!
I now want to live life as a truly liberated person. Amen.

God promises that He saves you.
You have to act like someone who was once lost
but have been saved – cooperate with God in every way.

It Will Go Well If ...

> "I will bless everyone who respects the Sabbath and refuses to do wrong."
>
> *Isaiah 56:2* CEV

We can take it for granted that obedience brings about a blessing. If we do what God asks, we'll reap the benefits – that's for sure! To live with integrity and justice, to love and to serve, to forgive and to reconciliate, to love God above all – all these things lead to joy, peace and prosperity. Just compare it to the option of doing evil, lying, hating, etc.

The point is obvious. In the Old Testament God gave His people the Law so that they knew what He expected of them. One aspect of the Law was to keep the Sabbath – to do no work on (what we know as) Saturdays, amongst other things.

The New Testament is clear that it isn't expected of non-Jewish Christians to keep to the Law of Moses and therefore we don't keep the Sabbath, practice circumcision, celebrate the Jewish feasts, etc. We lead a life that pleases God by the guidance and power of the Holy Spirit. Oh, what a good life, what a blessed life!

Lord, I want to live a life that pleases You! Amen.

If you do God's will by living a Spirit-filled life
and following His lead, He promises that you will reap
the blessed fruit. There is no better life than this.

Love Will Conquer

Let not the foreigner who has joined himself to the LORD say, "The LORD will surely separate me from His people"; and let not the eunuch say, "Behold, I am a dry tree."

Isaiah 56:3 ESV

The prophet prophesied something extraordinary – unbelievably radical! Remember, Jewish Law prescribed that people were to be ritually pure, which in practice meant abstaining from unclean things. For example, some people were ritually unclean (lepers, heathen, sinners, women periodically, men who were disfigured, etc.) and some items were unclean (non-kosher food like pork or shellfish, corpses, graves, carcasses of non-slaughtered animals, etc.). To touch any of these would render you unclean with the effect that you had to abstain from touching others or, more importantly, entering the temple grounds. You first had to become clean, or pure, again before you could approach God.

However, the prophet says here that this would change: in the new Canaan serving God would become less of an external matter and more a matter of the heart. Even those who were ritually unclean could go to God if their hearts were pure! The "pure in heart" – those who love and trust God – will definitely be included. They will be part of the people of God! The Lord looks further than mere compliance, He knows us deep within. Let's also look beyond the external things only – see the heart.

Thank You, Lord, for Your great love! Amen.

God promises that He sees the heart,
rather than just the exterior appearance of a person.
If your motives are sincere and you faithfully look to God for help
and salvation, you will definitely be rewarded for it.

Mutilated, yet Whole in God

"To the eunuchs who keep My Sabbaths, who choose the things that please Me … I will give in My house and within My walls a monument and a name."

Isaiah 56:4-5 ESV

Serving God in the new Canaan would change, said the prophet. Remember that some people were ritually unclean and therefore barred from entering the temple. Gatekeepers made sure that the heathen, sinners, lepers, women and others did not come into certain, non-designated, areas. The temple was holy ground – too holy for them!

This meant that such people were practically cut off from God – they couldn't sacrifice or pray in His house – and had to worship from afar. For example the eunuchs were considered unclean and permanently banned from God's presence.

That would change, said the prophet. As they were also human beings that could love God, God would not reject them. On the contrary, if they went to Him, He would write their names permanently in the temple – a wonderful honor! Yes, love wins over exclusion and rejection. Jesus also lived out this love, remember?

Lord, I sometimes experience rejection –
thank You for Your inclusion! Amen.

God promises that He looks at those ostracized by society
in a different way. Are you part of that group?
He looks at their heart. He loves them dearly.

Strangers, but Close in Him

"And the foreigners who join themselves to the LORD … these I will bring to My holy mountain."

Isaiah 56:6-7 ESV

In the new Canaan God will include those who were once rejected. The strict purity prescriptions of the Jewish Law excluded ritually unclean people from God's presence. For example, non-Jews were considered excluded from the covenant, not part of God's election and were therefore not allowed in the Jewish sections of the temple grounds. They had to stay in the *Court of the Gentiles*, even when they forsook their idol worship and turned to the God of Israel.

Signs above the different entrances to the temple warned non-designated people not to enter particular sections – punishable by death! However, Isaiah said this would change. There would come a time when everyone – Jew and Gentile – would be welcome.

It's wonderful, because it includes us: we are the non-Jewish nations that have turned to the God of Israel, not so? We also find Jesus reaching out with love to non-Jewish people: Romans, Samaritans, Phoenicians, etc. It angered His enemies but it really demonstrated the Father's heart. Remember that God loves all people equally! That includes me and you. With Him, we're never really strangers!

Thank You, Lord for Your love! Amen.

God promises that whoever sincerely seeks Him is welcome by His side. It doesn't matter what background, religion or belief you come from.

All People Will Praise Him

"My house shall be called a house of prayer for all peoples."

Isaiah 56:7 ESV

This chapter is a wonderful example of what we call Old Testament "universalism" – the growing conviction in the Old Testament that God is not just the God of the Jews, but of the whole world. At first Jews thought of God as their God only, that only they could be righteous and worthy, that God rejected the other nations. At times their thinking was very exclusive and even arrogant – but of course such superiority was the norm in ancient cultures.

The Lord confirms the following in this verse: He loves all people, He includes all people, the temple in Jerusalem is meant as a temple for all people. Jews did expect these things (and still do), but only in the time of the Messiah. The Messiah came in Jesus Christ and these things did happen!

God's people have been drastically expanded and now consist of believers all over the earth. One day, when you stand before the throne of God, you'll see brothers and sisters from every nation, tribe and tongue. Those men and women – the children of God all over the world – are our true kinsmen, our true people!

Lord, thank You for every true child of God,
every real brother and sister. Amen.

God promises that He loves each and every person –
man or woman, young or old, good or bad.
He wants to be every person's Father.

God Will Gather You

The Lord God, who gathers the outcasts of Israel, declares, "I will gather yet others to Him besides those already gathered."

Isaiah 56:8 esv

God is gathering in His people, said the prophet. All Jews are not automatically included – only those who really serve God and obey His commandments are included. The purpose of God with Israel's election was to create an example amongst the nations – to let His light shine, to draw the whole earth to Him. God is after all interested in the rest of the world as well. He therefore gathers His people from among the Jews, but also from among the non-Jews – all those who truly serve and worship Him.

Can you see how God and man work together? God is actively gathering His people and is looking for those to include. We again, are looking for God in our lives (if we do); we make a decision for Him and surrender ourselves willingly to Him. Both are equally important and true.

When you choose God, you realize and discover that He already chose you! If you want to be part of His people, know that He already included you in His people! Yes, how it works remains a mystery. Just take it as a fact.

Lord, I choose You – thank You for choosing me! Amen.

God choosing you and you choosing Him is two sides
of the same coin. God promises that He will choose you,
if you choose Him. Everyone who chooses Him
has already been chosen – no one is turned away.

You'll Inherit Everything

"But he who takes refuge in Me shall possess the land and shall inherit My holy mountain."

Isaiah 57:13 ESV

The Lord wanted the Jewish captives to turn to Him. Some of them had become ensnared by the idols of Babylon, but God invited them to return to Him for their salvation. God said that those who took refuge in Him would inherit the land. Literally it means that they would return to Palestine, and they did, but in Isaiah we also find a beautiful symbolism of the eternal Canaan. That is the land, that heavenly Jerusalem, which we want to inherit!

When the Lord says we should take refuge in Him, He means that He will be the One who does the saving, the rescuing. When we're in need, when we're lost we can only go to Him. He'll deal with the matter and bring us to where we need to be.

Why do we so often go through crises without hiding in Him? Why do we try so hard on our own to get to that Promised Land we have set our eyes upon? It's with Him and in Him that we'll get there! Let's decide again to go to Him with our needs and dreams and hopes. Let's share our whole life with Him! Our inheritance is in Him and nowhere else.

Lord, thank You that I can take refuge with You.
Hide me away! Amen.

If you choose God as your refuge –
in your everyday joys and fears –
you will be with Him permanently one day.
He promises that you will always be together.

God Will Bow Down

"I dwell in the high and holy place, and also with him who is of a contrite and lowly spirit."

Isaiah 57:15 ESV

The contrast in this verse is always so beautiful. God says earlier in this verse that He is "the One who is high and lifted up, who inhabits eternity, whose name is Holy," and that He dwells *in the high and holy place*. Then comes the contrast: God also dwells with those who are *contrite and lowly* – which means those who are humble before God. It makes us think of the beautiful verse Psalm 34:18 that says, "The LORD is near to the brokenhearted and saves the crushed in spirit."

Yes, the same God lives up on high and also down below in my heart! He is just as much God in His celestial temple as in the meager accommodation that my heart offers. He doesn't mind to take up residence with the humble – in fact, He is drawn to the lonely heart, the wanting soul.

God gladly "leaves" His heaven to bow down to us, to be near to us when we need Him the most! That's who God is: a Father who leaves everything and hastens to His child who calls on Him. In your need God is immediately there, by His Spirit – inside of you!

Thank You, Lord, for always being with me.
I want to be more aware of that! Amen.

God promises that He is personally residing with you through His Spirit. You can simply focus on Him – He is there! Your heart is His temple.

The Humble Will be Exalted

"… to revive the spirit of the lowly, and to revive the heart of the contrite."

Isaiah 57:15 esv

Humility, dependence and reliance on God are huge topics in the Bible. In fact, only people who possess these qualities find God, because they are the only people who look for God. Others believe that they don't need God and therefore never find Him.

Realization of our need for God is the essential start of the whole spiritual journey – the entry requirement, the *sine qua non*. Jesus therefore starts His whole ministry with these words: "Blessed are the poor in spirit (those realizing their dependence), for theirs is the kingdom of heaven" (Matthew 5:3). Yes, blessed are the humble and the needy … and not blessed are the self-sufficient, the independent, the self-righteous, the self-made and the arrogant, because they don't need and can never find God.

Humility does not only characterize the start of a life with God, it's also the defining characteristic throughout, since we never become less reliant on Him – only more so! Humility isn't inferiority or morbid feelings of guilt, it is knowing who God is and who I am, it is gratitude and awe. If that is our attitude God will fulfill these promises: the humble will receive strength, will experience mercy, will be exalted … the humble will know God!

Lord, keep me low before You
and extend me Your grace. Amen.

If you look up to God – humbly, dependent and needy –
He promises that you will experience His presence and assistance.
This is a fact. Proud people do not have that privilege.

The Oppressed
Will Receive Strength

"... to revive the spirit of the lowly, and to revive the heart of the contrite."

Isaiah 57:15 ESV

In the Bible we see time and again how God takes the side of the needy and the dependent – especially those who realize their need and trust God. We also see it with Jesus, who often reached out to the rejected and downtrodden and associated with them. He always gave such people back their dignity.

It's as if God is drawn to such people – His heart is with them! He's the God who's "near to the brokenhearted," who "saves those who are crushed in spirit," as the Psalm says. It's also the promise of this verse: the word that's translated "contrite" here can also be translated *broken, crushed, bruised, oppressed.*

Christians are indeed oppressed in many countries without religious freedom, but oppression is also felt in circumstances like discriminatory policies, financial hardships and humiliating relationships. Can you identify with that? If so, then God promises new life and new strength for today: you will get through the day, you will overcome the circumstances, you will be able to handle that person!

Lord, I need You so much in this situation!
Give me the strength to handle it. Amen.

God promises that those who need strength
will receive strength from Him – today and every day.
That goes for you too.

God Is Not Angry

"My people, I won't stay angry and keep on accusing you. After all, I am your Creator. I don't want you to give up in complete despair."

Isaiah 57:16 CEV

Old Testament believers had a great trust in God's mercy. They realized that they had broken His law and were guilty and deserved punishment. Of course they didn't know about Christ's atonement and just had to deal with the consequences of their sin. Remember that God's "wrath," which is so often mentioned in the Old Testament, isn't just His anger or ill temper – no, it's God's indignation with injustice and hatred. God wants things to be right!

After their mistakes the Jews relied on God not to stay angry for too long. They simply trusted that He would forgive them and bless them again. What beautiful faith in God's goodness! Fortunately, we know from the New Testament that Jesus Christ bore our sins and punishment completely. God's righteousness was meted out in full – to Him! Therefore there's no anger in God's heart towards us. Even though we sin, God is not angry. No, God is not angry.

*Thank You, Lord, that through Christ Jesus
I never experience Your anger – only Your love. Amen.*

God promises that He is not angry with you. If you belong to Him, you are already forgiven. God is angry with sin and what it does to people, and would like to move away from it.

If You Mourn,
He Will Restore You

"I have seen his ways, but I will heal him; I will lead him and restore comfort to him and his mourners."

Isaiah 57:18 ESV

The Jews in captivity experienced distance from God. Far from their land they were pining away. Luckily the 70 years they were to spend in captivity were almost over. God said that He intended to return them, but their hearts weren't right. Some didn't serve Him anymore. Many had decided to just stay in Babylon.

On the other hand there were those who were deeply troubled by their condition – their hearts were with God and they longed to be right with Him again. These are the people that God aims to work with; they are the ones He wants to restore!

In our usage the word "mourn" only has a negative connotation – we mourn when we have suffered a loss. In the Bible, however, it also signifies sadness for what is wrong, regret about sin. As such it means repentance – an attitude that is pleasing to God, because it leads to what is right. God meets with every repentant person and leads them back to Him! God is with all who mourn!

Lord, I am indeed sad about my wrongdoings.
Lead me back to You! Amen.

If you feel sad – about your life that is not right or because
you have experienced a loss – and you look to God,
He promises that He will bring you into His presence immediately.

You'll Get to Such a Place Again

"I will … give you comfort, until those who are mourning start singing My praises."

Isaiah 57:18-19 CEV

Praise is a spiritual discipline. We should be able to praise God in all circumstances. Do you remember Paul and Silas in the dungeon – shackled, but singing praises to God at midnight? Yes, it's possible. Still, it's not easy if conditions are bad. Then it entails a firm decision, faith, resolve, a sacrifice. It's warfare!

It benefits us so much, however, if we can praise God, especially in our dark places. On the other hand, when we experience blessing and prosperity, praise comes naturally – it joyfully springs from the heart!

In this verse God told His people that He knows they are in a dark space. There's little room for joy in their hearts. He promised to bring them back to a place where they could rejoice and praise again. Please accept in faith that you also will get to such a place again! You will look around you and see all the reasons for praising God! This we can proclaim with great conviction.

Yes, Lord, bring me to a place of praise! Amen.

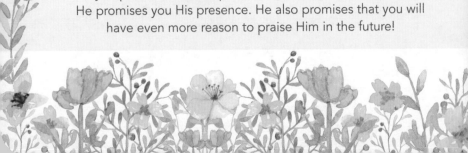

If you praise and worship God, regardless of your feelings, He promises you His presence. He also promises that you will have even more reason to praise Him in the future!

You'll Have Peace –
Far and Near

"Peace, peace, to the far and to the near," says the LORD.

Isaiah 57:19 ESV

What is this peace that God offers His children? It's first of all peace with Him – in other words the knowledge that we are right with God, finally and fully. Not because we have attained one or the other spiritual standard, but because we can fully accept and believe that Christ has made up for all that we lack before God. That is the radical meaning of the cross.

Secondly, we can have peace in the world with all its turmoil. Such peace doesn't come naturally to us, even as believers – we must actively practice it. The godless, however, do not have this peace at all, says this verse further on: they're like a tossing sea, never quiet.

True peace is like a calm and clear lake. To get to that inner calmness we need to surrender to God! It asks that we die to ourselves and to our own will and that we surrender to God's will. May you find that rest in the wonderful peace of God!

Lord, teach me to surrender to You –
to die to any self-centered will and passion. Amen.

If your "own self" – that is self-centered and wants to control everything – surrenders to God, and all resistance in you melts away before God's will, you will have perfect peace. God promises that.

Your Light Will Break Forth

"Then shall your light break forth like the dawn, and your healing shall spring up speedily."

Isaiah 58:8 ESV

The Jewish captives in Babylon were complaining about their faith. They felt it wasn't working out – they kept the law, they prayed, they fasted – but nothing happened! The Lord, however, said that they were fooling themselves. They only stuck to the outward trappings of religion – that's not what He asked for! To fast from certain foods or go through religious motions and prayers meant nothing to Him if they didn't stick to the rest of His will as well. They could just as well leave it.

True religion is justice and mercy: God wants His children to stop with injustice and oppression and start caring for one another. If they do such things, their light (or righteousness) will break forth "like the dawn".

The dawn breaks gradually, remember: first the eastern night starts to lighten up with beautiful red and orange colors. Then suddenly there's a bright stripe on the horizon and the sun comes up in its glory. Soon it is day – how wonderful! Keep on doing what God asks – that's the lesson. Keep on doing that. A new day will surely dawn.

Lord, what do You want me to do? Amen.

God promises that light will break through like the sun in the east. Nothing can stop it! Just continue to do the right things.

He'll Be in Front
and at the Back

"Your righteousness shall go before you; the glory of the LORD shall be your rear guard."

Isaiah 58:8 ESV

The Jews were very engaged with their religious duties: laws, feasts, prayers and fasts! God, however, does not necessarily find it all acceptable. Religion can be a powerful substitute for a relationship with Him! It can keep you busy with many things, but not necessarily the things that God requires.

Don't think that religion can be disregarded – no, religion has a very valid role to play, but when it remains busy with man-made things, it misses the point. So, what is it that God requires?

God asks for a changed heart: a heart that has yielded to Him, a heart full of love and kindness. Such a heart will never allow injustice or hatred, but will do only what is right. Hard-hearted, merciless or unloving people who busy themselves with religion are an anomaly – even an abomination. It's a completely wrong abomination. Only if we persist in love and humility will we experience God with us, in front of us, behind us, around us! Let's find God, not just religion.

Lord, I want to find You – nothing else! Amen.

The Bible says that religion can easily be sidelined, which can lead us away from God. However, if you focus on God alone, He promises that you will find Him.

You Will Hear: "Here I Am"

"Then you shall call, and the LORD will answer; you shall cry, and He will say, 'Here I am.'"

Isaiah 58:9 ESV

The Lord is not interested in religion as such, but in people. The role of religion is to teach people God's will and God's values and to deliver it – in certain set ways – to the next generation. Religion also provides ways for people to approach God.

All these things are very necessary. However, religion can sometimes come between us and God – defeating its own purpose! It can become a purpose in itself, which is wrong, because religion is not about religion, it's about God. How sad is it that people can busy themselves with religion – even defending what they believe is the true religion – but end up without Him?

Let's be clear: religion should take us into a relationship with God or it's a waste of time. Above all, seek Him in your life, find Him, talk to Him, listen to Him! When you cry to Him you'll start to recognize His voice, in one of many ways, saying, "Here I am!" Religion can help you with that.

Yes, Lord, I do want to know You and I
do want to hear Your voice! Amen.

If you sincerely cry out to God, He promises to answer you.
You will hear His voice. The best way to hear His voice
is to be in a relationship with Him.

Your Night Will Become Day

"If you pour yourself out for the hungry and satisfy the desire of the afflicted, then shall your light rise in the darkness and your gloom be as the noonday."

Isaiah 58:10 ESV

The Lord is talking to His people and says that true religion has to do with ending injustice and providing for those in need. Some people are very busy with religious duties, praying a lot and even fasting, but they're still without a heart for others. Such religiosity is fooling itself – it misses the point completely and it misses God. It stays in darkness, even though religion is meant to shine God's light around! However, when we start doing what God asks – out of a heart that loves Him – the darkness lifts.

Whenever we show compassion and humility, whenever we're willing to serve, oppose injustice and stand up for those who cannot, God's light begins to shine. We start to live like Jesus, because that's the way He lived! We "become" Jesus for others. God's light shines through us. Night becomes day – even in your own life.

Lord, I want to feel what You feel, see what You see and live the way You lived. Amen.

We may be deeply involved in spiritual things, but still miss the purpose of it all. We have to do the right thing, not just manage religion! Then God promises His light and guidance.

It Will Be in Your Heart

"You shall be like a watered garden, like a spring of water, whose waters do not fail."

Isaiah 58:11 ESV

This is a variation on the well-known promise of water in the wilderness. The prophet spoke of a "watered garden." Remember, their world was often dry. A cultivated and watered garden was something rare that could only be afforded by the rich.

In fact, the usual image of such a garden was something that was adjoined to the palace complex. Such a garden was walled in and had limited entry. Inside, various trees were planted in rows, with pathways laid out between them and benches provided to sit on. Water was channeled in ducts alongside. It was an absolute luxury to relax in such a garden, in the shadow of a tree, listening to the birds and the water flowing by.

By the way, this is also the picture we should have of the Garden of Eden – not the one we find in a children's Bible! This is the image that the prophet used when he said we would be like a garden that has its own fountain. It's also the image Jesus used when He said that the Holy Spirit would flow from our innermost being like a stream of living and life-giving water. Are you spiritually thirsty? The fountain is right there in your heart!

Thank You, Lord, for these beautiful images of rest,
recuperation and rejuvenation – in You! Amen.

If you live intimately with God and rely on His Spirit's guidance,
He promises that the Holy Spirit will flow from your
innermost being like a stream of living and life-giving water –
refreshing for everyone around you.

He Will Fix You

"You shall be called the repairer of the breach, the restorer of streets to dwell in."

Isaiah 58:12 ESV

Once the Jews returned to the land of Judah and to Jerusalem, they would restore the foundations of the city, build up the ruined walls, restore the streets and lanes, and rebuild the buildings that were torn down or burned out. The city would return to its former glory!

Today Jerusalem is known as the "Golden City", because its inhabitants are only allowed to build in a suitable style and may only use the yellowish sandstone that is found there. It's beautiful to see!

The emphasis in this verse is on restoration, which takes us to the concept of wholeness. In the origins of the word "whole", we also find the word "heal," and also the word "holy." Our word "salvation," for example, in Latin includes the concept of "healing."

God is the patient restorer, the Healer of souls, the One who saves us from destruction and brings us back to wholeness, which is akin to holiness. He will heal all your brokenness inside.

Thank You, Lord, for complete restoration in You. Amen.

God promises that He will heal you and make you well.
More than that, He will also make you a healer of others.
You have a lot of experience to offer.

You'll Find Your Joy Within

"Then you will truly enjoy knowing the LORD."

Isaiah 58:14 CEV

We already shared about the "joy of the Lord," but let's add something today. Remember that we can distinguish between "pleasure," which is found on the outside (when pleasant things happen to us) and "joy," which is found within us. It's important to realize that we can never find joy if we cannot find it inside of ourselves.

What can be found on the outside is pleasure and that's good – all of us need it in our lives – but pleasure is short-lived, and must be repeated again and again. It unfortunately has no lasting significance.

True joy though is on another level – it includes having self-worth, loving relationships, a meaningful life that adds value to others, and experiencing God's favor and blessing. These are things that money cannot buy! We can only find it inside of us, in our hearts, in our relationship with God – in knowing the Lord.

Lord, I want to find that joy that comes from You! Amen.

Pleasure is not wrong if it does not become an idol.
God, however, promises that true joy – joy of life –
can be found through a relationship with Him.

You'll Enjoy Your Father's Fruit

"I will feed you with the heritage of Jacob your father, for the mouth of the LORD has spoken."

Isaiah 58:14 ESV

It might look as though some people are just a self-made success: hard work or good luck made them come out on top! In reality it is the exception if it happens that way. According to research those that got to the top usually had a lot of help. Their parents, for example, were already involved in their particular field and could give them an advantage with the necessary exposure and contacts.

Those who made a lot of money had to have money to start off with – probably from the family. Those who studied far had the financial support for the (expensive) studies. Success often stands on the shoulders of previous successes, advantages or opportunities!

With these thoughts in mind, and with reference to this verse, let's go back to your father and mother. The Lord reminded His people that they would return to the land of their father Jacob. Generations before them have already lived in that land, worked its soil and built it up to a great state. Now they had to go and fill those people's shoes. You'll do well to appreciate what your parents did to get you where you are today. You are what you are because of them! Honor them. Try to fill their shoes.

Thank You, Lord, for my parents –
help me to honor them! Amen.

We stand on the shoulders of those who preceded us.
It is a great blessing. Whether you had help or not,
God promises that He will always be your Father who helps you.

His Hand Is Strong Enough

Behold, the LORD's hand is not shortened, that it cannot save, or His ear dull, that it cannot hear.

Isaiah 59:1 ESV

We now come to a chapter where the prophet really tore into the people – no holds barred! He confronted them with a list of at least 25 accusations: they were riddled with injustice, violence, malice, lies and treachery! They were a group of adders, they were weaving dangerous webs, their hands were defiled with blood, their sins were rising up to the heavens. It's because of those sins that God was so angry! Two things can be commented on here:

- Together with sin we always find its effects: sins have practical consequences and even forgiveness does not cancel those effects out. Also, sin causes a rift between God and us, but He will help us to turn away from that and start anew.
- On the other hand, we no longer carry the burden of sin's guilt before God. Jesus bore the punishment of all sin on the cross and (in principle) we are free – we just need to take it in faith.

Do you see that God's hand is strong enough for your sin-problem? Talk to Him about that.

Thank You, Lord, for intervening in our sin,
for taking the burden on Yourself,
for forgiveness, for a new start. Amen.

We are free from the guilt of sin, but have yet to deal with the consequences and impact. God, however, promises that He will help you through it.

Justice Will Lead to Favor

The LORD saw it, and it displeased Him that there was no justice.

Isaiah 59:15 ESV

We must never underestimate how important righteousness and justice is to God. In fact, if we're to summarize what God asks from us (except for a relationship with Him) it is justice and love. Even God can be described as just and loving.

Here God accused His people of having no justice among them. On the contrary, He found dishonesty and fraud, biased judgments, corrupt dealings, innocent people suffering and guilty ones getting away with it. Such things anger God!

You and I have to be 100 percent fair. If your enemy is right, you should acknowledge it – if your friend is wrong, he's wrong. Stand up for the truth and for those whose resources are few. Radically avoid all dishonesty, fraud, corruption or moral vagueness. Be unashamedly ethical! Walk a straight path, live openly and transparently and guard your integrity, character and testimony – even if it's unpopular. At least you'll have God's favor.

Lord, give me a righteous displeasure
of all forms of injustice. Amen.

God promises that He stands for righteousness and justice.
To be right according to the Bible also means that you
are true to God. In all this He gives His blessing.

Intercession Will Change Things

He saw that there was no man, and wondered that there was no one to intercede.

Isaiah 59:16 ESV

God was angry because of all the injustice He saw amongst His people – wholesale corruption, unfairness and exploitation for personal gain was common. Such things will never lead to prosperity. What angered God even more was that no one did anything about it – and no one came to plead before God! No one "interceded."

Intercession is a real and important topic in the Bible: it is to pray on behalf of someone else, someone who is not praying themselves. What's more, intercession is to fully identify with the wrongdoings of others as if it were our own, because it realizes the commonality of sin, our general brokenness. It pleads for God's forgiveness and mercy, because we are a sinful people!

In the Bible we see Moses, David, Daniel, the prophets and also Jesus Christ interceding on behalf of others – and we also see many examples of God intervening for the sake of an intercessor. Why would it work? We really cannot say, but the Scripture is clear: prayer changes things! Perhaps we should go down on our knees again …

*Lord, I wish to intercede
for the following things or people … Amen.*

God promises that all prayers are heard. He sees your heart, especially if you are advocating on behalf of others before Him. Such surrender moves God's heart!

God Will Work

Then His own arm brought Him salvation, and His righteousness upheld Him.

Isaiah 59:16 ESV

God doesn't wait on people before He acts. He sovereignly acts when and how He wants to act. He isn't a passive God, but an active God. He takes initiative. He takes control. He is working all over – it's impossible to keep track of what God is doing!

God is working in the world, in your country, in many places in your city, in your school and church (and also in other churches), in your boss's life, in your marriage, in your children's lives – and very powerfully also in your life!

What is God doing? Well, He is working to establish His kingdom. His Holy Spirit works through structures and circumstances, through His Word, and in the conscience and hearts of people. God is knocking loudly! People can either resist His work or they can submit to it, surrender to it, and cooperate with Him in what He wants to accomplish. Our task is to find out what God is doing and join Him there. Nothing else will work.

Lord, help me to forget my own will – and find Yours! Amen.

God promises that He is at work. He works everywhere, in all people. He is currently working in your life. It's your job to discern what He is doing and to join in.

East to West Will Glorify God

So they shall fear the name of the LORD from the west, and His glory from the rising of the sun.

Isaiah 59:19 ESV

In the Bible the east often stands for God: the Lord comes, as the new day, from the east. The Old as well as the New Testament expects the Messiah to return on the Mount of Olives, just east of Jerusalem, from where He will enter the city through the Eastern Gate (which is currently sealed).

Jesus Himself said of His coming that He will be worshiped from the east to the west. That doesn't mean that every single person will serve God, but that His servants will be spread out all over the earth.

That is already a fact: in the Far East the church is growing exponentially, as it is doing in Africa, and in the West the church is still strong. Also in Europe and in Muslim countries there is a church – in spite of opposition. When Jesus comes again, Christ's followers will be there! You and I as well, not so?

Lord, how can I contribute
to gathering Your church for the last day? Amen.

God promises that He will return for us.
But He is still waiting for the full number of believers to come.
You too can contribute to the church's global outreach.

November

The Spirit
Will Drive Out the Enemy

When the enemy shall come in like a flood, the Spirit of the LORD shall lift up a standard against him.

Isaiah 59:19 KJV

Our topic is still the Lord who will prevail over the enemy and bring His people home. The Jews were held captive by the powers in Babylon – the center of the whole world's occultism and idolatry. One can say that they were right there at the seat of the Evil One. In this verse the enemy is described in sinister terms, like a flood of darkness enveloping the earth. God, however, is not daunted and will intervene right into the pit of hell, by way of speaking, to save His children.

The message of the captivity is of course also a powerful metaphor for our spiritual bondage and salvation. Against the Evil One the Spirit of God stands, stopping the dark flood right in its tracks. Let's go immediately to the application: you and I need to live through the power of the Spirit! Then we'll conquer the enemy every day.

Lord, fill me with Your Spirit and give me
victory over the enemy. Amen.

God promises that His strength surpasses the power of evil by far.
If you recognize evil through the Holy Spirit and resist,
Satan will flee from you. He has no claim on you.

Turning Will Bring God

> "And a Redeemer will come to Zion, to those in Jacob who turn from transgression," declares the LORD.
>
> *Isaiah 59:20 ESV*

Conversion is a common theme in the Bible, but there's still uncertainty on what it means. Evangelical Christians have developed quite a tradition around it, for example that the minister ends his sermon with an "invitation," that people respond by putting up their hands and coming forward, that they then listen to a gospel explanation and pray a certain prayer. We have been doing it that way for years!

Of course it's just a method that may be suitable or not – it's not right or wrong – but it's interesting to note that in the Bible people came to God in many ways, but never in this way! Some just changed their behavior, others merely sat there weeping – one just said: "Remember me, when You come into Your kingdom" (Luke 23:42). Conversion is just – as the word suggests – to authentically turn to God, from wherever you stand, and to fully trust Him to be your Savior and Lord. How you come to God is not that important, but it is very important that you do come to God – because living life without Him will never be enough. Turning to God will bring Him into your life! In fact it will bring you right into a new life, because conversion is all about new living, new seeing, new feeling, new behavior. Yes, it's a whole new way of living.

Lord, I came to You in the past,
but I come to You again today. Amen.

We are naturally cut off from God by our sins and selfishness.
However, if you truly turn to God, He promises
to forgive all those things and give you a fresh start.

God's Covenant Is His Spirit

"... this is My covenant with them: My Spirit that is upon you, and My words that I have put in your mouth, shall not depart out of your mouth, or out of the mouth of your offspring, or out of the mouth of your children's offspring."

Isaiah 59:21 ESV

God made a covenant with Israel. It started with Abraham and was confirmed at Sinai, when they received the Law. The prophets, however, had good news – God would make a new covenant! Why would that be necessary? Remember that the problem of the old covenant (or Old Testament) was that it demanded compliance, but as humans we could never fully comply with God's perfection.

Now, in the new covenant, God will aid us into obedience by giving us His Spirit as a permanent endowment. His Spirit will take out our old heart of stone and give us a soft heart instead. His Spirit will write His law and His will right upon our heart (not on a stone tablet) – so that our heart wants to obey, and our mouth wants to confess Him as King. Jesus brought the new covenant by His cross and sent the Holy Spirit on Pentecost, completely fulfilling these promises. Let's be filled then with the Spirit! Let's walk by the Spirit – thereby staying in God's perfect will. That's the kind of surrendering that we need to do daily.

Lord, I want to walk by Your Spirit –
bear Your fruit in me! Amen.

By ourselves we cannot be like God, for we are sinners.
God, however, promises that He will put His Spirit in your heart,
and through Him change your heart and will and desires!

You'll Stand in the Glory

Arise, shine, for your light has come, and the glory of the LORD has risen upon you.

Isaiah 60:1 ESV

We need to share again about God's so-called "glory." I state it like this because the Jews saw God's glory as something specific, something separate. In Rabbinical thought the "glory" (*Shekinah*) or "mighty presence" of God was His observable manifestation. God sometimes sent His "glory" on those who had to experience Him. This "glory" was the fire in the burning bush, the pillar of fire that went before the Israelites, the lightning on Mount Sinai, the radiance on the "mercy seat" of the ark and the cloud in the temple, which shone so bright that the priests couldn't approach it. That light, said the prophet here, that glory, is rising over us!

There's a well-known testimony of a woman who had a near-death experience during an operation. As she met with family members who had already passed away, she saw that they all stood in a tangible white cloud. She asked them whether this cloud was God and one answered: "This isn't God; this is what happens when God breathes." She then thought to herself, *Wow, I'm standing in the breath of God.* Yes, perhaps we should not read too much into it, but it does remind us of the glory of God! One day we'll experience it for ourselves.

Lord, I pray that something of Your glory
will already be visible in me today. Amen.

God promises that you will experience His shining glory one day when you arrive in His kingdom. His holy glory is His love that would be physically experienced.

Your Children Will Be There

Your sons shall come from afar, and your daughters shall be carried on the hip. Then you shall see and be radiant; your heart shall thrill and exult.

Isaiah 60:4-5 ESV

In this beautiful chapter the prophet made wonderful promises about the future. When the people returned to their land tremendous abundance and prosperity would follow. Firstly, he said that their "sons and daughters" would return to them. He referred to the "lost" Israelites, because the Jews in captivity represented only a small part of God's people – a mere portion of the tribe of Judah. The rest of Israel was already gone – assimilated between the nations – but the expectation always remained that they would return.

What should be taken notice of in this verse, however, is the value of these "sons and daughters": they were mentioned as the first of the wealth that would be restored, as though they were the true riches. And aren't our sons and daughters worth more to us than all the possessions in the world? Aren't they our true silver and gold, our true wealth? Money and possessions will one day stay behind, but our children will join us in eternity. Pray for that and trust God for that! Also change your priorities.

Lord, thank You for my children.
Help me to invest in them more intentionally. Amen.

God promises that He will take every mother and father's prayer for their children into account. Such prayers are very precious to Him. You can bring your kids before God in prayer every day.

You Will Prosper

Your heart shall thrill and exult, because the abundance of the sea shall be turned to you, the wealth of the nations shall come to you.
Isaiah 60:5 ESV

The prophet predicted that the Jews would have great prosperity when they were back in their land. Trade would increase with the world and treasures from all over – gold, spices, exotic woods – would become commonplace. Ordinary Jews would share in the abundance.

What does it mean for us, for today? Well, we already (partially) live in that time and we can expect God's blessing. Yes, most definitely! God's blessing is the knowledge that He cares for us, that we will always have enough, that we needn't fear, that our destiny is wholeness, and that we will be in Him forever! What riches, what bounty! What peace and joy!

Unfortunately, this blessing doesn't intend to make every Christian, irrespective of circumstance, materially rich – if they would only take it in faith. Such an emphasis is foreign to biblical thinking about money. Money isn't the purpose of the gospel – salvation, liberty, righteousness, justice, peace, joy, love, caring, service – those are its purposes – and its riches!

Lord, bless me! Without Your blessing I am nothing. Amen.

God promises you prosperity and blessings.
Expect it, receive it, see it and honor Him for that!

Your Prosperity Will Honor God

"I will accept them as offerings and bring honor to My temple."

Isaiah 60:7 CEV

The Lord promised great prosperity when the Jews returned to their land. Everyone would share in it! This verse specifically states that it would happen for God's glory. Yes, prosperity and blessing is about God, but we often make it about us. We live in such an individualistic and materialistic culture that we believe that God's job is to supply us with money, possessions, health, happiness and so on. Why else would I have a God in my life? Unfortunately (or fortunately), the Bible doesn't reason that way.

In fact the Bible turns it around. In the Bible the world is broken and God is healing it – our job is to obediently work with Him in doing that! It all revolves around Him, not around us! However, when we seek the kingdom of God first, He will add *all these things* to us, according to His Word. There will be blessings, favor and abundance – but all to His glory, never ours.

Lord, help me to work for Your kingdom to come –
and then add to me all that I need. Amen.

If you put God's kingdom first in your life – His control, His reign –
He promises that you will have enough to live on.
You will not have to worry about it.

Your Doors Will Be Open

"Your gates will be open day and night to let the rulers of nations lead their people to you with all their treasures."

Isaiah 60:11 CEV

Oh, to live in a country where the doors can stand open day and night! There still are such countries and such places in the world, but for the most of us the doors – and often the security gates – must remain firmly locked. In ancient times their cities' gates also had to be closed for security purposes – they always had enemies and often had wars.

In God's future, however, there won't be a need for closed doors or gates anymore. Everything will permanently stay wide open – there will never be an enemy again! No crime, no hate and no violence! What a wonderful prospect! What is the lesson and promise for today, in our modern and often dangerous world?

Firstly, we still need to lock our gates. Yes indeed, we must be responsible. But we also need to realize that our precautions can only go so far. When you have done all that you can, you need to relax and trust God for the rest. We are not called to live in fear, but in faith and love. Open the gates of your heart!

Lord, help me to live safely – and freely. Amen.

God promises that He is with you. Do what you can to stay safe, but realize that believers do not have to fall into fear or neurosis.

Everything Will Be Upgraded

"Instead of bronze I will bring gold, and instead of iron I will bring silver; instead of wood, bronze, instead of stones, iron."

Isaiah 60:17 ESV

There is a saying that everything except hell is moving onto perfection. God is also working in our own lives by His Spirit: building us up and taking us forward. Everything that God does – or allows – is for our growth. Let's formulate it better: everything that happens with us is used by God for our development and growth. Everything is incorporated, everything works together for good!

See here how beautifully the Lord will upgrade the New Jerusalem: stone and wood will be substituted by iron and bronze (the suggestion is that iron and bronze will become as common as wood and rocks), silver will become as common as iron, and gold will be given in the place of every piece of bronze equipment that was looted from the temple by the enemy. Yes, whatever the enemy has stolen, God will reimburse – doubly so!

That's how God also works with us. We know we still have far to go – and grow – and still need to cooperate with God in many ways to get us to the image of Christ, not so? Yet, ask yourself: what is God busy doing in my life at the moment? What is currently happening? How is God using it?

Lord, I open myself up for Your work in me! Amen.

God promises that He is busy removing old things from your life and replacing them with new things. He is working through His Spirit to make you like Jesus Christ.

Peace Will Reign

"I will make your overseers peace ... violence shall no more be heard in your land."

Isaiah 60:17-18 ESV

Oh, to live in a world where peace is the norm, where violence is not heard of on a daily basis! Unfortunately, we often hear of violence – every day has its share of brutal attacks, suicide bombings, abduction of innocents, assaults, rape and murder. So many families are disrupted, displaced or bereft of children, fathers or mothers – trauma on trauma. Also, everyone following the news lives with the secondary trauma thereof – it might be best not to watch the news or read the papers again! Let's remember two important things here – one concerns our part and the other God's part:

From our side we need to become involved: we should donate, petition, protest, enlist in organizations and do what's necessary for peace. It's not just for us – it's for all, especially the vulnerable who are most affected.

Then we should pray for God's intervention: that our country will fear God, that good decisions will be made by governments, that the gospel will penetrate the world, and that peace will reign.

We are the children of God. We stand for the values of His kingdom! Let's pray and work together for peace – one day it will come, in His name.

Lord, I pray for this land – that You will be served
and that peace will reign. Amen.

God promises that you can experience prosperity
and peace in this country, because He will be with you.
Also work for everyone's peace and prosperity and pray for revival!

Another Sun Will Shine

The sun shall be no more your light by day … but the LORD will be your everlasting light.

Isaiah 60:19 ESV

The prophet looked at the future of the Jews in Babylon. They would be restored as a people in their own country, their temple would be rebuilt and the other nations would come and serve their God there. Peace and prosperity would reign. Then the prophet looked even further, right into a new dimension: he said on that day the sun and moon would not shine anymore – God Himself would shine over them! That makes us realize that he's talking about the next world, about eternity.

The book of Revelation also says that God Himself will shine over us in the "New Jerusalem" forever – it's something that can only happen in another dimension. In the meantime though, we already experience the symbols and shadows of that time, because the Messiah (the "Sun of righteousness") already came, the nations are already being added to God's people and the spiritual temple, God's Church, is already being built. And then – when this dimension spills over into the next – the whole city will be one big temple and God will shine over us as the sun. On that day we'll shine as well, the Bible says!

Thank You, Lord, for what lies in store for us –
half of which we've never been told. Amen.

God promises a future that you can't imagine lies ahead of you!
It should let you live without fear in this life.

Everyone Will Be Sifted

Your people shall all be righteous; they shall possess the land forever.

Isaiah 60:21 ESV

There will come a day, said the prophet, that everything will be perfect. God's people will be completely restored in their land and all its inhabitants will be righteous – no sinners will remain! The Bible is clear that eternity will have no place for sin, injustice, anger, hatred, suffering, loss or pain. Such things will not inherit the kingdom of God, according to the New Testament. All that is imperfect will stay behind! At the judgment God will sift out all sin – and sinners – and only then eternity will commence.

Let me ask you something: Will you survive the sifting of God? Are you righteous enough for eternal life? Well, of course not – no one is so righteous as to deserve eternal life. It was a trick question! All who inherit eternal life will do so because of Jesus Christ's righteousness and merit. Those who accept His love in faith have already passed through the separation; they have already been sorted with God's children, already been put aside for eternal life! That's the joy of being a Christian!

Thank You, Lord, that I'm reconciled,
and will not be judged anymore. Amen.

God promises that everyone belonging to Him
has already been judged with the judgment of the cross.
After death they will have eternal life. No judgment for you!

Its Time Will Come

"I am the LORD; in its time I will hasten it."

Isaiah 60:22 ESV

The Lord not only described the Jews' return, but also the whole epoch that would commence after that. That age would run into eternity itself, when God would come to live with His people. God said that at the right time He would introduce that age – "in its time I will hasten it."

Of course it happened, but take note how it happened: at the right time the Jews returned to Israel, but the whole promise wasn't fulfilled. At the right time the Messiah (Jesus Christ) came and inaugurated the new covenant: the Spirit was poured out, peace was proclaimed and the nations were coming into the kingdom of God. Yet the whole promise wasn't fulfilled – it is still continuing.

At the right time God will come and fulfill all promises finally and fully and establish the New Jerusalem forever. Do you see how God's promises are fulfilled every time in its time? So it also happens in our own lives: at the right time the right things will happen – in fact, at the right time God will hasten the things that need to happen. Every promise will be fulfilled – in its time! Pray for it, work for it and faithfully wait on God for it.

Lord, hasten Your promise to me – I wait on You! Amen.

God allows things to happen to you at exactly the right time –
not too early and not too late. You must trust Him.
He promises that He can be trusted with it!

The Spirit Will Come Upon You

> The Spirit of the Lord God is upon me, because the LORD has anointed me to bring good news.
>
> *Isaiah 61:1 ESV*

This last part of Isaiah is so beautiful – so full of hope and promise, so full of God's grace! Slowly read through these chapters in your quiet time. In this verse the prophet speaks about his own calling, but then Jesus applied it to Himself in His sermon in the synagogue of Capernaum. There He said: "Today this Scripture is fulfilled in your hearing" (Luke 4:21) – in other words, He says that He is the Anointed One that God sent to do the things listed here. The word "Anointed" in Scripture is the word *Christ* (Greek) or *Messiah* (Hebrew) – and that's who He is!

Remember now: we have the same assignment that Christ had, since we are called to finish His work. For that "Great Commission" Christ sent His Spirit onto the church. We now have the anointing of the Spirit, according to the New Testament. However, we should move in that anointing by spending time in God's presence and then by actively "walking in the Spirit." That entails a daily, deliberate decision to seek God's input, to surrender to His will and to live out His purposes with your life.

Lord, thank You for pouring out Your Spirit over me –
fill me completely! Amen.

God promises in His Word that all believers have the anointing of the Holy Spirit – you too. You need to be filled with the Spirit and continue to be filled. It's about commitment.

You'll Have Good News

The LORD has anointed me to bring good news to the poor.

Isaiah 61:1 ESV

The prophet wrote about his own call to announce the good news of the Jews' imminent liberation. Jesus then applied the same message to His call and the liberation from sin, bondage and oppression. Ultimately He commanded His disciples to take the same message further when He said: "Go therefore and make disciples of all nations" (Matthew 28:19). This message of Jesus is what the Bible calls the "good news," "glad tidings" or *gospel* – from the old English *godspell* (*god* = good, *spell* = story/tidings).

Yes, you and I are sent with the good news! For that we have been mandated by Christ and anointed by the Holy Spirit. The Spirit was given to the whole church on Pentecost, but we still personally need to be filled by Him and walk with Him daily. The bottom line is this: you and I are sent daily into our own specific world to act as messengers and witnesses. We bear His testimony at home, at work, at school, on the street, in the community, wherever we go! What is our message, our good news? *God loves you! It's worth everything to follow Jesus.*

Lord, make me a bearer of good news today. Amen.

God sends you today to spread the good news in your world. Just be faithful as a Christian – He promises to do the rest of the work in people's hearts.

You'll Bring the Difference

He has sent me to bind up the brokenhearted, to proclaim liberty to the captives, and the opening of the prison to those who are bound.

Isaiah 61:1 ESV

The Lord sends each of us into our own particular world to be a witness unto Him. Our message will be especially welcomed by all those in need, those who are brokenhearted, those in all sorts of bondage. It is especially meant for them! Jesus also reached out to the needy, the suffering and the vulnerable. He said they are blessed, because God will come to their aid. That is why Christians always put special emphasis on struggling people as well.

What constitutes the gospel for needy people? Shall we offer them a presentation on being saved? No, let's not – or at least not immediately. The gospel in such circumstances is supplying the need, comforting those who mourn, bringing freedom to those that are bound. That's what the Bible is saying here! True help and real change is the good news that we should bring! If God's children don't act out the gospel that they talk about, what empty gospel it is? No, let's bring the change; let's be the gospel of God's love! Later on we can also bring the gospel words.

Lord, help me to be the change that I believe in –
even in small ways. Amen.

The gospel is good news for the poor, hungry, blind and those committed to God. If you make a difference in these people's lives, you preach the gospel. God promises that He will honor it.

You'll Experience the Jubilee

... to proclaim the year of the LORD's favor, and the day of vengeance of our God; to comfort all who mourn.

Isaiah 61:2 ESV

The wording of this verse sounds like the description of the so called "Jubilee Year" in the Old Testament. Every fiftieth year had to be a special year in Israel, announced by the blowing of the ram's horn (the *shofar*). In that year the land and the people had to rest, debt had to be cancelled, slaves had to be set free and property returned to its original owners. That was God's way of restoring liberty, equality and dignity to all at least once per generation.

The Jubilee is not currently kept by Jews, as the twelve tribes are not in that land anymore. There is, however, a spiritual meaning: Jesus quoted this verse when He said that in Him the true, spiritual Jubilee had arrived – forgiveness of sin was proclaimed, as was liberation of bondage and the restoration of souls. Remember that the whole Old Testament is fulfilled in Christ. The Jubilee is a type, a symbol that points to Jesus, who represents the Jubilee in every way. The Bible says one day the *shofar* will sound: Jesus will come and an eternal Jubilee will break out over the earth forever!

Lord, thank You for the Jubilee that has come,
and the Jubilee that is still to come. Amen.

The spiritual jubilee already arrived with Jesus Christ.
If we do not live with jubilation in our hearts,
we miss something. But God promises you eternal jubilation.

You'll Receive Oil for Joy

… to grant to those who mourn in Zion … a beautiful headdress instead of ashes, the oil of gladness instead of mourning, the garment of praise instead of a faint spirit.

Isaiah 61:3 ESV

The Jews mourned in a certain way. When they heard the bad news they immediately tore their clothes, which orthodox Jews still do. We must remember that clothing in their day was scarce and valuable – to tear it was a great loss. The act, however, signified how little earthly things mattered to them at that moment. They also put on sackcloth (coarsely woven, heavy duty material made of goat's hair), threw ashes on their head, forsook all work and sat down – crying and bewailing their loss. All would hear and see it! They didn't care. Do you know what? That was therapeutically important.

Jesus said that those who mourn are blessed, because God will comfort them. He quoted these verses when He said His own calling is to wash the ashes from mourners' faces, give oil for their hair (which was part of their grooming), take off the mourning clothes and replace it with "a garment of praise!" Are you mourning? Take your time to grieve for your loss – it's so necessary – but then someday Jesus will come and take the sadness away. One day you'll feel a ray of joy again in your heart.

Thank You, Lord, for being with me
and changing my heart. Amen.

It is important and valuable that we mourn when we've experienced a loss. God, however, promises that you will appreciate the sunshine again someday.

You'll Be a Priest — and You Are

But they themselves will be priests and servants of the LORD our God.

Isaiah 61:6 CEV

The prophet was describing the peace and prosperity of the coming Messianic Era, when God Himself would come to stay with His people. During that time the priestly order would become obsolete. Remember that priests were intermediaries between God and man — they stood in God's presence on behalf of people and in people's presence on behalf of God. They offered up people's sacrifices and prayers to God, and made God's will and law known to people. However, when God Himself was present, the function of the intermediary expired. God could then be approached directly!

That is what happened when Christ came to us. In Him (Emmanuel — *God-with-us*) God came near. In fact, by His Spirit He came to stay right in us — directly available at all times! There's no need for a temple or for intermediaries anymore. That's why the Jewish temple was demolished after Jesus' death. According to the Bible, we have all become God's priests — a universal priesthood who come into His presence, offering His blood, not the blood of goats or lambs. We also stand as priests in God's sanctuary on behalf of others — praying and pleading for them. We may and we must! Do you now understand your priestly role better?

Lord, help me to fulfill a priestly role
in my family and community. Amen.

You are a priest and mediator of our God and your job is to intercede with God for people and to represent people in His presence. He promises that He is serious about you spreading the gospel.

You Will Multiply

Instead of your shame there shall be a double portion; instead of dishonor they shall rejoice in their lot.

Isaiah 61:7 ESV

The Lord promised that the Jews would have a double portion of what they lost during their captivity. He wasn't just referring to money, but also to their shame and degradation. Remember, in biblical times money didn't have the same value or function that it has today.

Today you can buy anything with money (or so we think), but in biblical times one's honor was the "currency" with which one got ahead in life. If a person or family lost their honor or dignity, it was never forgotten. Such a person was often avoided or ridiculed. Also, the embarrassment of the parents were held against the children and *vice versa*. The Jews were severely humiliated in having to leave their "holy" land to stay between gentiles and heathen. They felt forsaken – abandoned by their God.

God said here that the tables would be turned around – and how it did! While the Jews are still in their land 2,500 years later, the mighty city of Babylon is a mere ruin. Don't just look at the current status – look ahead and see what God can turn around!

Lord, thank You for multiplying my provision,
acceptance and dignity. Amen.

God promises to take away all shame and embarrassment from you,
and that He will bless you with honor and grace.
You are His beloved child after all!

He Will Soon Start the Celebration

> ... as a bridegroom decks himself like a priest with a beautiful headdress, and as a bride adorns herself with her jewels.
>
> *Isaiah 61:10* ESV

This verse is all about eager anticipation. The prophet said the coming salvation for the Jews was like a bridal couple that have already donned their colorful clothes, jewels, headdresses and tiaras, and were now just waiting for the ceremony to begin. In all Eastern cultures – up to today – brides and grooms are very lavishly adorned.

To bring it into our context we could say it's like a bride standing outside the church's door, together with her bridesmaids and inside the groom is waiting with his groomsmen. All that needs to happen now is for the church bell to ring, the door to open and the bride to walk down the aisle on the wedding march! The anticipation of that last-minute-waiting is what is captured here in this verse.

Have you ever seen pictures of a beautifully laid table, with golden plates, crystal glasses and silver cutlery – its empty chairs just waiting for the feast to begin? Yes, that's the metaphor that the Bible works with! The Bible tells us that the "Marriage Supper of the Lamb" is at hand. Everything is ready for the celebration to start, but the bell has not sounded yet. Why? The Bridegroom is still waiting on some more guests to arrive. In the meanwhile excitement is building!

Lord, I look forward to the eternal feast
that is promised to us! Amen.

God promises that the festival will start soon.
He wants more guests at His party.
You must please be patient – His angels are very busy inviting them!

It Will Be Inevitable

For as the earth brings forth its sprouts, and as a garden causes what is sown in it to sprout up, so the Lord God will cause righteousness and praise to sprout up.

Isaiah 61:11 ESV

The prophet used a plant metaphor here in order to demonstrate how naturally and organically God's righteousness would prevail. He said that fertile ground would produce plants and healthy plants would produce fruit. This happens all by itself – it's the way nature works! With God it's the same: His righteousness will prevail on earth – and in your life – by its natural authority. It's inevitable. Nothing will stand in its way.

The Bible uses another plant metaphor to describe a similar principle: "you reap what you sow." In other words, what you put into the ground will come up by itself – outside of your control – and bear fruit. What God has sown in our lives will work its way through and produce its results. That's a promise! If we keep doing the right things in the Lord, we eventually will receive its blessing. It's inevitable. However, when we continue with the wrong things, the results will only be disappointing. Lastly, remember that several seasons go by between sowing and reaping. Keep your faith.

Lord, I am waiting for the harvest –
and I will not lose faith! Amen.

God promises that there will emerge a crop for your seed.
Be patient, because the harvest does not follow directly
after planting. Leave the timing of the harvest with Him.

A New Day Will Dawn

For Zion's sake I will not keep silent, and for Jerusalem's sake I will not be quiet, until her righteousness goes forth as brightness, and her salvation as a burning torch.

Isaiah 62:1 ESV

The prophet said that he would continue to pray and prophesy until the Jews were delivered from Babylon. It was his calling and his burden. He referred to their salvation as a coming "brightness," probably meaning the dawn of a new day. He wanted to see them enter that tomorrow!

We must remember that we live our lives in seasons – extensive periods in our lives over which we have little control. Unplanned things can happen: you lose your work, you have to relocate, things happen in your family or with your health. God allows for it to happen. Still, we – as God's coworkers – also have a responsibility in these seasons:

- We need to work and do what we must do. Sometimes we wait on God to do things He is waiting on us to do!
- We need to pray. Prayer maintains the relationship with God, which is very important at all times. It also does more: we see here how persevering prayer breaks open the new dawn, the new era!

What is burdening your heart so much that you need to keep praying?

Lord, the following are the burdens of my heart ... Amen.

God promises that you can trust Him with your seasons, but you also have to live appropriately with it: distinguish the season and ask the Lord what its purpose is.

You'll Have a New Name

You shall be called by a new name that the mouth of the LORD will give.

Isaiah 62:2 ESV

At important moments in the Bible people get new names – Abram became Abraham after his covenant with God, Jacob became Israel after wrestling with God, Simon became Peter and Saul became Paul after meeting with Jesus. At this stage though the names of *Israel* and *Jerusalem* were reason enough for ridicule because Israel found itself cast between the heathen and Jerusalem was reduced to rubble. When things change around, however, they will have new names – according to God's promise. In Ezekiel the prophet said that the city's new name would be Yahweh Shammah – *God is there!* A beautiful name!

One day you and I will also have new names, according to the Bible. In Revelation we read that those who persevere will receive a white stone with a new name on it. That will be the name that God calls you by – a special name, lovingly used by Him, revealing how well He knows your heart. Would you like to know what your special name will be? Well, keep the faith, persevere to the end, receive your stone and read it yourself!

Lord, thank You for knowing me so intimately –
and loving me so deeply. Amen.

God promises that He has a special new name in store for you.
That's what He calls you! One day He'll show you.

You'll Be as Precious as a Gem

You will be a glorious crown, a royal headband, for the LORD your God.

Isaiah 62:3 CEV

In the future the Jewish people and their land would be restored, the prophet said in this verse. That restoration has already started, although many prophesies remain outstanding since we still live in that time. The Jewish people are still under God's blessing – although a small nation, have you seen the many scientists, inventors, artists, musicians and Nobel Prize winners they have had? The modern state of Israel also stands out in their region as a sophisticated first-world country.

One day Jerusalem – by which we mean the New Jerusalem – will be the capital of the world and shine like a jewel, according to this verse. God will form this city to be the crown of the world! Crowns in their day looked a bit different from the crowns we know – think of the headdress that a sultan wore: a golden band with a colorful turban, bejeweled by precious gems. The following is an amazing fact: according to Revelation the New Jerusalem stands for all of God's children, the whole church, His bride – for us! We are also precious in His hand, and you and I will also be – when God is done, for He's still working on us – like prized handmade treasures.

Thank You, Lord, for making something beautiful of my life. Amen.

You are very precious to God. He promises that you are a precious, handmade gem in His sight. You should value yourself.

Beulah: A Name for You

You shall no more be termed Forsaken, and your land shall no
more be termed Desolate.

Isaiah 62:4 ESV

The Jews thought that their God had forgotten about them, abandoned
them – like a man abandoning or divorcing his wife. In those times a husband could divorce or send away his wife if she brought dishonor to him.
Remember that it was a time in which honor was everything. For example,
a man commonly blamed his wife if she couldn't produce an offspring,
which was only one of many reasons for divorce. God, however, said that
He didn't abandon them – they deserted Him! Still, His promise was that
the relationship would be restored.

It's beautiful that they'll then be called *Hephzibah* ("My delight is in her")
and the country *Beulah* ("Married") – it makes us think of renewed marriage
vows, not so? Because of these names (given literally in the King James
Version), the beautiful name Beulah became popular for girls all over the
world. Let's take these meanings for ourselves: God says we are His bride,
His beloved, His wife. He delights in us. It shows God's longing for a deeply
intimate relationship with man – with me and you! Let's grow in such a relationship!

Thank You, Lord, for these beautiful names –
and Your beautiful heart of love. Amen.

God promises that He thinks of you like a groom
thinking of his bride: beautiful, as a loved one,
as someone to whom He promised allegiance.

God Rejoices Over You

As the bridegroom rejoices over the bride, so shall your God rejoice over you.

Isaiah 62:5 ESV

It is surprising and beautiful to see God's joy in this verse. We often see God as formal, even strict – loving, but in a reserved way. He has joy, but does He rejoice exuberantly? We don't see Him like that! Still, this verse hints at such joy. Take note of the context: God rejoices over us "as a bridegroom rejoices over the bride" on their wedding day.

Let's remind ourselves that a marriage in their times was the result of a long process. Negotiations by the parents started early, when the children were still young. A settlement over the dowry (the compensation paid by the groom to the bride's parents) was the first goal and after that the planning for the betrothal, which was a celebration on its own, could start. Probably a year after the engagement the wedding itself was celebrated as a feast of several days. Before that day the bride and bridegroom had little time to talk, spent no time alone and definitely had no physical contact. All those things had to wait for the wedding.

Can we understand the yearning that such a groom felt for her on that final day, or his joy over his bride, beautifully adorned like a princess, waiting just for him? Well, that is the joy that this verse is speaking of! Fantastic joy and longing is in God's heart for His bride! How wonderful is that?

Lord, it's astounding to think of Your love for us.
We love You too! Amen.

God promises that He desires an intimate relationship with you.
He invites you to open your heart to Him and share
your innermost thoughts with Him.

Your Bread and Your Wine

"As surely as you harvest your grain and grapes, you will eat your bread with thankful hearts, and you will drink your wine in My temple."

Isaiah 62:9 CEV

The sad background to this verse is the Jews losing their home country. Others came and captured their land, took over their vineyards and fields, and harvested them as their own. The Jews' wheat and grapes became others' bread and wine. It was terribly humiliating. Isn't that typical of what the enemy does? He comes to steal, destroy and break everything that others have built up. The Lord, however, promised that it wouldn't happen again. He said from then on what they sowed they would reap themselves: it would become their bread and their wine.

In the New Covenant this promise is fulfilled in Christ, because against Him no enemy can win, and from Him nothing can be stolen! His triumph over the enemy, and over sin and death, was on the cross and we find its symbols in the elements of Communion: whenever we eat and drink at the Lord's Table, the bread and wine confirms to us that God will forever be victorious, that God makes His promises true, that God will always supply our need. Even if you suffer setbacks, God's supply cannot run out!

Lord, thank You for compensating me
for the losses that I have suffered. Amen.

God promises that you will have enough to live on. Eventually you will experience abundance. You may ask the blessing of your own bread and own wine of the Lord – and then enjoy it!

You Will Clear Away the Stones?

Prepare the way for the people; build up, build up the highway; clear it of stones.

Isaiah 62:10 ESV

The prophet asked the people to start clearing away stones! He was referring to the highway that would be built – figuratively speaking – for the captive Jews to return to their land. It meant that God would provide a way back for them. It's that road that must be level, not rocky!

These images are very meaningful to us, because – spiritually speaking – we are also on our way to God. We know that those who don't serve God are still in the captivity of sin and need to return to Him. That road to God is already made – and His name is Jesus Christ. He is the Way to God, not just for salvation but also for the further journey that we need to take towards spiritual and personal maturity. Life is a journey, remember?

In this we do have a task and that is to "clear away the rubble," to use the prophet's image. We need to work on our habits, temptations, weaknesses, bad choices and other things that don't honor God. What are the "stones" in your own life? The Holy Spirit will show you. You can make a change, because the Holy Spirit will empower you! Don't stumble over the same things again and again.

Lord, help me with these stones on my way … Amen.

God promises that He is with you on your way in your spiritual life.
On the spiritual path, you also have a responsibility.
If you ask Him, He will show you the stones to roll away.

Let All See Your Banner

Raise a banner to help the nations find their way.

Isaiah 62:10 CEV

We already said that banners or flags were used in the old times to indicate the presence of the king, a regiment or a tribe. When the king, for example, was in his palace, or on the battle-field, his banner was flown. Some of their flags looked like ours, often with embroidered names on them, but others were longer and could be fastened to a spear or lance. Here the prophet said that the people should raise God's banner up high, because He is present and great things can be expected! Also, the "nations" needed to find their way to Him.

Similarly, we also need to raise God's banner to let people know that we serve Him. Flying His banner doesn't mean that you talk about God all the time. No, His banner is seen in things like a compassionate smile, encouraging words, being absolutely fair – by forgiving or helping. Your deeds will show whether God is present in your life! The Holy Spirit will then take it further – if someone initiates a conversation about spiritual matters, you can tell them your own experience. It's simple – just let the banner wave!

Lord, help me to wave Your banner today. Amen.

Your behavior as a child of God – where you find yourself –
is your testimony about Him, the banner that you show.
God promises that others can see it.

December

The Enemy Won't Escape

"I did this because I wanted to take revenge – the time had come to rescue My people."

Isaiah 63:4 CEV

As we read the promises and encouragement of God in Isaiah, we often also read about His wrath and vengeance. In the Bible, God's salvation and God's judgment always went hand in hand. On the day that God intervened to punish His enemies, He also saved His people. It's the same event. This literally happened when the Babylonians were defeated by the Persians and the Jews were able to go home. It also pointed to the Second Coming, when Christ would come for His children, but then also usher in the Last Judgment.

Let's consider this: who are God's enemies? Is it certain people? The unsaved? No, in the Bible it is most often the nations that opposed His people – not individuals. There is no emphasis in the Bible on God hating people or avenging Himself on individuals. No, God is against the forces of sin and evil that wreak havoc on humankind. Remember that in Eden, humans were never cursed by God because of sin; the earth became cursed and the snake was cursed for introducing sin. That is God's true enemy: the evil one! As for people like you and me, God loves us and wants to help us in this sinful world.

Thank You, Lord, that You are not angry with me.
You love me! Amen.

As people we are imperfect, and often sin against God.
He promises that He loves us and wants to help us in this sinful world.

His Steadfast Love Is Guaranteed

I will recount the steadfast love of the LORD, the praises of the LORD, according to all that the LORD has granted us.

Isaiah 63:7 ESV

In this verse we find a special word. It's found all over the Old Testament, but it's not well understood. The older translations translate it as "loving-kindness" – which sounds like a double dose of goodness – while the newer translations render the term as "steadfast love." Sometimes it's merely translated as *kindness*, *goodness* or something similar. The word refers to the fact that God will always be good or kind to us, that we will always experience His favor, love and blessing.

The reason for this unwavering affection is important, because it's the key to understanding the concept: it's not because we're so lovable or deserving – we're not – but because God has promised it! This word is often used in reference to God's covenant with Israel, of which we've become a part. Steadfast love is the covenant condition on God's side.

The wonder of God's steadfast love is that it's not conditional at all. While we stray away and become untrue, God remains true. He is not like us – His love for us never ceases, it remains "steadfast!" Even when we are completely undeserving of it, God's love can be counted on. He is always looking at His children with love, no matter what happens!

Lord, thank You for not reacting to my untrustworthiness.
Your faithfulness is the anchor of my life! Amen.

God promises you His kindness and goodness.
His loving allegiance is not about your worth or ability to love,
but about His promise. That is why it's forever!

Your Need Is His Need

In all their affliction He was afflicted, and the angel of His presence saved them.

Isaiah 63:9 ESV

This is a wonderful verse. The text is difficult to translate, but most translators decide on something like the above-mentioned. If the people are afflicted, God is afflicted – their need is His need! How wonderful is that? It's a definite biblical truth that the Lord takes His people's misery upon Himself – that their difficulties upset Him, even hurt Him. How can this be? Try to understand it from the perspective of His love. Remember, love includes pain, because love implies intense involvement with a loved one – with their well-being or suffering. Your children's pain is your pain, for example.

Another thing: love is not always reciprocated, love often brings disappointment. Yes, with great love can come great pain! The spiritual fathers realized that God must carry much pain in His heart, since God is love. What a wonderful and terrible thought. Although we shouldn't attribute too many human characteristics to God, we can be sure of this: God knows everything about love, even the pain that comes with it.

Lord, I love You too – I never want to disappoint
Your great love for me! Amen.

God promises that He will always love you, His child.
His love is always the same. However, He can be proud of you
or disappointed in your side of the relationship.

His Angels Will Save You

The angel of His presence saved them; in His love and in His pity He redeemed them.

Isaiah 63:9 ESV

God says His people's need is like His own need, which is why He's rushing to our rescue. He has great love and empathy for us! He sends the "angel of His presence" (or "angel of His countenance" or "angel of His face") to rescue us. This is precisely what the Bible says, but it remains uncertain what it means exactly. Is it the "Angel of the Lord," which is God Himself, or His "presence" (*Shekinah*), another angel? We're not sure.

Let's simply emphasize that God sends His angel or angels to save us – which is a common biblical fact, also here in Isaiah. Live with the awareness that angels share your room or office! They are there to protect and serve you – however incredible that may sound. Yes, they are "serving spirits," not under our control, but under God's control. They cannot be commanded by you, but how wonderful it is to know that they are there. Let that knowledge comfort you today.

Lord, thank You for the angels surrounding,
serving and protecting me today! Amen.

God promises that His angels are around you.
They keep you safe and serve you in spiritual ways.
Just knowing about their presence should give you much comfort.

His Spirit Is in You

Where is He who put in the midst of them His Holy Spirit?
Isaiah 63:11 ESV

In the Old Testament we read of God's Spirit being ubiquitously present: all over, life-giving and creative. When God (in the Old Testament) sent His Spirit to individuals, it was for a specific purpose: for example to creative people with a certain task, to a king or to the prophets. We see this in today's verse as well: the Spirit is put "in the midst" of the people, among them – on their leaders and prophets. However, the prophets predicted that, in future, God will pour out His Spirit onto "all flesh" – that His Spirit would freely live in all of His people's hearts. That is what happened at Pentecost!

In principle, the Holy Spirit is in every believer, because it is only through the Spirit that we can believe, repent and pray in the first place. However, we must also be *filled* with the Spirit – personally and uniquely engage with God's Spirit in order to live spiritually. Open yourself up to Him, receive what He gives you and work with the gifts that He wants you to use! Walk in the Spirit by being aware of God throughout the day. Practice and grow in this regard – we live in the era of the Holy Spirit, after all!

Lord, fill me with Your Spirit and teach me
to walk in the Spirit, I pray. Amen.

God promises that you can experience the greatness of His Spirit by opening yourself up to Him. It's something you have received and must do in faith.

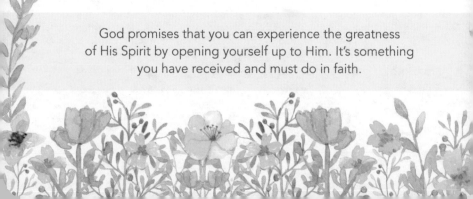

His Love Burns

Where are Your zeal and Your might? The stirring of Your inner parts and Your compassion are held back from me.

Isaiah 63:15 ESV

There are two interesting word choices in this verse:

God's "zeal" is the translation of the Hebrew word for *jealousy*, with the expanded meaning of *passion* or *fervor*, as in a passionate and consuming love. The prophet and the people wanted to know if God had lost His passion for His people – was He really like a husband who had lost all interest in His wife?

The translation of "stirring" literally refers to the *roar* or the *call* of God's innermost being – the place that they associated with our experience of emotions. The King James Version translates this with "the sounding of thy bowels." They want to know whether God was still affected or moved by the misery of His people.

In speaking like this, we know we're using very human images and metaphors for God, but it's the only way humans can speak about God! These rhetorical questions already have a biblical answer and that answer is a resounding yes. Yes, God *is* moved by our suffering! Yes, He keeps loving us passionately! Yes, at this moment God's heart *is* burning with love for you!

Lord, thank You for Your passionate love for me.
Help me to love You in the same way! Amen.

God promises that He is passionate about you –
He experiences a burning love for you. It is His intense desire
that you will be just as passionate about Him as He is about you.

He Is Still Your Father

Our ancestors Abraham and Jacob have both rejected us. But You are still our Father; You have been our protector since ancient times.

Isaiah 63:16 CEV

The idea of God as a "father" does occur in the Old Testament (like in today's verse), but only rarely. God was primarily seen as, well, God. Israel's covenant God was a strict God, but merciful in the end – much the way earthly fathers were in the old times, right? In those days fathers carried much more authority and demanded much more respect than we often see today. A father's word was final and children had no place opposing it! On the contrary, children kept on their father's safe side! Even though fathers could be unpredictable at times, children knew that ultimately their fathers loved them.

This is the way God was seen as well. Jesus, however, changed all of that. He lived in the most intimate relationship with His Father, whom He called *Abba* or "Dad." He spoke about His Father constantly and taught His disciples to approach and experience God as a Father as well. To the rabbis, this was wrong and upsetting. But we, as followers of Christ, may call God *Father* – yes, even *Abba* or *Dad*. After all, Jesus opened up this new relationship with God on the cross. Now God is *your* Dad – the perfect Father!

Thank You, Holy Father, that I may call You Dad! Amen.

God promises and confirms that He is your Father, and says in His Word that you can call Him *Abba* or *Father*. You may also be frank with Him, as children often are.

He Stays with You

O LORD, why do You make us wander from Your ways and harden our heart, so that we fear You not? Return for the sake of Your servants, the tribes of Your heritage.

Isaiah 63:17 ESV

The people had strayed away from God and it appears here as though they were blaming Him for this – He should never have allowed them to stray, He should never have hardened their hearts! Now He needed to return to them – repent from His ways, as it were! This sounds intense, but we know they didn't mean that God actively forced them into sin and was now punishing them for it. No, they meant that God had left them to their own devices and was now allowing them to experience the consequences.

Should He have stopped them? That's their implication, but in reality God will not prevent us from making wrong choices. From the beginning, He leaves us to our own will. That's the way He made us – with free will! It's intrinsically part of being human. It's wonderful, however, that God remains turned to us and stays with us even as we stray away. He stays with us! Wherever you stray, He is always right behind you – you can just turn around!

Thank You, Lord, that You're always with me.
Today I'm turning back to You. Amen.

God promises that He is with you. If you depart from Him, it's because you go astray. However, if you just stop and turn around, you will immediately find Him by your side.

You Will Meet Him There

You help all who gladly obey and do what You want, but sin makes You angry.

Isaiah 64:5 CEV

"Natural" religion is to try to just stay within God's will. For example, people may ask their pastor what they are allowed and not allowed to do – how much they may drink, how far they may take things physically – and then they (hopefully) stay exactly within that requirement. Then God will be happy, right? Others reason that obedience is difficult but you must just grit your teeth and push through – after all, pleasing God is hard work! Actually this is not what spiritual growth is about – it's simply human religiosity and it will always fail.

It is true that discipleship is not always pleasant (nor is it meant to be), but this verse says that it should become our delight. True religion is about a relationship with a loving God – a heart-to-heart thing. We don't do as little as possible for a loved one, do we? We do as much as possible! Love is all about pleasing that person and looking for ways to do it better! Yes, pleasing God is a delight! Deciding to please God is the point at which He will meet you, the turning point of your transformation. That's when you'll start becoming more like God, which is what spiritual growth is all about.

Lord, I want to do what You ask and I
want to delight in doing it, because I love You. Amen.

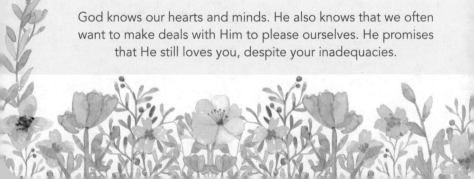

God knows our hearts and minds. He also knows that we often want to make deals with Him to please ourselves. He promises that He still loves you, despite your inadequacies.

You'll Receive New Robes

We are unfit to worship You; each of our good deeds is merely a filthy rag.

Isaiah 64:6 CEV

Our "natural" religion is to do good things and then to be very proud of ourselves: *see how spiritual I am, how obedient, how humble, how willing to serve, look at my gifts … God must be grateful for a believer like me!* Jesus was never impressed by people like this – just think of the parable of the Pharisee and tax collector in the temple.

In this verse from Isaiah we see the problem: human works are imperfect. Doing good works is necessary, but they remain limited, imperfect and sporadic. The Bible says that even our best works are like "filthy rags." To brag about them is just wrong and vain – even arrogant. We need to realize that we require God's help. Only when we turn away from our own good deeds and make Christ's "good deed" on the cross our own, we'll become acceptable to a holy God. Only then will our hearts be in the right place: humble and grateful. Put away your rags and receive His righteous robes! You only need to ask.

Lord, I know my devotion to You is lacking –
I need Your righteousness! Amen.

God appreciates the good work you do, but no human effort
is really worthy of eternity. He promises, however,
to allocate Christ's perfect work on the cross to you if you ask.

You Already Have a Father

But now, O Lᴏʀᴅ, You are our Father; we are the clay, and You are our Potter; we are all the work of Your hand.

Isaiah 64:8 ᴇsᴠ

Whose father is God, actually? Is He only the Christians' father? Well, no. He is also the father of unbelievers, Muslims and Hindus. Does it sound wrong to your Christian mind? Let's explain it like this:

In a general sense God, is indeed the Father of all, because He made everyone. This is precisely what this verse says: "You are our Father … we are all the work of Your hand." God made everyone in their own beautiful way and He loves them all equally, believer or non-believer.

However, not all accept or know God as Father. When we do, through Jesus Christ, we become His children in a more specific sense. In that sense, God is the Father of true believers – and He knows who they are. We needn't go around deciding for Him!

Think of the Prodigal Son. He had a father, but he turned his back on him, ventured far away and became "lost." Then he came to his senses, saying *I have a father*, got up and became reconciled with him. They were in the right relationship again, as a "father and son" should be – a true child! Where are *you* standing with regards to your Father?

Lord, I want to be a true child –
in a true relationship with You! Amen.

God promises that you can get up at any time
and return to your Father – no matter where you are!
You have a Father who constantly watches the horizon.

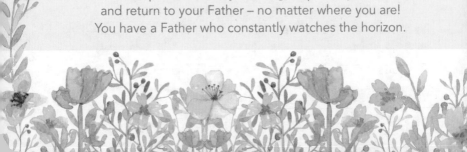

He Will Not Keep Silent

> Will You restrain Yourself at these things, O LORD? Will You keep silent, and afflict us so terribly?
>
> *Isaiah 64:12 ESV*

Here we have "rhetorical" questions again. A rhetorical question is a way of speaking in which the question does not necessitate an answer, because it's self-evident. When the prophet therefore asked "Will You keep silent?" there's a built-in, implied answer, because of the whole Bible context. The implied answer is a resounding *no – of course God will not keep silent!* He will definitely speak out, definitely answer!

Nothing is worse than God's deafening silence, or a partner's "silent treatment," not so? Where there's communication, there's still hope. Even the most direct and robust communication is preferable to mere absence (although we don't mean a shouting match), because communication is vital. Here is the good news: God always communicates! He teaches and shows and warns and encourages and comforts and leads and assures us of His love! Let's be right there with Him – let's join the conversation with everything we have!

Lord, teach me to listen, and help me to understand. Amen.

God promises anew that He has a message for you.
He did not withdraw and is not silent – He speaks!
Are you in a place where you can listen – can you hear Him?

God Always Reveals Himself

"I said, 'Here am I, here am I,' to a nation that was not called by My name."

Isaiah 65:1 ESV

The wonder of God in the Bible is that He doesn't conceal Himself – He isn't one or other secret God! On the contrary, God reveals Himself in different ways. He says here that He revealed Himself on His own initiative to Israel, a people just like many others: "Here am I!" He revealed Himself to Abraham, to Moses, David, Solomon and many others; He reveals Himself through His creation, through His Word, through His Son, Jesus Christ. He reveals Himself in our heart and in our conscience, in our circumstances and through others. God is always revealing Himself – it's His nature!

God is relational in His very being, always reaching out, always seeking to make Himself known to others: "Here am I!" He seeks those who are lost, knocks on the hearts of people – He whispers, He calls, He even shouts sometimes! He wants to draw your attention! God reached out to you in many ways since you were little – revealing Himself during all those years! He so wants you to enter into a relationship with Him.

Thank You, Lord, for seeking me out.
Find me, Lord – here I am! Amen.

God promises to reveal Himself to you, that He will show you who He is! You can experience His revelation in nature, in the Scriptures and in your heart. Search for it.

You Can Become Holy

"Keep to yourself, do not come near Me, for I am too holy for you."
Isaiah 65:5 ESV

In these last chapters of Isaiah the Lord confronted His people again about their sins. Here God referred to people who willfully disregarded His precepts, but still felt that they were better than others. For example, they told others to not touch them, because they were holy – sanctified – and touching others would make them unclean. Most probably they were priests working in the temple. The King James Version renders it with the words "I am holier than thou," which became a well-known phrase that referred to haughtiness and hypocrisy. There wasn't anything that angered Jesus more than the hypocrisy of the spiritual leaders of His day.

Hypocrisy is pretense: pretending to be spiritual, while everyone can see pride, selfishness, hardheartedness and a lack of love! Jesus said that it was far better to know your sin, to confess it and to ask for God's help than to pretend not to have it. Let's rather be real. Humility and authenticity is the beginning of holiness, nothing else. That's where we need to start. Remember that holiness is a lifelong becoming: becoming like God and becoming like Christ.

Lord, help me to become more like You.
I can never do it on my own –
work in me by Your Spirit, I pray! Amen.

People are not holy – holiness is a divine attribute.
Let us recognize our lack of sanctity and ask God
to make us more like Him. He promises that this is the way!

You Can Break Those Bonds

"I, the LORD, will make them pay for their sins and for those of their ancestors – they have disgraced Me by burning incense on mountains."

Isaiah 65:7 CEV

Do the sins of previous generations impact on us as individuals? Am I being punished because my granddad was wicked? It's difficult to imagine that God would exact retribution for sin in a way that's not fair, but that's not what the Bible means. What it means is that God works with people not only individually, but also corporately. He sees not only the person, but the family, the community, the nation. We should realize that we share our humanity, and the fact of sin, with our fellow humans, our family, our community. We are members of one body! In that sense, Granddad's sin is our family's sin, our sin!

Intercession is taking up responsibility for others before God – as well as for our family, our people and our generation. Intercession says: *Forgive us, Lord, for we have sinned!* This is the way that mature believers pray. Consider also the following: the effect of sin doesn't stop with any specific individual – it ripples through to others. If your grandfather was violent or abused alcohol, the effects would surely have had an impact on your dad – and through dad onto you, possibly. Take responsibility for your family, even for Granddad – break the bonds in Jesus' name and be free!

Lord, I am indeed part of a family and a community –
and I intercede for them today. Amen.

If you pray to God for your family, and ask God's forgiveness
and that He breaks those ties holding you back,
He promises to break every bond and shadow.

You'll Choose, He'll Choose

"My chosen shall possess it, and My servants shall dwell there."
Isaiah 65:9 ESV

The Lord warns His people that His judgment is near. When He intervenes on the last day, it will be the end of all sin, hatred, injustice, meanness, lies, fraud, oppression and exclusion. These are the things God hates and He'll deal with them – and with those who practice it. Yes, at the end – on Judgment Day – there'll be a great separation. Fortunately, there are also those who choose to serve Him, who seek His will, who trust in Him. They are the "remnant" with whom God will go forward, into eternity: the chosen ones, elected for salvation.

The word "choose" occurs twice in this paragraph in Isaiah: God chooses people and people choose God! Both are equally important and equally true: two sides of the same salvation truth! We can say that God choosing us is His part of salvation, and us choosing Him is our part of it. Another way would be to say that God's election includes our choosing for Him, freely and fully. Yes, it remains a profound truth and difficult to comprehend, but let's not water it down too much for the sake of our understanding – let's leave God's mystery to Him! Instead, let's focus on the biblical appeal: choose right, choose life, choose Him!

Lord, I choose You – I put you first!
Help me with this decision. Amen.

If you repent, God promises that you are chosen.
If you have accepted God as your Father,
God has adopted you as His child. One is evidence of the other.

Forget Fortune;
Rather Trust God

"You who forsake the LORD, who forget My holy mountain, who set a table for Fortune and fill cups of mixed wine for Destiny."

Isaiah 65:11 ESV

The words translated here as "Fortune" and "Destiny" refer to two idols, in Hebrew named "Gad" and "Meni," but they're not otherwise known and commentators aren't sure exactly who they refer to. Some think of the sun and moon, others of Jupiter and Venus, among other possibilities.

There is an early tradition, used in our translation here, that refers to Babylonian idols that control destiny, fate and fortune. That would mean that God blamed His people for praying to idols in order to better their chances in life. How sad – but it still happens! People trust their luck or rely on their "destiny" or "the universe" for their future. We know that mere chance or probability is a mathematical fact and simple games of chance cannot be seen as wrong. Our problem, however, comes when someone puts their trust in their good fortune, irresponsibly gambles with their future or makes "sacrifices" to blind luck such as gambling. It then becomes an idol – and a shortcut to losing what you had! Forget those things. Rather trust in God – He alone holds your future!

Lord, my fortune and happiness are with You. Amen.

Gambling is one of the fastest ways to lose your money, and can be quite addictive. It takes everything and gives almost nothing. God promises that your destiny is safe with Him.

Your God: Yes and Amen!

"He who blesses himself in the land shall bless himself by the God of truth, and he who takes an oath in the land shall swear by the God of truth."

Isaiah 65:16 ESV

Some Bible translations render the phrase "the God of truth" as "the God who can be trusted." It's also true, but ours is a joyful translation, because it renders the Hebrew wording well, which literally reads "the God of Amen" (*Elohe Amen*). The word *amen*, from a root meaning "firm" can mean *let it be so, it shall be so, surely, definitely, yes*, etc. *The Message* translates it eloquently as "Yes. Yes. Yes." Beautiful!

Amen is an utterance of faith and confirmation. How wonderful that God is our amen! Just as a firm *amen* confirms our prayers to God, so God confirms His promises to us with His personal *amen*! In the New Testament, Jesus Christ is also called *Amen, the faithful and true Witness* – in whom every promise is *yea and amen*. Yes, Christ is God's *Amen* to us, His final Word – His signature underneath all of His promises! He is the guarantee, the confirmation, the evidence of eternal love. Listen: if God promised something, you can know it's a given. It will be so, because He said amen to it!

Amen, Lord! Thank You for being faithful and true!

God promises that He is the yes and amen behind every one of His promises. He makes promises come true and He proved it when He came to earth and died on the cross. That's proof!

New Heavens and a New Earth Are on the Way

"For behold, I create new heavens and a new earth, and the former things shall not be remembered or come into mind."

Isaiah 65:17 ESV

What does the future hold for us, according to the Bible? Forget for now the complex End Time maps with all the predictions, comings and goings, wars and judgments. Throughout the Bible the following simple expectation emerges, including also here in Isaiah: God's people will suffer oppression, because the darkness always wants to extinguish the light. God will not forsake His people. At the climax of it all, God will personally intervene.

When He comes, on the Day of the Lord, it will be for the redemption of His people, but also a fearful day of wrath for His enemies. On that day God will separate the good from the bad.

Eternal peace with God will then commence for His people – and eternal death for the others. God will personally rule over us on a new earth in the New Jerusalem!

There are other details as well, but the above is the main framework. Jesus said that if we look around us, we'll see the signs of His coming: wars, disasters, false teachings, etc (Matthew 24:4-8). It means only one thing: the old is on the way out, the new is coming!

Thank You, Lord, for making all things new. Amen.

God promises that a day will come when the heavenly dimension will take over the earthly dimension and swallow it. Jesus will come, hold you tightly against His chest and wipe away every tear.

A New Jerusalem Is Coming

"Celebrate and be glad forever! I am creating a Jerusalem, full of happy people."

Isaiah 65:18 CEV

As Isaiah looked ahead into the future, he saw a brand-new world: one in which God would personally be joined with His people on earth. Remember that the end connects with the beginning – everything will be restored to its original condition and purpose! In Paradise, God walked with people in person – and He will do so again. Isaiah said that the future earth will be a "new" earth and heaven, a spiritual earth and heaven, with our current physical laws rendered invalid. Of that earth Jerusalem will be the center: the city of God, full of gladness and joy!

The book of Revelation takes this topic further and says that the New Jerusalem that descends from heaven is also the bride, the people of God. By the time Christ comes, His bride will be perfect in every way – "complete" in the sense that even the very last believer will have been included. Remember that it's only the bringing in of the nations into the Kingdom, which has prevented Jesus from returning. When the full and final count has been achieved, Christ's bride will be ready and the Marriage of the Lamb will commence – hallelujah!

Thank You, Lord, that I can be part of that city forever! Amen.

God promises that the "total sum" of believers is being collected in a hurry – all over the world! Once the last one has been collected, the New Jerusalem will be established on earth.

You'll Grow Old – Forever!

"Like the days of a tree shall the days of My people be, and My chosen shall long enjoy the work of their hands."

Isaiah 65:22 ESV

The prophet looked forward to the new era that awaited humankind – a new earth and heaven, and a new Jerusalem. According to these verses, everyone would live in their own house and eat from their own vineyard, a biblical image of prosperity and provision. This blessed life would never again be robbed from them by an enemy. God's favor would be seen in the longevity of His people. Old age is a biblical symbol of blessing and the prophets said that in that day a hundred years of age will count as being young!

This is another instance in which the end will be like the beginning, because the first generations in Genesis became equally old. The New Testament perspective changes, though, because our expectation is not to become very old, but to live forever. Remember that the Bible presents us with a continuing revelation: the New Testament gives us a clearer view on many things the Old Testament only alludes to. Let's conclude our thought for today: old age is a blessing from God. Ask Him to bless you with a long life! Yes, may you live in this world to a ripe old age, full of health and vigor, and may you live eternally with God in the next.

Lord, thank You that my life,
and my death, are in Your hands. Amen.

A long life is God's blessing. We are living in a broken world, but ask Him for that blessing! God promises a life that will be forever and ever!

God Will Be Nearer

"Before they call I will answer; while they are yet speaking I will hear."

Isaiah 65:24 ESV

When the new era commences, which the prophet can already see so vividly, God will come to stay with His people. He will personally dwell among them! Remember that the Jewish people had to approach God through their priests. A righteous Jew who was ritually clean could approach a priest in the temple with his need. The priest would then present his sacrifice and prayers to God.

That will change, according to God. When He comes to be with them, being directly available, the whole of Israel will become a priestly nation. God will hear their prayers before they are even spoken! How wonderful is that? Still, even more wonderful is this: that era has already started in Jesus Christ. As the Messiah, He introduced the Messianic Era, of which one aspect is the giving of the Holy Spirit to all people. Since Pentecost, therefore, God resides in every believer's heart! By His Spirit, He is nearer to us than we can even think, closer to us than our own breath! He knows our dreams and prayers and fears and frustrations – before we can even say it. What a privilege to live with God so closely. Start up the conversation – God is right there in your heart!

Thank You, Holy Spirit, for being part of me.
Guide me in Your ways, Lord. Amen.

God promises that His Spirit working in you is already praying
to the Father on your behalf. He is not only praying,
He is calling to God with unspeakable cries – for you!

It Will Just Be a Snake

"The wolf and the lamb shall graze together; the lion shall eat straw like the ox, and dust shall be the serpent's food."

Isaiah 65:25 ESV

Many prophecies in Isaiah refer to the "Messianic Era." That era started with the coming of the Messiah, Jesus Christ, but it hasn't yet finished. It will end when Christ comes again. Currently we live "between the times" – having received something of God, but not everything. The Kingdom has come, but it's still coming and is yet to fully come. Some prophecies are still not fulfilled. Well-known prophecies like these about the lion that lies down with the lamb cannot happen in this physical realm – it can only refer to the new, spiritual earth where there'll be no more bloodshed, killing or death. Only peace will reign!

Even the serpent will only eat dust, as he is commanded to do in Paradise (and as people thought snakes did). The meaning is that he'll no longer be an enemy of man, biting us in the heel. In Scripture the serpent is often a symbol or vehicle of the evil one, but in God's future he will just be a snake, for no evil will remain. Think about that future and accept that you'll see with your very own eyes how death is overcome, how evil is eradicated, how peace is established forever! This is God's promise. That makes us live with complete confidence!

Thank You, Lord, for victory
and peace in the future with You. Amen.

All homicide and enmity is abolished in the Messianic Era. You will experience total peace, be completely accepted and deeply loved. God promises that this is your future!

Nature Will Be Born Again

"They won't bite or harm anyone on My holy mountain. I, the LORD, have spoken!"

Isaiah 65:25 CEV

The prophets said that in eternity, nature will only know peace. The image of the lion that lies with lambs is a typical one. In today's verse, the Lord, speaking through the prophet, said that lions won't hunt deer anymore, nor kill humans. One can speculate about whether a lion would still be a lion, because a lion is designed in every way to be a predator! That, however, would be to miss the point.

These images are firstly symbols, indicating the time when there'll be no more decay, wear, erosion or loss, let alone bloodshed, violence, killing or death! There will only be vibrant health! That is the point. Let's not imagine it in the terms of our physical existence.

Jesus talks about a future life in which the body doesn't function in its physical capacity anymore. Paul says that the whole of creation is already groaning in anticipation, looking forward to the day when it is no longer subject to the fleetingness, the ephemerality of everything – awaiting its own rebirth. The day will come when God wipes the slate clean and starts anew – with a new earth and new heavens. Eternity will overtake that which is transitory, perfection will replace that which is flawed and life will remove all death when Jesus comes!

Lord Jesus, come! Amen.

God promises that eternal life will have a totally different order, that nothing will ever perish. Your spiritual body will consist of immortal light – no, do not try to understand it!

God Is Born in Hearts

"Heaven is My throne, and the earth is My footstool; what is the house that you would build for Me?"

Isaiah 66:1 ESV

It is Christmas Day and we've come to the last chapter in Isaiah. What a journey! Isaiah lambasted his people for their sins – the reason for their captivity in Babylon – but afterwards also promised God's deliverance. It happened just as predicted – read about the Jews' return to Judea in Ezra, Nehemiah, Haggai and Zechariah. The prophet, however, also looked farther into the future and foresaw a time when all sin would be removed and God would come in person to live with His people.

It will be a brand-new start with new heavens, a new earth and a new Jerusalem, which will be the center of God's presence. In that day, the city will no longer have a temple – it will be one big temple, because God will be everywhere. The prophet reminds the people that God cannot stay in any man-made structure because the whole of heaven is His abode and the earth is nothing more than His footstool, figuratively speaking. Here is the truth of this special day: there can never be an earthly temple anymore, for you and I are God's temple! Realize that the mighty King is pleased to reside in the humble abode of your heart. He chooses it far above any glorious edifice. What God seeks, above all, is a relationship.

I invite You, mighty King, into my heart.
Make me a worthy temple for Your presence! Amen.

God promises that He sees your life and heart as an appropriate
sanctuary in which to live. Through His Holy Spirit,
He makes you holy, little by little.

This Pain Leads to Birth

"Have you ever heard of a woman who gave birth to a child before having labor pains?"

Isaiah 66:7 CEV

The new world is coming, Isaiah says! The New Testament perspective on the End Times is strongly influenced by prophets like Isaiah, because its authors saw many Old Testament predictions come to fulfillment with the coming of Christ. The clear New Testament teaching is that the End Times were ushered in by Jesus, the promised Messiah, but that it's not over yet. Jesus Himself said that certain things first had to happen, and then He would return, in great power and glory. Then eternity would commence.

Among the things that must first happen are wars, disasters, false prophets, and a great tribulation such as the world has never seen before. He calls these things "birth pains," just as Isaiah describes them here. What does it mean? It means that painful things are happening around us and they might even get worse. However, they're productive pains, labor pains that will lead to all God's promises. Can there be a birth without pain? No – many things in a mother's body need to adjust to make way for the birth. It's very painful, but once the baby is there, it is all worth it! Change is always painful, but change is necessary – and the result will be worth it. That's a promise.

Lord, help me to see this situation through,
so that I can get to where I need to be. Amen.

You may experience all kinds of pain, but God promises that it is productive pain that will bring something new and produce something beautiful. See it through to birth.

A New Nation Will Be Born

"Shall a nation be brought forth in one moment? For as soon as Zion was in labor she brought forth her children."

Isaiah 66:8 ESV

The prophet says that childbirth is a process – and to birth a nation is a long process! It may take centuries and a lot of travail. Still, the new nation that God is going to bring forth – of which they're experiencing the birth pangs – will be born relatively quickly. Isaiah's expectation is that Jews from Babylon will return first and that they'll then be joined by the "lost tribes" of Israel. God will also include some of those of Israel who might be ritually excluded. Finally, people from all the tribes, tongues and nations of the world will be added as they come to worship the God of Israel in Jerusalem. In this way, God's people will come to completion.

Most of these things have already happened or are happening now, through Jesus Christ! We are living in a time when the nations are coming to God – through Christ – as never before. Millions of believers are entering God's kingdom from China, Korea and all over the East; the church is growing in Africa, South America and even in many "closed" countries. When God's new nation is completed and ready, Jesus will return! That's His promise.

Lord, thank You that I can be part of Your people.
How can I contribute in extending
Your kingdom even further? Amen.

God reigns and is currently building His church.
He promises to include everyone who wants to be part of it,
even you – and then the end will come.

In Jerusalem Forever

"As one whom his mother comforts, so I will comfort you; you shall be comforted in Jerusalem."

Isaiah 66:13 ESV

The New Jerusalem, which is introduced here in Isaiah, is also described in Revelation: with perfect dimensions, streets of gold, gates of pearl and so forth. Everything has symbolic meaning. Among other things, it's said that its twelve gates will always be open. In biblical times, cities' gates had to be closed at night or in times of danger. The point, of course, is that there'll never be any danger in God's future. With Him there (here in the image of a mother), everyone will feel completely safe.

Let's bring this truth home – for us, for today: that trust in God's protection, that feeling of safety can be ours now already. Our God is with us and our God can protect us. Our God will allow or won't allow what happens to us. What can people do – attack us, hurt us, even kill us? Yes, things may or may not happen; but whatever happens, even in the worst scenario, we'll end up safely with God – in His Jerusalem, forever and ever! This is our security, our safety and our protection. No unbeliever can have it. No attacker, weapon or bullet can take it from us. On the contrary, it frees us to truly live, fearless and confident!

Lord, thank You that I am safe in Your care –
now and forever. Amen.

God promises that you are safe forever.
No real threats remain. With Him you are assured of
an eternal future, free from pain and loss.

All Will See Him in You

"I will send them to announce My wonderful glory to nations that have never heard about Me."

Isaiah 66:19 CEV

Isaiah is called the "gospel" of the Old Testament because it deals so intensively with the topics of salvation, the coming "Servant of the Lord" and the nations that will be added to God's people. Here we see it again: right at the climax of the book, it's the prophet's expectation and prayer that all on earth would know God, and would love and serve Him. He foresees how Jewish "missionaries" go into the world to announce God's glory everywhere. Isaiah concludes his book with a great vision for the whole world, just as the gospels do.

The Jewish people have never reached out to the world in this way, because they're still waiting for Messiah to come. For us, however, the Messiah already came in the form of Jesus Christ. His Great Commission was to send us out as witnesses into the whole world. This is our task at the moment. Every Christian is involved, because every Christian is sent. You are sent as well! Your world is your family, workplace, school, neighborhood and community. Your mission is to go and live the gospel of Christ in the most radical sense. How? By proving your discipleship through your love. That will be the sign, Jesus said (John 13:35).

Lord Jesus, help me to radically
love others today and always. Amen.

God sends you into your community to preach His gospel. Who knows, perhaps you will be called to other places, people and languages. He promises to be with you through all your days – until the very end!

All Will Serve God

"From new moon to new moon, and from Sabbath to Sabbath, all flesh shall come to worship before Me, declares the LORD."

Isaiah 66:23 ESV

The prophet's vision, right here at the end of Isaiah, is of "all flesh" worshiping God. How wonderful! God is the God of all; He loves all equally and made provision in Christ for the salvation of everyone. You and I are already the fruit of this vision, because we're among those non-Jewish people who worship the God of Israel! We do not worship in the Jewish way, because the earliest church in Jerusalem taught that non-Jews such as us are not obliged to first become Jews in order to become Christians.

Let's join the vision of the prophet, right here at the end of his book, his grand climax. It's the same vision that John had in his book of Revelation (and see it in your mind's eye): thousands and thousands of believers, from every tribe and tongue and nation, joyfully gathered before God's throne, clothed in white robes, rejoicing and waving palm leaves! They are the ones who have run the race, who have crossed the finishing line, who have kept the faith. They have overcome in Jesus' name. They have lived and died and lived again to reach the goal – God Himself! Oh, shall we meet before the throne of God?

Lord, I want to be in that number before Your throne.
I trust You for that in name of Jesus Christ. Amen.

It's a wonderful privilege to be a child of God.
He promises you anew today that you will
have eternal life if you serve Him.

Always Jesus!

The scroll of the prophet Isaiah was given to Him. He unrolled the scroll and found the place where it was written, "The Spirit of the Lord is upon Me, because He has anointed Me to proclaim good news to the poor."

Luke 4:17-18 ESV

It's the end of another year and we've concluded a wonderful journey through Isaiah. It's really surprising how these ancient words, which were written to encourage God's people at least two and a half thousand years ago, can still ring so true today. Why is that so? It's because we're also human: we, too, ask questions about God; about suffering, life, death and the meaning of it all – even though we live in a time and culture that would've been unimaginable to people in biblical times. As fellow humans, we share an innate longing for God, for significance, for love!

Another reason why we still read and find comfort in these words is because of Jesus Christ. He is the One about whom the prophet Isaiah wrote: the "Servant of the Lord," the Anointed One or Messiah. This Jesus attested to personally when, centuries later, He read from Isaiah in the synagogue, and announced that the prophecy was fulfilled in Him. Many didn't believe Him, but some did – and so do we! We know that once we personally and decidedly follow Christ, we can never return. He becomes our inspiration, our reason, our goal, our life! On this significant day, make the decision every Christian needs to make: *This year for Jesus! Always Jesus!*

Yes, Lord Jesus – always You! Amen.

Thank God that He has been with you through this past year.
Ask Him to guide you as you enter the New Year.
He promises you hope and a good future!